DRUGS, CRIME AND CORRUPTION

Also by Richard Clutterbuck

ACROSS THE RIVER (*as Richard Jocelyn*)
THE LONG LONG WAR
PROTEST AND THE URBAN GUERRILLA
RIOT AND REVOLUTION IN SINGAPORE AND MALAYA
LIVING WITH TERRORISM
GUERRILLAS AND TERRORISTS
KIDNAP AND RANSOM
BRITAIN IN AGONY
THE MEDIA AND POLITICAL VIOLENCE
INDUSTRIAL CONFLICT AND DEMOCRACY
CONFLICT AND VIOLENCE IN SINGAPORE AND MALAYSIA
THE FUTURE OF POLITICAL VIOLENCE
KIDNAP, HIJACK AND EXTORTION
TERRORISM AND GUERRILLA WARFARE
TERRORISM, DRUGS AND CRIME IN EUROPE AFTER 1992
INTERNATIONAL CRISIS AND CONFLICT
TERRORISM IN AN UNSTABLE WORLD

Drugs, Crime and Corruption

Thinking the Unthinkable

Richard Clutterbuck
Security and Political Risk Consultant
and Honorary Research Fellow
University of Exeter

 NEW YORK UNIVERSITY PRESS
Washington Square, New York

First published in the U.S.A. in 1995 by
NEW YORK UNIVERSITY PRESS
Washington Square
New York, N.Y. 10003

Library of Congress Cataloging-in-Publication Data
Clutterbuck, Richard L.
Drugs, crime and corruption : thinking the unthinkable / Richard
Clutterbuck.
p.   cm.
Includes bibliographical references and index.
ISBN 0–8147–1524–9 (cloth). — ISBN 0–8147–1529–X (pbk.)
1. Drug traffic,   2. Drug traffic—South America.   3. Drug
traffic—Great Britain.   I. Title.
HV5801.C5645   1995
363.4'5—dc20   95–13890
                                                         CIP

Printed in Great Britain

Contents

List of Tables

Preface

Drug trafficking has elbowed its way uninvited into all the four books I have written in the past five years on terrorism, crime and international conflict. Almost every criminal gang and most terrorist movements are partly or wholly financed out of the $500 billion the world spends each year on drugs on the streets, most of it in the affluent cities of the USA and Europe.

Drug trafficking provides a constant circulation of criminal money, as will be described more fully in this book. Of the world's $500 billion, $3 billion (£2 million) is spent by drug users on British streets each year. They acquire 90 per cent of this by petty crime, for example by breaking into homes and cars to fund their addiction. Of the £2 billion, less than 1 per cent goes to the Latin American and Asian farmers who produce the drugs; the other 99 per cent goes entirely into the hands of criminals, through the street dealers, distributors, importers, and exporters to the drug barons. Each hopes to make 50 or 100 per cent profit – some, like the Colombian barons, much more.

The criminals use this money to finance a lavish lifestyle but also, more important, to build up huge assets which they use for intimidation and corruption to manipulate politicians worldwide as a means of extending their power. Their aim is to run the part of the world they live in, as the Mafia have done for years in Sicily, for their own benefit and enrichment.

Damaging as drugs are to addicts, the aggregate damage done to innocent members of the community by the crime they generate is far greater.

The cure must lie in the main consumer countries, the USA and Europe, rather than the drug-producing countries in Latin America and Asia. This was brought home to me in two consultancy assignments in Peru in 1991 and 1994. Peru grows 60 per cent of the world's coca, mostly processed and marketed by the multibillion dollar drug cartels in Colombia. These cartels have for years financed the vicious Shining Path terrorist movement in Peru and have spent even more on corrupting both Peruvian and Colombian society.

Drenching the Peruvian peasants' coca fields with poison will
not solve this problem. So long as our drug users are willing to pay
for them, the growers, the barons and the criminal gangs will find
ways to provide the drugs on our streets. The same arguments
apply to opium and heroin.

So how do we stem the flow? Certainly not by carrying on as we
are. If we hope to do so by police and judicial suppressive
measures, we will have to make them strong enough to work. If
the price for this in erosion of civil liberties would be too high,
then we will have to explore the other three alternatives –
decriminalization, licensing or licensed legalization, or a
combination of the four. The British government's Consultation
Paper, *Tackling Drugs Together*, published in October 1994, invited
debate to develop a working strategy. In this book I have assessed
these four alternatives with their pros and cons to contribute to
that debate.

I owe special thanks to Commander John Grieve of the
Metropolitan Police; to Nicholas Dorn and John Witton of the
Institute for the Study of Drug Dependence (ISDD); and to
Simon Baker and his friends in the Hong Kong Police. In Peru I
was enormously helped by the British Ambassador, Keith Haskell,
by his Defence Attaché, Colonel Van der Noot, and the rest of his
team; also by Police General Antonio Vidal, Army Generals
Sinecio Jarama and Alfredo Rodriguez; Lieutenant-Colonel Otto
Guibovich; and Dr Enrique Obando. I have also quoted a lot
from the excellent case studies by Jon Silverman in his *Crack of
Doom* and especially from the extensive research into drugs and
the mafia by Alison Jamieson. They do not necessarily agree with
each other or with me, so they must not be blamed for my
conclusions.

Exeter   RICHARD CLUTTERBUCK

List of Abbreviations

For foreign acronyms and in other cases where it is judged to be more helpful to the reader, an English description (in parentheses) is given instead of spelling out the words.

ACJANL	Andean Commission of Jurists, *Andean Newsletter*
ACJDTU	Andean Commission of Jurists, *Drug Trafficking Update*
ACPO	Association of Chief Police Officers
AIDS	Acquired Immune Deficiency Syndrome
AP	(Centre political party) (Peru)
APC	*Annual of Power and Conflict*
APRA	(Leftist political party) (Peru)
ASF	Automated Search Facility (Interpol)
BCCI	Bank of Credit and Commerce International
BKA	(German Police Intelligence Service)
BND	(German Foreign Intelligence Service)
CAT	Community Action Trust
CDCU	Central Drugs Coordination Unit
CELAD	(European Committee to Combat Drugs)
CGSB	(Simón Bolívar Guerrilla Coordination) (Colombia)
CICU	Crack Intelligence Coordinating Unit
CID	Criminal Investigation Department
CIS	Commonwealth of Independent States
CJA	Criminal Justice Act, 1988
CSA	Controlled Substances Act, 1970
CTR	Currency Transaction Report
DC	(Italian Christian Democratic Party)
DDU	Drug Dependency Unit
DEA	Drug Enforcement Administration (USA)
DINCOTE	(Peruvian police anti-terrorist unit)
DNA	(Genetic molecule in body fluids)
DTOA	Drug Trafficking Offences Act 1986
EDU	European Drugs Unit
ELN	(National Liberation Army) (Colombia)
EMZ	Emergency Military Zone (Peru)

EPL	(People's Liberation Army) (Colombia)
EU	European Union (formerly EC)
Europol	European Police Office
FARC	(Armed Revolutionary Forces of Colombia)
FATF	Financial Action Task Force
FD	(Centre Left coalition) (Peru)
G7	Group of Seven (Canada, France, Germany, Italy, Japan, UK and USA)
GDP	Gross Domestic Product
GNP	Gross National Product
HIV	Human Immunodeficiency Virus
HRP	Harm Reduction Policy (drugs)
ID card	Identity card
INLA	Irish National Liberation Army
INCB	International Narcotics Control Board
INSCR	International Narcotics Strategy Control Report
Interpol	International Police Organization
IRA	Irish Republican Army
ISDD	Institute for the Study of Drug Dependence
IV	Intravenous (drug injection)
JLP	Jamaican Labour Party
KGB	(Former Soviet secret police)
LSD	(Synthetic hallucinogenic drug)
M19	(Colombian left-wing party)
MDMA	(Ecstasy – hallucinogenic drug)
MIR	(Bolivian centre-left party)
MLCA	Money Laundering Control Act 1986 (USA)
MNR	(Bolivian centre-right party)
MT	Metric Tonne
NA	Narcotics Anonymous
NATO	North Atlantic Treaty Organization
NCIS	National Criminal Intelligence Service
NDIU	National Drugs Intelligence Unit
NHS	National Health Service
NRA	National Rifle Association (USA)
OCR	Optical Character Reading
PACE	Police and Criminal Evidence Act 1986
PEPES	(People persecuted by Pablo Escobar) (Colombia)
PNC	Police National Computer
PNP	People's National Party (Jamaica)
PTA	Prevention of Terrorism Act

RC	*Rondas Campesinas* (Peruvian village guards)
RCIO	Regional criminal intelligence office
RCS	Regional crime squad
RISCT	Research Institute for the Study of Conflict and Terrorism
SB	Special Branch (British police intelligence)
SFRC	Senate Foreign Relations Committee (USA)
SIN	(National Intelligence Service) (Peru)
SL	*Sendero Luminoso* (Shining Path) (Peru)
SUA	Shan United Army (Myanmar)
THC	Tetrahydrocannabinol (active ingredient in cannabis)
TREVI	(EU Ministerial Security Committee)
UIC	(Italian Exchange Bureau)
UFF	Ulster Freedom Fighters
UN	United Nations
UNFDAC	UN Fund for Drug Abuse Control
UWSA	United Wa State Army (Myanmar)
UVF	Ulster Volunteer Force
VAT	Value Added Tax

Part I
Introduction

1   Are We Losing the War?

Who pays the peasants, the smugglers, the dealers . . . ? You do, stupid! You pay in your stolen cars and stolen car radios; your break-ins; your muggings; your children's brushes with the underworld of drug related crime.
Matthew Parris in *The Times*, 15 August 1994

DRUGS AND CRIME

The people of the world spend about $500 billion a year on buying drugs in their streets. This is more than the Gross Domestic Product (GDP) of all but the seven richest countries in the world.[1]

When an addict spends £66 ($100) for a gram of cocaine or heroin in London or New York, less than 1 per cent goes to the farmer in Peru or Afghanistan who produced it. More than 99 per cent goes into the hands of the criminal gangs who distribute it.

In Britain, a hard drug addict spends on average £33,000 ($50,000) a year on drugs;[2] of about £3 billion ($4.5 billion) spent annually on drugs, 90 per cent is funded by crime; about 50 per cent of the theft and burglary is to pay for drugs, mainly by breaking into homes and cars and selling the radios and video recorders for cash at street markets and car boot sales. In the USA, 50 per cent of the 25,000 homicides each year are drug related. The suffering caused by the crime is now greater than that caused by the drugs.

Consumption of drugs is increasing year by year, particularly of cocaine (including crack) and of synthetics – amphetamines, MDMA (Ecstasy) and LSD. The proportion of young people taking drugs suggests that the total will go on rising. Half a million people spent £700 million ($1 billion) on Ecstasy at 'raves' in the UK in 1993, at about £18 ($27) per dose.[3]

The US government spends billions of dollars every year ($8.6 billion in 1993),[4] on attempts to encourage or coerce the countries where cocaine, heroin and cannabis are produced to reduce their supplies. This, however, is attacking the wrong target. So long as

3

people on the streets of the affluent countries are prepared to pay for them, the farmers will go on producing drugs and the criminal gangs will go on distributing them. The cure must lie at the demand end.

It is estimated that 50 per cent of the world's illicit drugs are sold in the USA.[5] There are millions of addicts in and around the opium-growing countries in Asia, but they do not pay the inflated prices extorted by criminal gangs in the West. In the European Union (EU), Italy consumes the most drugs in proportion to the population, in which the mafias play a big part, but Britain, to her shame, is second in the league. The present anti-drug measures in the West are clearly not succeeding. Radical alternatives need to be considered to overcome the problem and especially to cut off the huge flow of drug money, almost all from addicts on Western streets, into financing organized crime.

This book looks first at the producing countries; then at the money laundering whereby the cash paid on the streets is converted into apparently legitimate assets for the criminal gangs; and finally at the consumers, assessing some of the radical measures which may be needed.

THE PRODUCERS

Virtually all the coca and opium and most of the cannabis are grown in Third World countries. One has been selected for a case study in depth in Part II – Peru, which grows 60 per cent of the world's coca, and best illustrates the interplay between drug trafficking, corruption, crime and terrorism in a producer country. Peru has suffered from the world's most vicious terrorist movement, financed by drugs, and has dealt with it by intelligence techniques from which there is a lot to learn. A common thread through this book is that, for defeating terrorism, corruption and crime, including drug trafficking, intelligence is the key.

Part III describes not only the operation of the Colombian cartels in processing and distributing the cocaine, but also the conversion of cocaine into crack, which is almost entirely done in the consumer countries.

Part IV examines, more briefly, the production and distribution of heroin, cannabis and the synthetics.

MONEY LAUNDERING

Part V examines the techniques of money laundering. About half the cash taken from drugs sold on the streets stays in the hands of the domestic criminal gangs which import, distribute and sell them. Most of this is laundered by concealing it amongst the takings of cash-intensive businesses such as fast food, betting shops, casinos, scrap yards and antique dealers, whence it finds its way into banks, stocks and property (mainly luxurious houses, fast cars, works of art and jewellery) having the appearance of legitimately earned profits.

The other half is laundered by a more complicated process to be legitimized as the assets of multinational corporations which provide cover for multi-billion dollar drug trafficking by the Colombian cartels and the big heroin and hashish traders in Asia. This involves the manipulation of the now highly computerized international banking system, especially including banks in 'fiscal havens' which have institutionalized banking secrecy and act as hosts for the criminal takings of bogus corporations with no questions asked. When money is passed electronically in and out of two or three of these in succession, to end up in a respectable bank or property in Europe or the USA, its original source is virtually impossible to trace.

These chapters also look at the laws and international conventions enacted to detect money launderers and to confiscate their assets, and at why they have so far not proved very successful.

THE CHOICE FACING THE CONSUMER COUNTRIES

Part VI looks briefly at some of the big consumer countries, notably the USA and in East and West Europe; also at the methods being tried in the Netherlands to decriminalize the consumption of drugs; and at the working of the Italian mafias and their influence in developing organized crime in other countries, which is growing at an alarming rate in Russia and East Europe.

Part VII is a four-chapter case study of drugs and associated crime in the UK. In October 1994, the British government issued a Consultation Document, *Tackling Drugs Together*,[6] which set out a programme for developing and implementing a new anti-drug strategy over the period 1995–8 and invited comment and debate on it. This book is intended to be a contribution to that debate.

Britain, as an island, offers the best opportunity for research and experiment into radical alternatives for tackling drugs on an international scale. There are four possible lines of approach.

The first option is more drastic suppression. Can we tighten up the laws and police powers for suppressing drug trafficking so that they really do work, which at present they clearly do not? Should we punish the importers and distributors more severely, particularly for repeated offences? Can we find ways of increasing the low rate of conviction of the guilty? Can we protect witnesses and juries from intimidation and corruption? Can we prevent professional drug traffickers from repeatedly entering the country with false passports? Is there a case for applying some of these measures to other serious crimes, such as those involving cruelty and abuse of children, and for persistent offenders? And would drastic measures do more harm than good by eroding civil liberties?

The second option would be to follow the Dutch approach and decriminalize the possession of drugs for personal consumption, though not to legalize drug trafficking.

The third option would be to extend the current licensing of doctors at the Drug Dependency Units (DDUs) to prescribe and provide drugs in the treatment of addiction. This extension would aim to give compulsory treatment to addicts who are considered to be a danger to the public or who finance their addiction by crime, also to convicted criminals who are addicted or who take to drug abuse in prison.

The fourth option would be to continue this extension of licensing so that eventually drugs could be imported under government control by licensed importers direct from the growers and sold, heavily taxed and under strict regulation, by licensed retailers – as we do with alcohol. Would this be likely to lead to a massive increase in drug abuse? Would it send a dangerous signal to teenagers – that drug abuse is acceptable? Would it undercut the criminals – from drug barons to street dealers – and drive them out of business, saving us from the crime which drug trafficking generates? If we were to try this option, unlicensed import and sale of drugs should remain a criminal offence – as it is with alcohol. In particular, making drugs available or peddling them to children would need to incur the heaviest penalties.

It would be unwise to confine our experiments to any one of these four options – drastic suppression, decriminalization, licensing and legalization under licence. The aim, as set out in the Consultation Paper, should be trial and development over the period 1995–8. Licensing, for example, could be extended gradually, always keeping open the means of reversal if it were leading to an unacceptably large increase in drug abuse. Many of the more drastic measures, needed in any case for other forms of serious crime, would be available for dealing with people who tried to bypass the licensing system and to fill the inevitable demand for drugs by teenagers, unable to get them from licensed sources.

It would also be essential to guard against allowing any relaxation in the availability of drugs to embarrass our neighbours, a problem not wholly solved by the Dutch; also to negotiate amendment of some of the provisions of UN, Council of Europe and European Union Conventions to which Britain is a party, in order that we can pursue and evaluate alternatives to solve a world problem.

Chapters 21 and 22 of this book examine the feasibility and pros and cons of each of these alternatives, to stimulate debate and chart the way for research, trial and assessment. Since present methods are manifestly failing, we should approach this debate with an open mind, if necessary 'thinking the unthinkable'.

Part II

Cocaine and Terrorism in Peru

2 The *Mistis* and the Shining Path

INCAS, *MISTIS* AND COCA

The Shining Path, one of the most vicious terrorist movements in history, was conceived in 1962 and born in 1970 in the Inca country of Peru.

For 90 years before the Spaniards came in 1532 the Incas, a small tribe based around Cuzco in Peru's Andean Highlands, governed an empire extending 5000 km down the Andes from Colombia to southern Chile. This was a remarkable form of civilization which developed independently from others. The king (the Inca) was regarded as divine and headed a pyramid of government which ruled autocratically down to every village. Communications – roads, bridges and tunnels through the mountains – were good, the climate was temperate and the soil was fertile. Property was communally owned and there was a tradition of communal labour. The people were required to give a proportion of their crops and labour to the state in exchange for protection, with a well-organized system of control and distribution of water supply and of reserves of food. Three basic laws, against theft, laziness and deceit, were brutally enforced, though in general justly and without corruption, by a powerful army. They did not discover the idea of writing so administration was conducted by word of mouth and recorded by a complicated system of knotted ropes. The Inca and his nobility were able to live a luxurious and leisured life, which supported a culture of arts and artefacts which, for their time, bear comparison with any in the world.

The Andes Mountains in Peru rise to a peak of about 22,000 feet but the Incas lived mainly in the temperate slopes and valleys between 7000 and 12,000 feet. To the west are the lower foothills in which most of Peru's rich mining areas (for copper, silver, gold, lead, zinc, iron and other metals) are situated. These were also developed by the Incas, whose gold and silver were a particular

11

attraction for the Spaniards. Further west is the coastal region, including Lima and the port of Callao, which is mainly arid desert, kept cool by the Pacific Humboldt Current. To the east of the spine of the Andes, the ground falls away into the basin of the Amazon River, whose upper tributaries provide the soil most suitable for the cultivation of coca. Throughout their history, the Andean Indians have chewed coca leaves to relieve hunger and thirst and to make tea. Coca for these and other legitimate purposes, for example, for manufacturing medicines, still accounts for 10 per cent of Peru's coca production, the other 90 per cent being exported for illicit use as cocaine.

The Inca empire was overthrown in 1532 by Francesco Pizarro, leading 170 Spanish infantry, cavalry and artillery, who trapped and massacred an Inca army of 7000 by sheer nerve and guile. Under ruthless colonial rule, the Andean (Indian) population was reduced from 9 million to 600,000 in the following 100 years.[1]

When Peru became an independent republic in 1824, she was still governed by a small Spanish elite, using the classic techniques of 'divide and rule'. They had developed a growing *mestizo* (mixed blood) population who were taught Spanish and regarded themselves as Peruvians as distinct from Indians. They were known to the Andeans as *mistis*, a term whose overtones imply an educated petty bourgeoisie. The *mistis'* ability to read and write Spanish and their technical and administrative skills gave them an economic advantage over the Quechua-speaking *campesinos* (peasants). In army parlance, the white Peruvians were the officers and the *mistis* were the sergeants and the clerks, determined to maintain their position. Only 15 per cent of the population are now classed as 'Europeans' (though the majority of even these have some Indian blood), 37 per cent *mestizos* and 45 per cent mainly Quechua-speaking Indians, who have always resented the privileges of the *mistis*.[2]

The twentieth-century Quechua Indians, descendants of the Incas, have some remarkable characteristics which make them, despite their poverty, much more effective as human beings than other Latin American rural and shanty town populations. First is the tradition of communal action. This is reflected in the manner in which they organize themselves when they decide to migrate from the rural areas to Lima, which is now surrounded by some 5 million people in shanty towns. These, known as *pueblos jovenes* (young towns) are of a markedly higher standard than the shanty towns around other Latin American cities.

The Peruvian custom is for the people of a rural district to form a collective intention to migrate as a community. They thereupon elect a committee to organize this. The Lima hinterland is largely desert and the committee of a community planning to migrate go discreetly in advance to select a piece of unoccupied land, taking into account its prospects for water supply, access to work, and so on. They usually mark it out in 90 square metre plots, one for each family, with space for road systems, workshops and markets. There may be as many as 1000 families, with 5000 men, women and children planning to migrate. The committee then organize buses to collect these families, all bringing their possessions and rolls of matting for temporary shelter. During the night, they conduct a well-organized move, each family being directed to its allocated plot. Next morning, the police find the land occupied by a tent city of several thousand people.

The Peruvian government and municipal authorities have a wise rule that they will negotiate with squatter communities only through elected committees. If the committee members have done their reconnaissance, investigation and planning well, they will usually be able to negotiate approval for the settlement and title to the land. They will then organize a factory for making bricks on site, for which fortunately the soil is well suited. Within a few weeks, most of the families will have built brick houses at very little cost. The more enterprising ones will acquire a means of earning a living, such as an ancient taxi, truck or bus. Hernando de Soto has estimated that 90 per cent of Lima's public transport is provided by this 'informal sector', which pays no taxes and provides cheap competitive services; they also provide a large share of other urban services such as food markets and repair workshops.[3]

Within a year or two, most of the *pueblos jovenes* contain some two-storey houses, a rudimentary road system and an active array of shops, markets, garages, workshops and small factories. Most are eventually connected to public utilities such as water, sewerage and electricity. The people are poor and some live by begging, petty crime, or hawking on the streets of Lima, but the majority find other ways of earning a living, thanks to their own collective efforts.

A THIRST FOR EDUCATION

Another striking characteristic of the descendants of the Incas is their strong desire for education as a means of getting a better life. For most of Peru's history, the white rulers provided no facilities for the *campesinos* to learn Spanish, in order to maintain the advantages of the *mistis* and thereby keep their loyalty. This policy changed from 1960 onwards. In the 20 years from 1960 to 1980, the percentage of 18–25 year olds pursuing secondary education rose from 19 to 76 per cent. This placed Peru fourth in educational take-up amongst Latin American countries in 1980, having been fourteenth in 1960. This was accompanied by substantial economic growth, which averaged 5.5 per cent per year from 1949–70.[4]

This advance was not achieved without set-backs. In 1968 there was a *coup d'état* by a military junta which ousted the reformist President Fernando Belaunde Terry, and installed General Juan Velasco Alvarado in his place. This in itself was a familiar pattern of politics in Peru, which had been ruled by military juntas in the periods 1930–9 and 1948–56, and again briefly in 1962–3.

The junta which seized power in 1968 differed from the others in that its politics were radical. Its declared objective was a 'revolution from above' to pre-empt a revolution from below. Its politics can best be described as 'national socialist'. Like Hitler, Velasco used populist policies to arouse nationalist support. He broke up the *haciendas*, dispossessing the big landowners, to whom the previous government had delegated much of the local administration on feudal lines. Some estates were taken over as government cooperatives and others distributed between individual *campesinos*. (The landowners – the historic white elite – survived and regained much of their power and prosperity by acquiring control of many of the commercial enterprises in Lima and the mining areas.) Velasco also gained patriotic support by nationalizing many foreign enterprises, especially those owned by US corporations, which had invested $600 million in the country. The totalitarian governments of China and the USSR publicly applauded Velasco – just as the Soviet Communist Party in the early 1920s had applauded Hitler.

Though Velasco's measures were initially popular with the *campesinos*, it soon became clear that he had no intention of helping them to progress to equality with the *mistis* – the very revolution his measures were designed to pre-empt. He introduced censorship, closed a number of newspapers and radio stations and acquired 51 per cent of the stock of the three privately owned television stations. In 1969 he decreed that free education would be restricted to those who passed specific entrance grades. This struck a raw nerve with the Indian population, who saw it as a plan to perpetuate their subordination. He also threatened to close the San Cristobal de Huamango University in Ayacucho, in the heart of the Andean Highlands, which had been founded in 1677, closed in 1885 and reopened in 1959 – and where there was a little known Communist philosophy professor, Dr Abimael Guzman.

Nationalization, large-scale government intervention and alienation of foreign investors inevitably began to wreck the economy and alarmed the junta, who in 1975 dismissed Velasco and appointed General Francisco Morales Bermudez Cerrut as president. But the economy continued to decline, arousing growing frustration with the reversal of the rising expectations of 1949–74.[5]

ABIMAEL GUZMAN

This was the background against which Dr Abimael Guzman, an ideological Maoist, began in 1962 the long process of recruiting and organizing a system of cadres for what was to become *Sendero Luminoso* (SL), the Shining Path, in the Andean villages, emanating from the University of San Cristobal del Huamango in Ayacucho.

Guzman was born in 1934, the illegitimate son of a prosperous middle-class merchant. He was an outstanding student at school and university, where he obtained a doctorate. His theoretical ideology had been fired in 1960 with a desire for practical action after he had taken part, while still a PhD student in Arequipa, in a census designed to assist the relief effort amongst the victims of a devastating earthquake. He was enraged by what he saw of the squalor in which poor families on the fringes of the city lived, revealed when their miserable dwellings were laid bare by the earthquake.[6]

In 1962, at the age of 28, he was appointed to the philosophy chair in Ayacucho, where he was soon surrounded by a devoted band of student disciples, mainly of *mestizo* or Indian stock, to whom his lucid exposition of puritanical Maoism and his quiet intellectual passion aroused an intense response. At the same time, the Peruvian Communist Party, of which he was an active member, put him in charge of youth work.[7] Marxism was a fashionable doctrine amongst his fellow academics and Guzman persuaded them to set up a teacher training school in which cadres were recruited and trained to go out and spread his gospel in the Andean villages and towns, and to organize the people to interact with the university, especially with the student organizations[8] as a means of arousing the indignation of the students about the injustices inflicted on the poor. This long and patient build-up of his cadre organization was the first stage of the Maoist strategy of People's War, and Guzman began it 18 years before the Shining Path was ready to launch its armed struggle.

In 1965 the Peruvian Communist Party, already riven by schisms, made a disastrously unsuccessful attempt at a revolution sponsored by Cuba, using Che Guevara's 'guerrilla foco' theory – a theory finally discredited and abandoned after Guevara's own failure and death in Bolivia in 1967. Guzman and his pro-Peking section of the Party declined to participate, already recognizing its flaws. He was at this time beginning to organize a military wing of the party and, as his arrest seemed imminent, he was ordered by the party to go underground, and they sent him to cadre school in China. The Cultural Revolution was just beginning and his enthusiasm intensified. At the same time, he received thorough instruction in the People's War doctrine, including courses on 'open and underground work' and 'explosives and demolition'.[9]

The military take-over by General Velasco in 1968 further split the party. Velasco's national socialist measures were warmly applauded by Fidel Castro but Guzman rejected him as a fascist and saw the danger posed by the initial popularity of his reformist activities in reducing the revolutionary fervour amongst the masses, especially breaking up the *haciendas* and giving the land to the *campesinos*. Guzman, however, made the most of the junta's abolition of free education for those who had not already had some education. He commented: 'they knew that when the sons of workers and peasants open their eyes it endangers their power and wealth'.[10] Thousands of striking students, teachers and workers rioted in Ayacucho and the neighbouring town of Huanta, some throwing rocks and petrol bombs. About 20 people were killed, many of them children. The army restored order, but judged it wise to repeal the education decree. Guzman was imprisoned for a few months in Lima and then paid a second visit to China.[11]

THE FOUNDATION OF THE SHINING PATH

In February 1970, after further furious rows in the Peruvian Communist Party, Guzman carried the majority with him and formed a new 'Communist Party of Peru by the Shining Path of Jose Carlos Mariategui' – the full title of SL. Later he added 'and Marxism, Leninism, Maoism and the thoughts of Chairman Gonzalo'. 'Gonzalo' was the war name adopted by Guzman but he was also known by his students as 'Dr *Puka Inti*' (Quechia for Red Sun).[12]

Then, and throughout his campaign, the majority of his cadres had some form of university education and were found from the urban provincial middle class and from disaffected members of the intellectual elite.[13]

Thereafter, the build-up of the cadres continued through the 1970s, when SL was able to harness the disillusionment of the *campesinos* with Velasco's agrarian reforms, whereby the landlords had been replaced by bureaucrats sent from Lima to run the former *haciendas* as state cooperatives. The smaller estates had been distributed to a new class of 'rich peasants' (in Maoist terminology). The ordinary *campesinos* had no more say in their lives than they had had under the feudal system.

By the late 1970s Guzman was suffering from a painful skin complaint which was to plague him for the rest of his life – psoriasis – which was apparently exacerbated by long periods in high altitudes. In 1976 he resigned from his chair at Ayacucho and operated increasingly from Lima, where he had many cultured and artistic admirers from the 1960s who were living comfortable bourgeois lives and were happy to accommodate him. After another brief spell in prison in January 1979 he went underground. His 1979 police mugshot remained his public image until his capture in 1992.

The photographs used by SL propaganda posters were very different from the usual portrayal of a guerrilla leader in combat uniform carrying a gun. Guzman was almost invariably pictured in a suit carrying a book and wearing glasses, as the students who became his cadres had known him. This was the image which also most appealed to the *campesinos* and those who had migrated to the *pueblos jovenes* around Lima, longing for education for their children to lift them out of the rut.

The Maoist organization in the *pueblos jovenes* and urban areas had developed fast in the 1970s and by 1979, police intelligence reported that about 500 'people's schools' were operating in Lima alone. There were also reports of students and *campesinos* doing shooting practice in the jungles and the dunes in coastal areas around Lima; and there were reports of thefts of explosives and detonators from the mines. In April 1980, police intelligence warned the government that SL would launch its armed struggle in the following month.

These warnings were largely ignored but proved precisely accurate.

3 Coca Enters the War

THE START OF THE ARMED STRUGGLE 1980–1

In 1979 Guzman and his Central Committee had taken the decision to launch the armed struggle in 1980 and they chose 17 May, the day before the presidential election which was to bring Belaunde back to power. This was the first democratic election since General Velasco's military coup had ousted Belaunde in 1968. SL selected polling booths and ballot boxes as their first targets, to show contempt for the bourgeois democratic process. They selected the town of Chuschi, capital of a district about 30 km south of Ayacucho.

Chuschi was a small town of about 6500 inhabitants. On 17 May 1980, four masked students from the university in Ayacucho, armed with non-functioning pistols, entered the town hall, tied up the registrar, seized the registration book and the ballot boxes and burned them. New ballot boxes and voters' lists were delivered next day and the elections proceeded without further incident. A purely symbolic start.

For the remainder of 1980 the armed struggle continued in a very low key, with a number of bomb attacks both in the Andes and in Lima, a total of three people being killed. In 1981 there was a sharp escalation of the bombing campaign. In the first six months of that year there were over 800 bomb attacks on public buildings and rural police posts and there were nearly 50 bank robberies in Lima. By the end of the year there had been over 1200 terrorist attacks, but still only four people were killed, bringing the total for 1980 and 1981 to seven.[1]

Most of those killed were police officers or, in a few cases, victims chosen to gain approval from the villagers. In Chuschi, for example, two 'enemies of the people' publicly executed were cattle thieves from a neighbouring village.[2] It is clear, with hindsight, that SL spent 1980 and 1981 building up their support organizations in the villages and Lima, training their 'People's Guerrilla Army' and, perhaps more important, raising funds by bank robberies and extortion of protection money.

19

During 1980 and 1981 the police arrested some 500 people whom they classed as 'terrorists'. Some of them no doubt were but others were probably just villagers who were suspected of sympathizing with SL – which a large number of *campesinos* at this time clearly did, as a result of Guzman's painstaking agit-prop during the previous 18 years. On 22 June 1981 the Cardinal of Peru, Archbishop Juan Landazur, accused the police of torturing political detainees,[3] the first of many such accusations.

THE ESCALATION OF VIOLENCE 1982–4

In March 1982 Guzman's armed struggle entered a new phase; his People's Guerrilla Army launched a major offensive, operating in company-sized units of 100 or more. A well-coordinated attack by three columns of guerrillas numbering 450 in all attacked and held the security prison in Ayacucho, freeing 100 SL militants.[4] The bombings continued, with a particular concentration on electric power, resulting in the first of the many black-outs which were to plague Lima and other cities for the next ten years. Above all, they intensified their 'People's Justice', carrying out public trials and executions of officials, including the Mayor and Deputy Mayor of Ayacucho. Other victims were politicians, union leaders, school teachers, business people, individual *campesinos* who did not coop-erate with SL and leaders of local organizations such as the *Rondas Campesinas* (vigilantes for collective defence against banditry).

One such 'people's trial' was vividly described by a female witness:

> They stood the man in the town square, calling him a traitor and a coward. Then, in front of everyone, they cut off his head with a knife. Five minutes later they did the same with his pregnant wife. Then they said: 'Whoever does the same thing will receive the same punishment; we have 100 eyes and 100 ears; we know everything'. Frightened local officials in the highlands resigned *en masse* and teachers, judges and others whose names appeared on the SL hit list fled the region.[5]

Despite this barbarity, however, there was no doubt that Guzman still had a great deal of popular support at this time. In September 1982, over 30,000 people turned out for the funeral in Ayacucho of Edith Lagos, a young guerrilla commander killed by the police.[6]

In all, 170 people were killed in 1982. This was less than 4 per cent of the number who were to be killed two years later in 1984 but it was enough to provoke government counter-measures.

Up till the end of 1982, President Belaunde did not take the threat seriously, regarding it as within the capacity of the police to handle. He had steadfastly refused to allow the armed forces to take any part, presumably for fear of facilitating another military coup. On 29 December 1982, however, he declared a state of emergency in the three worst affected departments, Ayacucho, Huancavelica and Apurimac, and deployed 1000 troops in the area.[7] These were the first Emergency Military Zones (EMZs), which by mid-1980s were to incorporate 60 per cent of the population of Peru. In the EMZs, the civil and police authorities were subordinate to the army general who became, in effect, a military governor of the zone.

In 1983 and 1984, SL spread their activities more widely in the rural areas and intensified their bombings in Lima. The total killings by the two sides totalled 2807 and 4319 respectively in these years. Then the military actions in the EMZs took increasing effect and the killings declined to 697 in 1987 (see Table 3.1).

Between 5 and 10 per cent of those killed were members of the armed forces and the police (348 in 1989 and a peak of 455 in 1992). It is probable that the numbers killed by the security forces and the terrorists were roughly equal. Claims by the army that,

Table 3.1 Numbers Killed in the Terrorist War in Peru

1980	3	1988	1986
1981	4	1989	3198
1982	170	1990	3452
1983	2807	1991	3180
1984	4319	1992	3101
1985	1359	1993	1692
1986	1286	1994	640 (estimate)
1987	697	Total	27 894

Source: Peruvian government figures

for example, they had killed '80 terrorists' in a single ambush were usually interpreted by the public as meaning that they had shot 80 people believed, rightly or wrongly, to be terrorist supporters.

PRESIDENT GARCIA 1985

On completion of President Belaunde's five-year term, Alan Garcia Perez was elected president and took office on 28 July 1985. Garcia's party, APRA, was originally formed in Mexico in 1924, dedicated to ending the exploitation of American Indians and the elimination of US imperialism, also to the institution of a planned socialist economy and nationalization of foreign enterprises. By 1985 it had become a centre party advancing moderate socialist policies. It was also widely regarded as corrupt.

Garcia, at 34, became the youngest president in the western hemisphere. He was energetic and charismatic and had considerable appeal to the Indians. He also appreciated that it was necessary to retain the support of the army. His party was condemned as 'reformist' by SL, who disrupted voting in the EMZs, rejected overtures for talks, exploded the first car bomb in Lima and bombed APRA offices.

Garcia aroused the resentment of the army in August 1985 by forcing the resignation of three generals, including the comman-der-in-chief of the armed forces, as he held them responsible for some of the human rights violations of which the army was accused. He also conceded to SL demands to give convicted terrorists political status in the prisons, including the right to administer their own cell blocks (a mistake made by the British government with IRA prisoners in 1972). This meant that SL commanders could run their blocks as barracks, organizing military training and political classes throughout the day without interference. The prison staff never entered these blocks and were responsible only for those containing common criminals and for the security of the prison perimeter.

In some cases, prison staff also connived at a remarkable system of 'substitution'. An SL prisoner could arrange a few weeks' holiday by changing clothes with one of his visitors, who took his place in the SL prison block for a period agreed with his jailers. These deals were usually made with junior members of the prison staff, though the higher ranks were no doubt aware of the system.

Sometimes this may have been done out of genuine sympathy with the prisoners but it was probably used more often as an insurance policy against being put on SL's hit list.[8]

These substitutions also helped SL in several other ways. It enabled them to keep close touch with all their militants in that prison, getting reports on their attitudes and likely future performance. The SL hierarchy could give instructions for training and indoctrination. They could maintain the morale of the militants and reward them for loyalty. And – perhaps most important – they could smuggle weapons, ammunition and explosives into SL blocks.

On 18 June 1985, SL prisoners took advantage of a prison officers' strike to take a number of staff hostage in the SL blocks in the three major prisons in Lima – the Santa Barbara Women's Prison and the men's prisons at Lurigancho and El Fronton. President Garcia ordered the armed forces to restore order. At all three prisons the prisoners resisted with their small array of improvised grenades and the weapons which they had smuggled in or taken from the hostages.

At Santa Barbara the air force was in overall command and mounted an efficient operation, including one entry from the roof and two others through holes blasted in the walls. They killed three women prisoners in recapturing the prison. The army was more ruthless in recapturing Lurigancho and killed 124. The Marines recaptured El Fronton, which is on an island, and killed 135 prisoners.[9] The public generally deduced that, in view of the disparity of weapons, most of the 259 who died at Lurigancho and El Fronton were probably killed after they had surrendered.

This wholesale slaughter did immense harm to the reputation of the army and handed a permanent propaganda weapon to SL, who commemorated their martyrs on every anniversary thereafter.

GUZMAN TURNS TO COCA FOR FINANCE

By 1987 the army in the EMZs had made considerable inroads into SL's logistic organization, which was still based in the southern highlands in the departments of Ayacucho, Huancavelica and Apurimac. So SL opened a new front in the upper reaches of the Amazon basin in the Huallaga Valley. Here, the area planted with coca had increased from 1000 hectares in 1975 to over 100,000, with more than 200,000 families growing coca.[10] SL signalled their arrival in May 1987 with an attack by 200 armed men on a police post, killing 15 policemen.[11]

Initially, they levied a 5 per cent 'revolutionary tax' on the coca paste sold by the *campesinos* to the traffickers who exported it to Colombia. At a conservative estimate, this may have yielded about $30 million a year.[12] This was later supplemented further by the drug barons paying a facilitation fee of $10,000 to $15,000 for providing an airstrip for each take-off by an aircraft carrying coca paste out of the valley. This will be described more fully in Chapter 5.

In April 1989, General Alberto Arciniega took command of the army in the Huallaga Valley and, from the start, took a completely new line. He knew that the coca growers amounted to 80 per cent of the population of the valley, and deeply resented the harassment they were receiving from three different quarters: from crop eradication teams organized and financed by the US Drug Enforcement Administration (DEA); from SL, who extorted money from them and tried to enforce their alternative government at gunpoint; and from the army and the police, from whom they feared torture, disappearance or death if they cooperated with SL.

On his first day in the valley, Arciniega assembled the population of the small town of Uchiza and ordered them to replace the SL flag with the red and white national flag of Peru. They pleaded that, if they did, they would be massacred by SL. He replied that, if they continued to fly the SL flag, he would attack them with his helicopters but that if they flew the Peruvian flag he would protect them. He made it quite clear that all his efforts would go to eradicating SL from the valley and that he would not interfere with their production and export of coca paste.

As a result, he received unprecedented popular support, which yielded the intelligence which is the only means whereby a regular army can make contact with a guerrilla army in the jungle. In his seven-month tour of duty, he claimed to have carried out 320 helicopter operations, had 44 clashes with SL columns and inflicted 1100 casualties. There were allegations that the army still carried out human rights abuses and that disappearances increased, but Arciniega had a charismatic personality and the great majority undoubtedly supported him. Towards the end of his seven months, 30,000 *campesinos* gathered in Uchizo on Armed Forces Day and cheered his assertion that the fight was against SL, not against the growing of coca.[13]

Arciniega's success story soon got around the army and others copied his methods, many of them resenting the way the USA applied pressure on the army to respect human rights by restricting aid money. Some probably felt that the growing of coca should be discreetly encouraged, as it brought huge amounts of money, albeit illegally, into Peru; and that it was unfair for the USA to criticize Peru's toleration of cocaine production when they were failing to take effective action against their own consumers at home.

Following directly from this attitude came the growth of corruption amongst army officers happy to accept bribes from the drug barons to turn a blind eye to the outgoing flights carrying cocaine paste, as will be described in Chapter 5.

GARCIA'S LEGACY

President Garcia's five-year term ended in 1990. Peru's constitution at that time barred the retiring president from standing for a second term (though this has now been changed). The two main parties, Belaunde's AP and Garcia's APRA, had both been discredited in the period 1980–90, with widespread public unease about corruption and incompetence, and in 1990 the voters rejected them both and elected Alberto Fujimori, who stood for an entirely new party. This election will be discussed in Chapter 4.

Garcia's presidency was economically disastrous. As with the 'national socialist' military regime of 1968–80, his state intervention caused massive inflation which reached 7000 per cent when he handed over in 1990.

His record in the war against SL was a mixed one. By backing commanders like General Arciniega who turned a blind eye to coca production, he had in some places secured better relations between the army and the population. This, however, had been negated by accusations of abuse of human rights, of which the prison massacres of 1986 were a glaring example. On the other hand the public, both in Lima and the countryside, were well aware that human rights violations by SL – torture, kidnap, public executions and massacres – were a lot worse.

Although the number killed in the terrorist war fell from its peak of 4319 in 1984 to 697 in 1987, it rose again to 3198 in 1989 and 3198 in 1990. More important, SL had expanded its area of activity; it had secured an ample source of funding from the drug traffickers; and its political and military organization had reached its full maturity. There was, in fact, a very real threat of SL causing a total collapse of government and having in place a structure capable of taking power.

THE STRATEGY AND ORGANIZATION OF THE SHINING PATH

By the end of President Garcia's term of office, the Shining Path had reached its peak, both in its organization and in its finances.

Abimael Guzman was a puritanical disciple of Mao Zedong and based his strategy on the Doctrine of Protracted War which Mao had expounded in the 1930s. Guzman in the 1980s saw things in broad historical terms. He envisaged that the revolution in Peru would take about fifty years in five phases:[14]

1. Agitation and propaganda
2. Sabotage and the first guerrilla actions
3. Generalization of the guerrilla war
4. Establishing support bases and liberated areas
5. Civil war, with the guerrillas controlling the countryside around the cities, in which the final collapse of government would be brought about by armed uprisings.

He spent 10 years on Phase 1 (1970–80) – or 18 years if we include the period 1962–70 when he began to politicize trainee teachers and send them out to the towns and villages to carry out the patient process of agit-prop amongst the *campesinos* and the school children as described earlier.

In 1970 he created his formal party structure, tentatively at first, and in 1982 he moved into Phase 2 with the systematic terrorization and murder of local government officials and their collaborators.

By 1984, he had moved into Phase 3 and in 1987 he extended his support bases into the coca-growing areas in the Huallaga Valley – Phase 4 – which led in turn to a massive new source of finance from the Colombian drug barons.

In July 1988, he gave a prolonged interview to *El Diario*, a Lima newspaper acting as a mouthpiece for SL, and it published 41 pages in which he analysed the ideology, organization, strategy and tactics of his movement. He said that his original estimate of 50 years had been pessimistic and that it was already time to carry the war into the cities, Lima in particular. In other words, he sounded the call to advance into Phase 5.

He had by then moved himself and his Central Committee into Lima, and he ran this more or less in combination with the Metropolitan Committee which directed operations in the city itself and the surrounding *pueblos jovenes*.

This was the situation when President Fujimori took over from President Garcia in 1990.

4 President Fujimori and the Capture of Guzman

PRESIDENT FUJIMORI

The presidential election held in two ballots on 8 April and 10 June 1990 was contested by three candidates: Luis Alvaro Castro from Garcia's APRA party; Mario Vargas Llosa, a world-renowned novelist leading a coalition of centre parties (including AP) calling itself *Fredomo* (FD) Alliance; and Alberto Fujimori, a businessman of Japanese descent, who had recently formed a new party of his own, Change 90.

In the first ballot, Vargas Llosa led with 28 per cent of the vote, 3 per cent ahead of Fujimori, with the APRA candidate third. To most people's surprise, Fujimori won the run-off on 10 June with a comfortable 63 per cent of the vote. Unfortunately for him, however, in the congressional elections, held on 8 April before Change 90 had got fully into its stride, his party won only 16 per cent of the seats in the Lower House and 19 per cent in the Senate. So Fujimori took office on 28 July in face of an overwhelmingly hostile Congress, dominated by bitter and angry FD (AP) and APRA members.

During the presidential election, there had been much mud slinging at Fujimori and he was at one time at risk of being declared ineligible to stand on account of some property deals which were against the law. The challenge was handled by his lawyer, Vladimiro Montesinos, who managed to get the case settled satisfactorily. When Fujimori took power he appointed Montesinos as head of the National Intelligence Service (SIN); he was also a close adviser to the president on other matters. Montesinos was a shadowy figure, virtually never seen in public, who had been cashiered from the army as a captain and was alleged to have been involved in corrupt deals connected with drug trafficking. He was also believed to have a powerful influence on the appointment of senior army officers.

Fujimori's most immediate concern, however, was to tackle the country's economic troubles, including the 7000 per cent inflation bequeathed by Alan Garcia. He wisely chose Dr Carlos Bolona, a brilliant young businessman who had got his doctorate at Oxford, to be his finance minister. Inflation was brought down to 56 per cent by 1993 and business confidence was rapidly restored.

Fujimori, however, was frustrated by blocking tactics in Congress, and by the ineffectiveness and corruption of the judiciary. To be fair, the judges suffered constant intimidation and many were murdered if they refused to bow to the combination of threats and bribes. To borrow a phrase coined in Colombia, they were offered the choice between silver and lead. As a result, less than 10 per cent of terrorist cases had been coming to trial at all, the judges having ruled that there was 'insufficient evidence to proceed'. In those that did come to trial, there were many perverse acquittals, and allegations that some of the accused were convicted on the tacit understanding (again enforced by 'silver or lead') that they would be quietly released after serving a short period in prison.

On 5 April 1992, with the support of the army, Fujimori dissolved the Congress, suspended the judiciary in a 'self coup' (*autogulpe*) and ruled by decree, pending fresh elections based on a new constitution. The result of this coup was a surge in Fujimori's popularity. The public as a whole, and especially the poorer sections of it, shared his exasperation with the corruption and incompetence of the country's administration and with the traditional parties, the Congress and the judiciary, who had offered them no protection against domination and violence from all quarters, both in rural and urban areas.

Fujimori temporarily replaced the judges by military courts; in 1993, when the civilian judiciary was restored, judges and witnesses sat behind one-way glass so that neither the accused nor the public could see their faces.

In October 1993, Fujimori narrowly won a referendum, with 52 per cent of the vote, for a new constitution giving stronger powers to the president and removing the bar on the incumbent standing for re-election. A new Congress was elected which endorsed his presidency as legitimate. This, among other things, led to the US government resuming its aid programmes, which had been suspended since the 1992 coup.

WHY GUZMAN SHIFTED TO LIMA

Politically and economically the country seemed to be on the road
to recovery. There had, however, been a very tricky period in the
months immediately following the coup, in the summer of 1992.
SL, as described earlier, were concentrating their efforts overwhelmingly on Lima and, with business people and the middle
classes alarmed by giant bombs in the heart of the business district
in Miraflores, there was a serious risk of a collapse of government,
probably accompanied by a military coup, or possibly by an SL
seizure of power like those in Cuba in 1959 and Nicaragua in
1978.

There may have been one or all of three reasons why Guzman
decided to shift his focus to Lima: first, his assessment as published
in *El Diario* in 1988 (see p. 27) that the time was ripe to move into
Phase 5 of his revolutionary plan; second, his desire to seek relief
from his skin complaint, psoriasis; and third, because his second in
command and mistress, Elena Iparraguirre, was urging him to
bring the revolution to its triumph in Lima while he was still
young enough to enjoy power. Guzman's late wife, Augusta, had
been a passionate Andean Marxist who wanted SL to continue
the revolution where its roots lay – amongst the *campesinos* in the
Sierra – even if it took 50 years. It may be no coincidence that
Augusta died in November 1988. Guzman, seen in a video later
seized in a police raid, implied in an emotional eulogy over her
corpse that she had committed suicide; but there were others who
believed that she had been murdered.[1]

THE CAPTURE OF ABIMAEL GUZMAN

In June 1990, the police raided a house in Monterrico, a middle-
class suburb of Lima, where they suspected that Guzman had
been living. Guzman had, in fact, left the house a short time
earlier, but the police found another video tape, recording a party
with some of his friends. It showed him dancing with Elena
Iparraguirre to the music of *Zorba the Greek*. In the background
were a number of recognizable friends including a former nun
called Nelly Evans. This was the start of a classic police
intelligence operation which led to his capture in 1992.

Nelly Evans came from a rich family, had a British grandfather and carried a British passport. She had entered the order of the Sisters of the Immaculate Heart of Mary and became captivated by the ideas of liberation theology. She left the order and married a former priest but her marriage broke up when she became increasingly involved with SL. The police came to suspect that she might be the movement's accountant, and her friendship with Guzman was confirmed by the video. The police therefore stepped up surveillance of her.

Six months later, one day in January 1991, she became aware that the police were following her. By that time Guzman was indeed living in her house. She deliberately diverted her route and played for time, knowing that Guzman would guess why and leave the house, which he did. When she arrived home the police followed her in and found evidence of Guzman's recent presence. She was arrested and remains in prison but, once again, they had missed Guzman.

They then turned their attention to others believed to be friends of Nelly Evans amongst the radical chic community in Lima. One of these was her niece, a ballet dancer called Maritza Garrido Lecca. Maritza, born in 1965, was the youngest of a large well-to-do Catholic family: she had herself at one time wanted to be a missionary amongst the *campesinos*, but she developed exceptional talent as a dancer at school and embarked on the disciplined life of a ballerina. She married young but left her husband when he began to take issue over her friendship with another man. She had considerable success in classical ballet and might have become Peru's leading ballerina but she became disillusioned with it, regarding it as repressive and bourgeois. After a visit to Cuba in May 1986, she came back enthusiastic about the power of contemporary dance to further the revolution, and began to work for SL, initially on open-front tasks such as distributing leaflets. She began to perform in propaganda ballets and to teach contemporary dance in the *pueblos jovenes*. Then she moved in to live with her aunt, Nelly Evans, and their relationship was noted by the police. Later she took a second husband, an architect called Carlos Inchaustegui, who was also involved with SL. They set up house in another middle-class suburb, at 459 Callo Uno, Los Sauces, in which she converted the ground floor into a studio for teaching contemporary dance. Upstairs were a number of rooms, in which she accommodated Abimael Guzman, Elena Iparraguirre and two other women who were members of his Central Committee staff. In all, there were six people living in the house. Unusually for such a substantial house in a prosperous suburb, there was no telephone. All calls were made from public call boxes to avoid the risk of telephone tapping. Presumably to avoid the risk of appearing unusual, there were no armed guards in the house nor, apparently, anyone watching out to detect evidence of police surveillance.

In November 1991, a new commander, General Antonio Ketin Vidal, was appointed to DINCOTE, the police anti-terrorist intelligence service. Vidal was a dedicated professional police officer; a *mestizo* of humble origin, he went to university and is himself an intellectual, a student of philosophy with a love of classical music. In his young days he had been in love with a ballerina and they had wanted to get married but she had insisted that he must leave the police. He decided that he could not abandon his career and remained unmarried until 20 years later. He never heard from his ballerina again until the day after he had captured Guzman and his friends, when she telephoned to congratulate him and told him that he was right to stay in the police.

He took command of DINCOTE a few months after the arrest of Nelly Evans and his prime task was, of course, the capture of Guzman. This became increasingly urgent in the summer of 1992, with bombings in Lima and confidence in the army eroded by accusations of corruption and violation of civil rights, giving rise to a real fear that the government might collapse. Vidal realized that it was vitally important that Guzman's prestige should not be further reinforced by another police raid which failed to catch him.[2]

For this reason he decided to rely on a patient and unobtrusive intelligence operation to detect for certain where Guzman was and to ensure that he was there at the time the raid went in. He decided to keep the entire operation on a strictly need-to-know basis and, in particular, not to give any details of his progress to his superiors. He was sure that, with a mixture of impatience, a desire to take a share of the credit and to make the most of the publicity splash, some of them would try to rush the pace and prejudice the final and most delicate stages of the operation.[3]

Because of Maritza's link with Nelly Evans, Vidal had been discreetly watching her house for several months before he decided on the moment to raid it. He had sent some of his police agents to obtain jobs as gardeners in a nearby park, and as street cleaners and refuse collectors, as well as detailing others to shadow Maritza whenever she left the house. The absence of a telephone aroused their suspicion and they also noticed that the curtains of the upstairs rooms were kept permanently drawn, day and night. They observed that Maritza was buying much larger quantities of food and drink than would be consumed by two people, yet no one other than herself and her husband, and the young dance students who went in and out of the ground floor studio, was ever seen to enter or leave the house. They also saw her buy shirts and sweaters for a big fat man, as Guzman was, whereas her husband was small and slim. But it was the rubbish bin which finally convinced Vidal that Guzman was there, for the rubbish included empty packets of Kenacort-E cream for the treatment of psoriasis. As further confirmation, there were many stubs from Winston cigarettes, which a blow-up of the *Zorba the Greek* video had revealed were the brand which Guzman smoked. Vidal mounted his raid on Saturday 12 September 1992 four days after the rubbish was spotted.

Deliberately or otherwise, Vidal picked a time when nearly all the hierarchy above him would be at a party – a reception for a visiting British Cabinet minister, Kenneth Clarke – at the residence of the British ambassador. In retrospect it became clear that none of those at the party had any idea that there was an important operation in progress. Fujimori himself was away on a fishing trip.

Vidal's surveillance that evening confirmed that the occupants of the suite upstairs were still at home, with the lights on. Vidal, in plain clothes, parked in a small unmarked car in a side street from which he could watch.

At this point they had a piece of luck; one of Maritza's uncles, Celso Garrido Lecca, was Peru's most distinguished composer, and was planning with his partner, Patricia Awapara, to produce a ballet of *Antigone*, for which he had written a score. Celso was himself a fashionable Marxist, though not connected with SL and unaware of his niece's involvement. The ballet was to have an allegorical message about military repression in Peru and Maritza had enthusiastically agreed to dance the title role. On an impulse, Celso and Patricia decided to go and discuss the ballet with Maritza. At 8 pm they parked their car and knocked on the door to see if she was at home. Maritza was not expecting visitors and she took some time to come down. They were about to leave when she came to the door and called out to ask who was there. Recognizing her uncle's voice, she opened the door and let them into the dance studio where they talked about *Antigone* for half an hour. The police raiding force were ready, disguised as cleaners and as a courting couple in an adjacent café, and when the door was opened to let out the visitors they pounced. Pinning Celso, Patricia and Maritza to the studio floor they burst into the upstairs rooms and arrested all the four people there, including Guzman, who was watching television. None was armed and the only shot fired was when Elena Iparraguirre, the only one to resist, was beating her fists against the leading policeman. She hit his gun, which fired accidentally and grazed one of his fellow policemen.

A few minutes later they were joined by General Vidal, who addressed Guzman courteously and shook his hand. Guzman, who was clearly expecting to be summarily shot, responded equally courteously, saying that even if they killed him they could not kill his ideas, which had now spread throughout the country, and that the revolution would prevail. But the interrogation had begun on a civilized note and continued in that atmosphere in the car and back in Vidal's office.

From there, Vidal had the arrest reported to the broadcasting stations, so it went out publicly before his superiors were aware of it. Vidal feared that, if the authorities knew first, they might have Guzman shot before the news became public. Vidal was convinced that far more value would be gained from Guzman alive, and subsequent events have confirmed this. Vidal also, with a respect for the law, did not wish to be party to a summary execution without trial.

Vidal was decorated and given a reward, which he gave to a charity, and he was promoted to higher rank, with responsibility for police personnel and training. The cynics commented that, in a society like that of Peru, there were people who had reason to fear what a first-class and embarrassingly honest police intelligence chief might unearth.

THE REPENTANCE LAW

In the immediate wake of Guzman's capture, another 200 SL leaders were captured, some from documents found in his headquarters. Following this, a measure which had been introduced on the recommendation of General Vidal in May 1992 – the Repentance Law – began to take dramatic effect. This law was derived from laws and procedures which had originally been devised by the British in Malaya in the 1950s.[4] Captured or surrendered terrorists or supporters were 'turned' – that is, in exchange for cooperation in the war against the terrorists they were promised leniency, generous rewards, protection and, if they wished, a new identity. This went further than the age-old practices of leniency or plea bargaining offered by most judiciaries to criminals who give 'state's evidence'; it asked for positive cooperation in the war and gave much higher rewards. The Italians followed a similar technique in the war against the Red Brigades in 1991–3 and then applied it equally successfully against the Mafia.[5] General Vidal had been most interested to learn about this experience in 1991.

Under the Peruvian Repentance Law, SL members and supporters who gave information of particular value in identifying terrorists or their whereabouts and eroding the terrorist organization were able, not only to get reduced sentences (usually half or one-third) or sometimes a full pardon without going to trial at all; they were also guaranteed secrecy and protection; also, if they were judged to have earned it, a new identity, with their families, in a different area or country, with the financial resources to start a new life. The rewards for really good inside information could be very large, but would cost far less than, say, an extra helicopter and would be much more cost effective.

One of Fujimori's most courageous and successful measures was the arming of the village defence forces, the *Rondas Campesinas* (RCs). These had originally been formed by local initiative by the *campesinos* over ten years previously, as a 'home guard' to protect themselves against cattle thieves. They had applied for legal registration in August 1980 but this was refused by President Belaunde.[6] Fujimori issued them mainly with shot guns, because these were lethal only at short ranges. To many people's surprise, this did *not* result in a leakage of weapons to the terrorists (in contrast to the experience with the Popular Forces in Vietnamese villages in the 1960s). This was because the RCs greatly valued their weapons as a deterrent to thieves as well as for defence against terrorists. By early 1992 there were 526 villages with armed RCs and another 1117 had applied for arms.[7] Another dividend was that – particularly after the capture of Guzman – the RCs provided a useful source of intelligence for the army and police, once they had become confident that SL were on the way to defeat.

The best intelligence of all, however, came from the surrendered terrorists themselves, again reflecting British experience.[8] By August 1993, 400 terrorists had surrendered under the Repentance Law[9] and the numbers escalated fast. The number of full-time terrorists in the SL columns in the Huallaga Valley fell from 1000 to 250 in the 12 months from January 1993 to January 1994;[10] it was announced on 2 June 1994 that 3095 SL terrorists had surrendered in the previous two years.[11] The annual number of people killed in the war fell from 3101 in 1992 to 1692 in 1993 and about 500 in 1994 (see p. 21).

Abimael Guzman was sentenced to life imprisonment. He retained his revolutionary aims but he declared that the phase of the world revolution which began in 1848 had come to an end with the collapse of Communism in Russia and East Europe in 1989 and that the time had come to suspend the armed struggle in Peru. After making a number of television statements to this effect, and writing three letters to President Fujimori, he submitted a long paper of some 6000 words which was published in the press; in this, he analysed the previous 150 years and the coming 50 years and explained how the revolution would eventually triumph if there were now a period of peace.

His view was accepted by most of the *Senderistas* in prison and a proportion of those still at large, increasing numbers of whom came in to surrender. Some militant groups, however, carried on their campaign of bombing and assassination, one in the northeast in the Huallaga Valley which continued to provide the bulk of SL's funds, and the other in the southern highlands in the original heartlands around Ayacucho. Known as *Red Sendero*, these were under the leadership of Oscar Ramirez Durand, who used the war name 'Feliciano'.

This split, and Guzman's readiness to discourage his followers from continued violence, can be put down to the way he was treated on his first capture by General Vidal. Thereafter the decision to continue the dialogue with him with a view to saving bloodshed proved far more beneficial than torturing and executing him, which would have made him a martyr and achieved nothing. By 1994 it was clear that Guzman's pronouncements from his prison cell were the biggest single factor in dismantling the Shining Path.

HUMAN RIGHTS AND CORRUPTION

The war against SL was always a dirty war and will remain so as long as it lasts. The worst offenders were the terrorists but this does not excuse those on the government side who accepted bribes or violated human rights, nor undo the harm they did.

The terrorsts' control of the population rested on their reputation for ruthlessness in torturing, maiming and killing people who opposed them, or who openly collaborated with the government as local officials in rural villages or *pueblos jovenes* or impeded SL in other ways. An example was given on p. 20.

Many people who become terrorists are first involved in revolutionary movements as genuine idealists, motivated by compassion for the deprived and hatred of oppression. When the movement uses terrorism many such people leave it but others become brutalized and rationalize their killing. The ballerina Maritza who housed Guzman in Lima was an example and her friends could hardly believe the change in her. She was reported by one of them to have said: 'we may kill a child in a car bomb but we are working for a society where no child dies – and at the moment thousands die. It's a war. There's no other way.'[12]

Of the average of just over 3000 people killed in the conflict in Peru every year from 1989 to 1992 (see p. 121) about half, 1500, were recorded as 'civilians' and the remainder were 300–450 soldiers and 1200 'terrorists', because the army and police class all those they kill as 'terrorists'. To take the figures for 1992 as an example, government statistics showed that 455 army and police personnel and 1482 civilians were killed by terrorists. There is no reason to doubt these figures and the public was well aware of the massacres carried out by SL. But the statistics also showed that 1151 'terrorists' were killed by the army and police in that year.[13] While some hundreds of these undoubtedly were terrorists, many people in the villages and *pueblos jovenes* claimed to have seen with their own eyes that several hundreds of others were ordinary people whom the army merely regarded as SL sympathizers, willing or unwilling. The stories they told, to Peruvian journalists and to visiting researchers from the Red Cross or Amnesty International, gave rise to much domestic and international indignation and to cuts in foreign aid on account of violations of human rights.

Some of these violations were proved beyond doubt. The massacre of 259 prisoners in Lurigancho and El Fronton Prisons

in 1986 was described on p. 23. Another case was the murder of
nine students and a professor at La Cantuta University, who
'disappeared' in July 1992. Following a tip-off from a dissident
army officer, a group of journalists dug up the remains of the
bodies including a severed head, and found a key which fitted the
locker of one of the missing students.[14] There was strong forensic
and circumstantial evidence linking the incident to nine army
officers who, in February 1994, were charged and tried in a
military court. Two officers were sentenced to twenty years in
prison and the others to terms of between one and five years.
There was some public suspicion, however, that these had been
made scapegoats for people much higher up and President
Fujimori's popularity rating dropped to its lowest level since
before the 1992 coup.[15]

Corruption is endemic in Peru, as it is in many other countries,
rich and poor. In underdeveloped countries, this is almost
inevitable in the context of their economies. The business and
other middle classes, who travel and deal with business people and
officials from the countries which invest and trade in Peru expect,
not surprisingly, to have a lifestyle comparable with that of people
of similar status in North America and West European countries;
in fact they may feel that they would be humiliating Peru if they
did not. On the other hand, the much lower Peruvian GNP per
capita is reflected in the tax revenue so, for public servants at
least, the government budget just cannot afford this. Moreover,
the administrative structure is not efficient enough to extract
anything approaching the taxes which the law lays down. In
Peru, the tax take is supposed to amount to 14 per cent of the
GNP. Before Fujimori took over, the inland revenue authorities
were managing to extract only about 8 per cent. This has been
considerably raised but is not believed to be anywhere near the 14
per cent it should be. Business people can organize their
companies to pay themselves and their staffs reasonably high
salaries, and find ways of 'creative accounting' to avoid paying the
taxes that they should. This is not so easy for the public sector.
The consequence is obvious.

At the other end of the scale, millions of *campesinos* live close to
subsistence level and pay no taxes at all. As was described in
Chapter 2, several million settlers in the *pueblos jovenes* live by an
informal economy providing Lima's transport and other services
without records or accounts and pay no taxes. The government

has little option but to accept this, as otherwise many more would starve or be driven to crime and prostitution. And, of course, the bus and taxi corporations and many of the high street shopkeepers have been driven out of business so there is no tax revenue from them either.

One result of this is that the salaries the exchequer can afford to pay generals and colonels in the army and police are considerably less than those of secretaries and chauffeurs in the prosperous business sector, and only a small fraction of what the business people themselves can earn. A two-star general in 1993 was paid $284 (£189) per month basic pay including benefits; he was also provided with a car, military chauffeur and steward. If he chose to forgo the chauffeur and steward, he could in addition draw their wages of $53 a month each (itself hardly a wage to inspire undying loyalty from the soldier in the ranks!), raising the general's total receipts to $400 (£277) per month. To put this in perspective for British readers, the general could choose between £44 or £64 a week – both considerably less than the British state old age pension. It is no surprise that this drives some of them to corruption but, in the prevailing circumstances, there is no way of paying the public sector any more. Corruption in the police and the army, as well as facilitating international drug trafficking, inevitably also results in extortion from the public, which adds to the unpopularity already caused by abuses of human rights. It is a complex problem.

Corruption had been given a big boost by a policy introduced by President Garcia. In order to control the army, Garcia terminated the system whereby they promoted and appointed their own senior officers, and he vested the government with the power to co-opt and appoint higher commanders who were prepared to go along with his left of centre ideology. It was alleged, however, that he chose corrupt generals in the knowledge that their loyalty could be assured by the threat of public exposure and prosecution.

The policy of co-option was continued by President Fujimori and later extended under his constitution to promotion of all generals and admirals. The commander general (head of all three armed services), instead of serving a fixed term, may now remain in command for as long as the president chooses. Advice on promotions and appointments comes from the National Intelligence Service (SIN), headed by Vladimiro Montesinos, which is alleged to monitor senior officers by telephone tapping. The system caused a division within the higher and middle ranks of the army between the co-opted officers and the 'institutionalists' who resented the degree of political control of the army. As in Garcia's day, allegations of corruption and human rights violations continue, especially against Fujimori's chosen commander general, Hermoza, against whom there was an attempted military coup led by dissident army officers in November 1992.[16]

The opportunities offered by army corruption have also been fully exploited by the drug barons who, thanks to the billions of dollars paid each year for cocaine by addicts all over the world, have plenty of money from which to pay the bribes. The effect of this on drug trafficking is discussed in the next chapter.

5 Cocaine Production in Peru

THE PERUVIAN COCA PLANTATIONS

Peru exports about 700 metric tonnes (MT) of washed basic cocaine paste each year. Figures for the prices paid for the paste and for pure cocaine by brokers, importers and dealers vary enormously. There are many reasons for this. The cocaine content of coca leaves varies from 0.72 per cent in Bolivia to 0.28 per cent in Colombia, with Peru in the middle at about 0.53 per cent.[1] Costs of transport by aircraft, boats or couriers, in bulk and in small smuggled packages, vary; and so do the sizes of payments to terrorists, corrupt police officers, soldiers, and officials in countries down the line. The price which consumers are prepared to pay on the streets also varies, depending on the perceived degree of dilution (on which the buyer may be misled), and on the effectiveness of police control exercised in different countries. The figures given in this chapter, therefore, provide only some typical examples, to illustrate the enormous escalation in price from the grower to the consumer.

Whatever figures are used, it usually works out that less than 1 per cent of the street price goes to the farmer who produces the cocaine paste and more than 99 per cent to criminals acting outside the law (terrorists, traffickers, corrupt officials, smugglers, brokers, importers, distributors and dealers) from the coca growing areas to the streets of Europe and the USA.

Estimates of world production vary enormously.[2] They generally agree, however, on the breakdown within the Andes. Peru provides 61 per cent of the cocaine paste, Bolivia 21 per cent and Colombia 18 per cent. To produce pure cocaine the cocaine paste is refined in laboratories in Colombia (75 per cent), Bolivia (15 per cent) and Peru (5 per cent) with 10 per cent elsewhere.[3] The Colombian drug cartels, now overwhelmingly the Cali cartel, dominate the distribution worldwide. Marketing and exporting are mainly done by apparently legitimate multinational corpora-

41

tions organized on mafia lines, which also carry out legal business of various kinds to provide cover for producing and selling drugs and laundering the proceeds. These multinational corporations are usually headed by Colombians, resident either in Colombia or the USA, where there is a large immigrant Colombian community.

Washed basic cocaine paste contains between 70 per cent and 90 per cent pure cocaine. The refined product is transported to the USA and Europe as pure cocaine powder, to get maximum value into the packages to be smuggled. The importers, distributors and dealers then commonly 'cut' it, that is, dilute it with cheap white powders such as glucose, flour, bleach or talcum, both to inflate the receipts and to make it safer and more amenable to use. The cut cocaine sold on the streets is usually between 30 and 60 per cent pure. Some is converted into 'crack' by a process which will be described in Chapter 9, as it is done almost entirely in the consumer countries.

Well over half the coca produced in Peru has traditionally been grown in the Upper Huallaga Valley (see Chapter 3) in the vicinities of Tingo Maria and Tarapoto. The Huallaga River is a tributary of the Amazon, passing through fairly high tropical jungle. Due to military pressure and to a fungus which attacked the coca plants, more of the production has recently moved lower down the Huallaga and further into the highlands.

PRODUCTION OF COCAINE PASTE

Approximately 120,000 hectares (300,000 acres) are believed to be under coca cultivation in Peru. Coca has always been a legal crop, used by the Andean Indians as freely as alcohol and tobacco in other countries. But the traffickers in illicit cocaine offer a price which makes coca by far the most profitable crop, between twice and eight times more profitable than cocoa, four times more than rubber and forty times more than maize.[4] Coca and cocaine exports, at the prices paid to exporters, illicit and legal (e.g. for medical use), may account for 35 per cent of the total exports of Colombia and Peru, and some say as much as 80 per cent of Bolivia's. For all these reasons, attempts to encourage crop eradication and substitution for coca have met with at best half-hearted support by Andean governments and hostility, sometimes violent, by the *campesinos* who grow it. This hostility is egged on by the drug traffickers and by the terrorists whom they finance.

In Peru, four crops of about 125 kg of coca leaves are harvested each year per hectare, that is, 600 kg of leaves per hectare per year. The *campesinos* can sell the leaves for about $2 per kg or $1200 per hectare. They generally convert them, however, first into coca paste and then into washed basic cocaine paste, which reduces the weight by 100 to 1, that is, to 6 kg of the paste per hectare. The farmers have to pay the labour involved in processing so they charge about $400 per kg of the washed basic cocaine paste; thus for 6 kg they get about $2400 per hectare per year – double what they would get from selling the leaves unprocessed.

Peru's 120,000 hectares produce a little over 700,000 kg of washed basic cocaine paste per year, most of which goes to Colombia for refinement.

The first stage of processing is labour intensive; the coca leaves are soaked in paraffin or petrol and trampled by the feet of *pisadores*; this precipitates the alkaloids and produces coca paste containing about 40 per cent pure cocaine. The trampling is a traditional ritual in the Andes, in which the *pisadores* chew some of the paste and end up in a high state of euphoria.

The next stage is for this coca paste to be treated with sulphuric acid and potash of permanganate, which further reduces the impurities. The resulting washed basic cocaine paste is then sold to the traffickers to be flown to Colombia.

The final refinement into pure cocaine requires the use of ether and acetone. Nearly 12 kg of ether are needed to process each kg of the paste, producing 700–900 gms of pure cocaine.[5] This can be a dangerous process, which is why the *campesinos* do not normally do it themselves. Ether is volatile and, on reaching a critical vapour percentage in the air, becomes highly combustible or, in confined spaces, explosive; it can be set off by a spark from a hobnailed boot on a stone or by an electric light switch. The refinement is therefore generally done in properly equipped and controlled laboratories, 75 per cent of which are in Colombia.

FLYING OUT THE PASTE

The export of paste from Peru to Colombia involves the first stage of the clandestine and criminal processes which end up with illicit cocaine or crack being sold on the streets. The paste is bought by *traquateros* (traffickers) who operate around the villages, trying to dodge the police and the army (other than those who have been bribed). The *traquatero* haggles to pay the lowest price possible and is part of a Peruvian-based trafficking organization whose leader, a minor 'baron', arranges transport and sells the paste in bulk to a Colombian cartel, sometimes for as much as ten times the farmer's price – $3000–4000 per kg.

Out of his profit, the Peruvian baron pays the pilots of light aircraft to fly the paste to Colombia; he also pays a bribe either to Peruvian army officers or to the Shining Path terrorists – or both – to 'facilitate' the use of airstrips, protecting them while the aicraft land, load and take off, usually at night. In the Huallaga Valley in 1994 there were about 82 such airstrips, of which 14 were controlled by the army (i.e. with resident army posts), another 10 known and patrolled by the air force and about 58 clandestine – a varying number, because on flat ground an airstrip for light aircraft can be very quickly made.[6]

The average facilitation fee in 1993 was $15,000 per landing. For this, the terrorists would prepare and secure an airstrip or a corrupt army officer would turn a blind eye to the use of an existing one.

Up till 1994, the largest of the Peruvian *traquatero* organizations in the Huallaga Valley was led by Demetrio Chavez Penaherrara (war name 'El Vaticano') who was arrested in January 1994 in Cali, the headquarters of the largest Colombian drug cartel. He had been selling some 60,000 kg of paste per year to the cartel. He was normally resident in a luxurious and well-guarded country house in Campanilla, close to the Huallaga River but, fearing arrest, he had fled to Cali, where he hoped to become a Colombian citizen. When arrested, he was found in possession of $60,000, presumed to be intended for a bribe to gain his freedom if needed.[7]

El Vaticano's arrest may have been one of the factors which accelerated the shift of coca planting from the Upper Huallaga Valley down the river and up into the highlands. He led the biggest of eight rival 'firms' which between them organized about a hundred gangs of *traquateros*. One of his brothers, Elias ('Lan Chile') is believed to have taken over his firm (eight other brothers were in prison). The other seven firms continued to operate, the next largest run by a Colombian, Waldo Vargas

Arias, also exporting from the Upper Huallaga Valley, averaging 40,000 kg per year. The other six operated several hundred miles further south, around Ayacucho and in the province of Madre de Dios, bordering Brazil and Bolivia.[8]

The payments to the pilots of the light aircraft and the bribes to the army officers or the terrorists, though lucrative to an individual, were small in relation to the profits of the *traquatero* organization. The average light aircraft carried 300–400 kg of paste. Compared with the *campesinos'* price of $400 per kg, the pilot received about $30 per kg or $9000–12,000 per flight. Even after paying the costs of his aircraft, this could leave him more from a single flight than from a full year's normal salary.

BRIBERY OF PERUVIAN ARMY OFFICERS

A corrupt army officer could earn a lot more for himself than that. A *commandante* (lieutenant-colonel) could sometimes receive the whole facilitation fee, with no costs for him to pay – $15,000. His basic salary in 1994, with benefits, was about $2400 a year plus some perks such as an army car with driver and petrol, so $15,000 could amount to about six years' salary in a single night. More commonly, however, the fee would have to be shared out with others in the know; but in a six-month tour of duty in the valley he could expect to be involved in quite a lot of flights. There were several flights out every night.

President Fujimori was elected in 1990 with a mandate to tackle corruption. (Was any president ever elected without claiming such a mandate?) Since the judiciary and the Congress themselves contained many corrupt members, he was able to make little progress until he suspended both in his coup in April 1992. In 1993, 32 army officers were charged with corruption and other drug-dealing offences, of whom 13 were serving prison sentences by February 1994, when another 55 were named as under investigation.[9]

This military corruption by the drug barons became a regular feature from 1987 onwards after a number of senior officers had adopted a policy of condoning the production and export of coca paste in order to secure the cooperation of the *campesinos* in defeating the SL terrorists (see pp. 24–5). Many *campesinos* would try to satisfy both sides, cooperating with whoever was threatening them, but in the end most came to realize that their best hope was to support the side which seemed likeliest to win, as the only way to be rid of the war. Army commanders who helped them to sell their most profitable crop sometimes achieved spectacular successes against SL, gaining prestige, promotion and credit for 'winning the hearts and minds of the people'.

It was a small step from this to corruption of junior officers and it was rumoured that some senior generals, officials and ministers were a party to this and rotated officers who were willing to cooperate, giving them short tours of duty in the coca areas with the expectation of earning enough to acquire comfortable houses in a safe residential area in Lima, to buy new cars and to build up a healthy bank balance for securing the future. Some of the ministers and senior army officers may have believed that there was no other way of getting people paid a pittance to take on the dangerous life of an army officer in this war at all. Junior officers who became corrupt were also thereafter vulnerable to coercion, like corrupt generals appointed under Garcia's 'co-option' system (see pp. 39–40). Possibly some of those charged in 1993 and 1994 were chosen as scapegoats because they did not play ball.

The Huallaga Valley was a two-star general's command. As explained in Chapter 4, the salary of a two-star general in 1994 (commanding about 10,000 men), including benefits in cash and in kind, was $284 a month ($2400 a year), or $400 a month ($4800 a year) if he went without his chauffeur and steward.[10] A lieutenant-colonel got about $250 a month and a soldier or police officer in the ranks only $50–60, on the basis that he would get part or all of his food and accommodation free. None of them could hope to live or keep a family on that, so they had two options: to supplement their income by 'moonlighting' – doing half a day's work for the army and a part-time job – or, more likely, using the opportunities inherent in the job for corruption. When on active service in the field, the moonlighting option was not available. The surprising thing is that there were any uncorrupt officers at all!

It is a fair assumption that, of the estimated $150 million paid per year by the *traquatero* barons for facilitation of cocaine paste flights to Colombia, about half went to corrupt army officers and the other half, about $75 million, went to finance the SL terrorists, their main source of funds from 1987 onwards.

THE EFFECT ON PERU'S ECONOMY

Peru's Gross Domestic Product (GDP) in 1993 was about $25 billion.[11] The world production of cocaine was estimated at 900–1200 MT per year, of which 61 per cent came from Peru,[12] that is, around 70,000 kg per year. The average price paid by the Colombian refiner (under direct control of the cartel) to the Peruvian *traquatero* firm, up to $4000 per kg, brought in a total of about $2.5 billion, that is, roughly 10 per cent of the GDP. The estimate of $2.5 billion is conservative, because additional bribes were probably paid direct by the cartels to Peruvian politicians and officials. Looked at another way, Peru's legitimate exports (metals, fish meal, etc.) are about $3.5 billion a year.[13] The illicit export of cocaine paste therefore adds 60 per cent over and above the legitimate exports.

It could be argued that this is a boon to the economy. It provides a better income for coca-growing *campesinos* than they would get from other crops. Overall, however, it does more harm than good. Though some of the illegal money is ploughed into the Peruvian economy, much of it is laundered and invested abroad or spent on imported luxury goods. Having 10 per cent of the money supply circulating illegally and unaccounted for disrupts the economy and fuels inflation. The corruption of politicians, judges, army officers, police and other public officials does both social and economic damage and finances crime.

Later in the book (Chapter 22), the case for licensing the purchase of cocaine and other drugs by the consumer countries will be examined. One of the arguments for doing this is that the legitimate payments to *campesinos* ($400 per kg) would continue but the huge profits acquired by the *traquateros* and the cartels would be cut out. Thus the producing countries such as Peru would gain the legitimate benefits from growing a profitable crop without the far greater infusion of dirty money, corruption and crime.

LESSONS FROM PERU

Peru was selected for this case study because it illustrates the interplay between drug trafficking, corruption, terrorism, counter-insurgency and crime.

As in every conflict, criminal or political, intelligence is the key battle-winning factor. General Vidal's capture of Abimael Guzman was a classic example of a good intelligence operation. Overnight, it transformed the conflict from one that the government was in serious danger of losing to one that it became almost certain to win. It was accompanied by the Repentance Law, a measure whose success had been proved in Malaya and in Italy, against both terrorists and the mafia. The result was an escalating flow of surrendered terrorists who can provide the best intelligence of all if handled wisely. Rewards, incentives and confidence in future protection and security were crucial in encouraging both surrendered terrorists and people in the towns and villages to take the risk of giving information. This was also one the most important dividends from President Fujimori's bold decision to arm the *Rondas Campesinas* in the Andean villages.

The Peruvian experience underlined the need for a joint civil–police–military direction for this kind of war at national, provincial and district level. The military control in the EMZs was not ideal, but the weakness of the civil structure and leadership was probably such that the army was the only organization capable of taking charge.

The army paid a heavy price for its failure to curb the minority of officers who violated human rights, using disappearances, torture and murder in the hope af achieving success. The French proved in Indo-China and Algeria that if the security forces act outside the law they will irrevocably alienate the population.

Peru has also illustrated the very difficult problem of eliminating corruption when the national exchequer cannot afford adequate salaries for public servants, especially army and police officers. When drug trafficking and organized crime make profits that totally eclipse the salaries which the state can pay, corruption seems almost inevitable. Yet it can be as counter-productive as violation of human rights in alienating the population.

There is no easy solution to corruption. Velasco's national socialism (Nazi for short) did not help. Nor did Belaunde, nor Garcia. Nor did Communism, which Karl Marx sincerely believed would sweep away the inequities of feudalism and capitalism, but in practice, whether Stalinist, Trotskyist or Maoist, has in practice created even greater privileges for its *nomenklatura* and even greater abuse of power, so that too is now discredited. Guzman, Augusta, Nelly Evans and Maritza all began, like Marx, as idealists – it was 18 years before Guzman's movement killed its first victim – but the atrocities which followed benefited no one. Nor will corruption be cured by pious scolding from the Western states whose addicts provide the money for it. Corruption is the symptom rather than the disease.

The disparity between the wealth of the *traquatero* barons and of public servants underlines the responsibility of the affluent consumer countries to cut the huge sums of money flowing from the drug users on their streets, 90 per cent of which is found from the fruits of their own crime and 99 per cent of which goes into international organized crime, mainly the multinational drug cartels which poison the economic, political and social life of the Andean countries. Ultimately the cure lies in cutting the demand, either by suppression or by bringing down the grossly inflated price of drugs on the streets by decriminalization, licensing or legalization The choice between these will be discussed in the final chapters of this book.

Part III
The Colombian Cartels

6 Bolivia

THE RICHEST COCA LEAVES IN THE WORLD

Bolivia's coca leaves contain 0.72 per cent pure cocaine, so are nearly twice as rich as Peru's and over 2.5 times as rich as Colombia's. Bolivia's coca is therefore the most popular for chewing and making coca tea in the world. Leaves and paste are freely sold in the shops. Much of the refined cocaine is also bought for manufacture of pharmaceutical products worldwide. A higher proportion of Bolivia's coca crop is used for legitimate purposes than that of Peru or Colombia and the possibility of banning the domestic use and export of coca products, unlikely in Peru or Colombia, is inconceivable in Bolivia.

In contrast to Peru, Bolivia sends only a quarter of her cocaine paste to Colombia. Most of the rest is refined in Bolivia's own laboratories and exported by many routes. Some goes via Brazil, Paraguay, Argentina, the Antilles, the Caribbean or Mexico and some direct to the USA and Europe.

Bolivia, with a population only one-third that of Peru, exports 200,000 kg of cocaine paste or pure cocaine per year, compared with Peru's 700,000 kg. This has an approximate street value of $20 billion in London or New York. Estimates of the money that this brings home vary from $2 billion to $4 billion a year. This is because no one can be sure how much of the $20 billion is taken by middlemen since the structure of distribution is more diffuse than that of the Colombian cartels. Since Bolivia refines so much of her own cocaine, the $4 billion figure is quite possible – half the size of the GDP and four times the value of legal exports.[1]

BOLIVIAN POLITICS

Until 1981, Bolivia suffered chronic political instability, having had more than one military coup for every year of her existence as an independent country. General Luis Garcia Meza's coup on 17 July 1980 was the 189th since independence in 1819 – 189 in 161 years. That coup was financed by a drug baron who was a cousin of Garcia Meza and it is alleged that most of his year in office was devoted to developing the drug trade.[2] His government lasted only until August 1981, since when there have been three elected presidents in turn. President Jaime Paz Zamora, of the centre-left MIR party was elected in 1989 and there was then another peaceful democratic transition to President Gonzalo Sanchez de Lozada of the centre-right MNR on 4 August 1993, so there was in 1994 a hope that, after 15 consecutive years of elected presidents, Bolivia may at last have established a stable democracy.

The large export of cocaine products at high prices from such a small country with few other resources has distorted the economy, bringing in many times more foreign exchange than all Bolivia's legitimate exports put together.[3] This, however, is all dirty money and a large part of it is laundered and converted into foreign property and stocks or banked in foreign banks. As this cash flow is subject to no kind of tax or accounting, corruption is rife and at least two recent presidents have been blatantly involved in corruption.

ATTEMPTS TO ERADICATE COCA

Coca plants are hardy and not generally susceptible to herbicides. The only effective one is Trebuthurion, usually known as Spike, but environmentalists point out that it also seriously damages other plant and animal life and can also damage human health; it has thus far been used only for brush clearance in the USA on land that is not intended for growing crops. The Bolivian growers deter spraying by growing alternative rows of coca and other plants. Coca will also grow in the shade, so it can be concealed from aerial photography. It requires prohibitive time and labour to dig out coca roots in remote areas not easily accessible to mechanical plant. Cutting back the foliage merely has the effect of pruning and stimulates future growth.

The main coca growing area in Bolivia is the Chapare Valley in the Cochabamba Department, about 250 miles east of La Paz, on the eastern slopes of the Andes Mountains. Other coca areas are further east in the Beni and Santa Cruz Departments. Although drug traffickers in these areas are increasingly carrying arms, the scale of violent crime and terrorism has never been comparable with that in Colombia and Peru.

The USA has tried to coerce Bolivian governments by making economic aid conditional on the eradication of coca production from a specified acreage each year but these targets have generally not been reached. Some 30,000 Bolivian peasants and their families cultivate 40,000 to 60,000 hectares of coca, earning more than they could from any other use of the land. Crop eradication and harassment of coca production arouses intense hostility and, if carried out persistently and ruthlessly, could prompt an escalation of violent resistance, both by the drug traffickers and by terrorist movements seeking local support, as the Shining Path did in Peru.

For this reason, and because of the huge flow of dollars (albeit dirty money) into Bolivia from the cocaine trade, no government is ever likely to make more than token gestures towards reducing it. The only cure, as with every drug-producing country, will be to cut off the money being poured into the criminal drug trafficking gangs by addicts in the consumer countries. Whether this can best be done by suppression of the demand or by changing the law will be discussed in Chapters 21 and 22.

7   Colombia

A HISTORY OF VIOLENCE

Colombia has the most consistent record of democracy in Latin America, yet she has had – and still has – a higher level of violence than any of her neighbours, and since the late 1960s has been the centre of the world's cocaine trade. Colombia is prosperous, with rich agricultural and mineral resources; she is the world's largest producer of coffee, which accounts for 51 per cent of her legal exports; she is the fourth largest gold producer and a major producer of oil.[1] She is one of the few Latin American countries which has not had to reschedule her foreign debt, though this is partly due to the billions of dollars entering the country from the cocaine trade.

The population comprises 20 per cent Europeans, 58 per cent *mestizo*, 14 per cent *mulatto*, 7 per cent Afro-Asian and only 1 per cent pure Indian, so there is no equivalent of the large areas of traditional Indian culture in Peru. Colombia has, however, an unequal society, in which 4 per cent of the population own 68 per cent of the cultivable land and 13 million of her population live in poverty.[2]

The violence in Colombia has historically been between adherents of the two political traditions – conservative and liberal. The country became independent in 1819 and from 1840 to 1903 there was a prolonged civil war, reaching a peak in 1899–1905 in which as many as 130,000 people may have died.[3] An even bloodier civil war, again between conservatives and liberals, occurred between 1948 and 1957, in which 200,000 were killed. This, known in Colombian history as *La Violencia*, at last had a cathartic effect, and the two parties formed a National Front in which they agreed to alternate four-year presidencies. This operated peacefully for 16 years (1957–73). Since 1974, there has been normal competition between the parties. In May 1994 the Liberal candidate, Ernesto Samper, was elected with a 1.5 per cent majority over his Conservative opponent and the result was accepted with a good grace, despite accusations that Samper's campaign was funded by the Cali drug cartel.

This political courtesy is in stark contrast to the violence still prevalent in Colombian society, in the early 1990s averaging nearly 30,000 killed every year – 28,000 in 1993. The kidnap rate was also by far the highest in the world, averaging 1450 a year from 1990 to 1992.

On 30 April 1994, a Colombian minister announced that in 1993 10 per cent of the world's recorded murders took place in Colombia (28,000), more than in the entire USA (25,000). Of the 28,000, 8 per cent were by drug traffickers, 10 per cent politically motivated and 82 per cent as a result of domestic or social violence (i.e. 'normal crime').

THE GROWTH OF THE COCAINE TRADE AND TERRORISM

The explosion of world drug addiction began in the 1960s, leading to a situation in which Colombia refines and exports 75 per cent of the world's cocaine. The emergence of the Colombian drug cartels which organize this trade will be described in the next section.

At the same time, a number of political terrorist movements emerged. In 1964, inspired by Che Guevara, came the National Liberation Army (ELN); next, in 1966, the Armed Revolutionary Forces of Colombia (FARC). A number of others appeared of which two – M19 and the People's Liberation Army (EPL) – accepted a peace plan in 1990; their representatives have entered Parliament with some success but a splinter group of EPL dissidents broke away and continued terrorist activities.

In the mid-1990s the three surviving terrorist movements are allied in a loose federation, the Simón Bolívar Guerrilla Coordination (CGSB) which was formed in 1987. The largest is FARC, with 7000–8000 guerrillas operating in 64 fronts, mainly in rural areas. Next largest is ELN, with 2000 guerrillas in 26 fronts and 6 smaller urban groups. ELN mainly targets the oil/gas and mining industries but, like FARC, was trying in 1994 to build up its strength in urban areas. The EPL dissidents, numbering 100–200, operate mainly in northern provinces, assassinating members of the EPL majority who laid down their arms to join the lawful political process.[4]

FARC is heavily involved in violent activities in alliance with the drug cartels. Its 64 rural fronts also act in a semi-overt way to exercise alternative government. Its attitude to foreign multi-national subsidiaries is different from that of ELN, and is aimed at establishing a reputation as 'guardians of the people'. FARC activists first check whether the people welcome the foreign company operating in the area because it will bring jobs and prosperity. If that is so, FARC will advise local officials, such as the mayor and police chief, to 'ask' the management of the enterprise to employ a large proportion of junior managers and staff, as well as manual labour, from the local community; also to subcontract transport, construction and other services to local firms. It is made clear to them that, if they comply, they will have no trouble from FARC, and this undertaking is generally honoured. If the company fails to respond, however, the next activists to call will probably wear guerrilla uniforms and will warn of the consequences of defiance.[5] Provided that FARC's action brings local employment, it will gain popular support. If it does not, then violence will follow, both against the foreign company and against Colombians who cooperate with it.

THE RISE AND FALL OF PABLO ESCOBAR

The two main Colombian drug cartels are based in Colombia's second and third cities, each with a population of 1.6 million; Cali (200 miles south-west of the capital, Bogotá) and Medellin (150 miles north-west). The cartels were formed from competing drug trafficking gangs, to avoid them fighting each other.

The Medellin cartel was dominant until 1991. Its principal leader was Pablo Escobar who, at his peak in 1989, was assessed by *Forbes Magazine* to have accrued a personal fortune of $3 billion.[6] Like FARC, he and his fellow drug barons used their money and power to build up a base of popular support on Mafia lines (see Chapter 16). In Medellin, for example, they cultivated a Robin Hood image, taking money by selling cocaine to the *gringos* and Europeans and spending it on welfare in the poorer parts of the city, financing schools and hospitals, building local football grounds with floodlights, and so on. A Medellin drug baron owned one of Colombia's leading professional football teams. There were few people in Medellin who were not involved in some way in the activities of the cartel, or who did not at least have relatives who were – including most of the police. Escobar could, up till 1991, live and walk freely in large areas of Medellin, knowing that the people would warn him and if necessary protect him from police activity; he was confident that the police would not dare to mount an operation against him anyway.

The same applied to the luxurious ranches in which he and his fellow barons lived in the rural areas. No attempt was made to conceal these. Escobar, for instance, ran a 'game park' on one of his, for which he imported giraffes, Indian elephants and hippo-potamuses.[7] The locations of these ranches were well known, but the *campesinos*, willingly or from fear, maintained a warning screen for miles around them. The ranches had strong defended perimeters and garrisons to guard them and each contained its own airstrip.

The laboratories in which the cocaine paste imported from Peru and Bolivia was refined were defended on similar lines. One of the rare occasions on which such a laboratory was successfully raided was in October 1984, on the banks of the Yari River, not far from the Peruvian border. Several hundred Colombian police landed by helicopter and secured the perimeter after a two-hour battle. They then repulsed a counter-attack by an estimated force of 100 men from a guerrilla base nearby. The police seized 13.8 tons of cocaine with a street value of at least $1.2 billion, along with 44 buildings including 10 cocaine-processing laboratories, 6 months' food supply for 80 people and 7 aircraft, with a runway equipped for night landings.[8] This was, of course, only a fraction of their refining capacity and of their annual production of cocaine. But it does give an idea both of the scale of the cartel's operation and of their confidence that they were secure from attack.

By 1989 there was a very real fear that the drug barons, and especially the Medellin cartel, were in sight of gaining *de facto* control of the government in Colombia,[9] just as the government in Palermo at this time ruled only with the permission of the Sicilian Mafia, who also had a measure of control, through corrupt and intimidated politicians, of the majority party in the Italian government. The Mafia and the Colombian cartels worked in the same way, using money as a means of exercising power, which would open the way to make more money and, eventually, to achieve absolute power. It did not seem inconceivable that Pablo Escobar might soon be able to exercise control over one or even both of the main political parties, who would then run candidates approved by him for the presidency and supported by a majority in Congress also in his thrall; he would similarly have been able to control the appointment of judges and make them act as he wished – all by a mixture of corruption and intimidation.

This end was pursued by the combined use of money and guns. It began with the judges; they were offered generous bribes if they did what they were told, with a warning of assassination or kidnap of themselves or their families if they did not. As in Peru (see Chapter 4) cases were being dropped, perverse not guilty verdicts returned or token sentences passed with the understanding that they would be quietly remitted after a short time in prison. Faced with the 'choice between silver and lead' a number of judges felt that they had little option but to pay one or other of these prices.

The same choice was offered to politicians and others with power in the bureaucracy or business. With 30,000 people murdered every year, no one doubted the reality of the threat. The murder rate in Medellin was in 1988 the highest in the world – one every three hours in a city with a population of 1.5 million. Thirty judges were murdered between 1985 and 1988.

In May 1985, Ronaldo Lara Bonilla, the courageous 38-year-old justice minister who was responsible for the 1984 raid on the Yari River cocaine laboratories, was assassinated. He was shot in his car by a gunman on a motorcycle who, on arrest, revealed that he had been paid $20,000 to shoot the minister on account of his anti-drug activities.[10] President Betancur declared a state of siege under which drug dealers could be detained without bail and tried by military courts. The drug barons announced that, if their business was interfered with, they would cause 1800 businesses to close down and arm a guerrilla force 1800 strong.

Betancur and his successor in 1986, President Virgilio Barco, nevertheless maintained the state of siege and, as part of their plan, they announced that they would implement their dormant extradition treaty with the USA. This was particularly feared by the leaders of the cartels, all of whom could be implicated in drug trafficking into or through the USA, where many of the Colombian multinational corporations acting as cover for drug trafficking or money laundering were based. If Escobar and his ilk were to be arrested and imprisoned in Colombia, they were confident that their accomplices outside could quickly bribe or terrorize the authorities into releasing them. If imprisoned in the USA, however, they could not apply this pressure and might well stay in prison for the best part of their lives. So when the government announced the intention to implement the extradition treaty, Supreme Court judges began to receive daily threats of death. Not being as heavily guarded as ministers, they caved in, announcing that the treaty was 'unconstitutional'.

In January 1897, a nationwide police operation netted 350 suspects, 72 of whom were described as 'big fish' whose extradition had been requested by the USA. Within a few days of these arrests, a former Colombian justice minister, Enrique Parejo Gonzales, was shot and seriously wounded by unidentified gunmen in Budapest, where he had been appointed Colombian ambassador in August 1986, in the belief that in Hungary he would be safely out of reach of the drug traffickers' hit squads. The message was no doubt noted by many other ministers, judges and officials concerned about their future. This was one of Colombia's lowest points, but President Barco maintained his courage and determination through the rest of his term, and he turned the corner.

The decline of the Medellin cartel was set in motion by the president's reaction to the assassination on 18 August 1989 of Luis Carlos Galan, the ruling Liberal Party's candidate for the presidential election in 1990 when Barco was due to complete his five-year term. Galan was a popular candidate and there was a surge of public support for a crackdown by the government. The same day, President Barco and his Council of Ministers enacted a decree for emergency powers, which included some drastic and effective measures. They used their powers to reinstate the procedure for extradition to the USA. They enforced the provision in the constitution empowering the Council of Ministers to order the arrest and detention of suspected dangerous criminals, so that they would not have to leave that responsibility to corrupt or intimidated judges. They authorized preventive seizure of criminally acquired assets, with severe penalties for those who assisted their concealment.[11] Suspected drug traffickers and terrorists could be held incommunicado for up to seven days. More protection and resources were provided for the judiciary. Juries were abolished where intimidation was likely and judges were appointed with territorial jurisdiction.

These measures had an immediate effect. Between 18 August 1989 and 20 March 1990, 15 drug traffickers had been extradited and a further 12 were awaiting extradition; 11,500 arrests had been made, 1800 weapons seized, 300 aircraft grounded and 1370 properties occupied. Large quantities of cocaine base and chemicals for processing were seized and hundreds of laboratories were destroyed. Of all the world's cocaine seizures in 1989, 80 per cent took place in Colombia itself.[12]

At the same time, military and police operations were stepped up against the heavily guarded ranches in which the top drug barons normally lived. On 15 December 1989, one of the three most wanted leaders of the Medellin cartel, Jose Gonzales Rodriguez Gacha, was shot dead, with his son, when police raiding his ranch pursued them by helicopter as they tried to escape in a truck.

On 27 May 1990 Galan's replacement as Liberal candidate, Cesar Gaviria, was elected president. He took office on 7 August and continued to pursue the anti-drug campaign with the same vigour. On 22 November, the 'Extraditables', an association of drug barons liable for extradition, offered a cease-fire during the Constituent Assembly elections in December. They said that 200–300 senior drug traffickers would surrender if President Gaviria would undertake not to extradite them to the USA. Gaviria accepted this on condition that they confessed to some of their crimes and served sentences for these in Colombia. In January and February 1991, the three Ochoa brothers surrendered on these terms; one of these, Fabio, was the third of the most wanted leaders of the Medellin cartel, with Escobar and the late Rodriguez Gacha. It was believed that Gacha organized the supply of the cocaine paste, Escobar supervised the production of the pure cocaine and the Ochoa brothers were responsible for distribution and finance.[13] The Ochoa brothers were also prominent as Robin Hood style benefactors in Medellin, famous for breeding the finest stable of trotting horses on the continent.[14]

Prolonged negotiations then took place whereby the top man of all, Pablo Escobar, surrendered the day after the Constituent Assembly had voted to end the extradition of drug traffickers to the USA. It was reported that bribes had been paid to 37 members of the Assembly.[15] Escobar was incarcerated in a specially constructed 'prison', of a design which he himself had approved. This was secure from the outside, but inside Escobar lived the life of a millionaire, surrounded by his aides ('fellow prisoners') with prison staff doubling up as servants – rather like a captured medieval king awaiting ransom. The reason for his surrender may, in fact, have been that he himself feared assassination and preferred to direct the elimination of his rivals from within a secure base, which he duly did. Some of the government may have been quite happy about this, as Escobar knew better than they did where these people were. Escobar communicated and received visitors freely, and continued to direct the operations of the Medellin cartel. He was no doubt confident that he could escape as soon as it suited him and he did so after a little over a year in captivity, in July 1992. He and his entourage left *en bloc* and went underground in Medellin, in an area where he could rely on the population to harbour and screen him.

He resumed terrorist operations with increasing violence, but his control was no longer monolithic. A number of his enemies formed an organization called PEPES (People persecuted by Pablo Escobar) and there was much bloodletting, both between factions and in attacks on the police and the army. After 16 months of this, the police located his home, by telephone tapping, and raided it on 16 December 1993. Escobar was shot dead on the roof of a neighbouring house as he attempted to escape; his age was 44. The police estimated that he had himself been directly responsible for the deaths of more than 1000 civilians and 500 police officers.

COLOMBIA AFTER PABLO ESCOBAR

Pablo Escobar's brother Roberto Escobar inherited the leadership of the Medellin cartel but was himself still in prison in 1994, along with four other cartel leaders.[16] They were attempting to negotiate deals, both with ELN guerrillas, who had for a long time operated in conjunction with Escobar's 'drug mafia', and with the Cali cartel.

The Cali cartel had always been bigger than the Medellin cartel but used less violence. It was headed by the brothers Gilberto and Miguel Rogriguez Orijuela and Jose Santacruz Londono. Most of its leaders were successful middle-class businessmen running large corporations with overtly legal commercial activities within which they concealed their drug trafficking and money laundering with discretion.[17] When coercion was needed it was generally done by corruption and by infiltration of the corridors of power. Even before the Medellin cartel began to get into trouble in 1991, the Cali cartel controlled 70 per cent of the cocaine trade in Colombia. After the deaths of Pablo Escobar and Rodriguez Gacha and the surrender of the Ochoa brothers, the Cali cartel was able to take over whatever it chose.

In 1994, pressure increased on the Cali cartel. On 24 January, Jesus Elisio Ruiz Diaz was arrested in Switzerland and extradited to the USA. He was believed to lead a network earning an average of $12 million a week ($600 million a year) by cocaine sales in New York. His previous Cali boss, Ramiro Herrera Buitrago, was already serving a prison sentence in the USA.[18]

Then in Colombia on 25 March, the police killed Carlos Alberto Urdinola who, with his two brothers, Ivan and Julio Fabio, controlled the Cali operations in the Northern Cauca Valley.[19] Three weeks later, on 12 April 1994, his brother Julio Fabio Urdinola himself surrendered after negotiations which his lawyer had begun in December 1993.[20] He was initially sentenced to 22 years in prison but this was reduced to 5 years under the Colombian equivalent of the Repentance Law.[21] Other leaders were also believed to be negotiating similar deals.

There was some suspicion that, after such long negotiations, a deal might have been made with Julio Fabio Urdinola on the lines of that made with Pablo Escobar in 1991 but, in view of the Escobar experience, it seemed unlikely that he would be given the opportunity to resume his activities. If he were to prove ready to continue to cooperate, he would be in a position to persuade other members of the cartel to surrender. If so, the Colombian government might be willing to reward him for doing so.

The British did this in 1958 with Hor Lung, the second in command of the Communist guerrillas in Malaya (his commander, Chin Peng, had already moved to China and stayed there). Hor Lung came in to surrender unexpectedly and was permitted, under discreet supervision and protection, to contact his subordinates, one by one, and he secretly induced nearly all of them to accept the surrender terms. He took great personal risks but in so doing he earned not only his freedom, but also a big enough reward ($80,000 at 1958 prices) to start his own timber business. This thrived and he lived on quite openly in the same area, with no apparent anxiety. He seemed generally to be respected for having saved hundreds of lives, and brought to an end 12 years of bloody conflict which almost everyone by then wanted to end. Few people in Malaya doubted that the practical benefits to the public, including the guerrillas and their supporters, far outweighed any moral scruples about pardoning and handsomely rewarding a former terrorist leader.[22]

The Peruvian government had studied the British experience and in 1992 began the process of applying it, with devastating effect in the war against the Shining Path terrorists (see pp. 34–6). The Italians took a similar approach, both against the terrorists and against the Mafia from 1980 onwards (see pp. 135–6). It remains to be seen how far the Colombians will follow suit to exploit the successes they had against the drug cartels in 1993 and 1994.

The Colombian government in 1994 were strongly urging the consumer countries, especially the USA, to legalize cocaine, to cut off the flow of money to the cartels and other criminal organizations. The arguments for and against legalization are discussed in Chapter 22.

8   Cocaine Distribution

EXPORT FROM COLOMBIA

Most of the cocaine produced in the Andes is consumed in North America or Europe, though there is a disturbing increase in consumption in Latin America itself.

The 25 per cent refined outside Colombia comprises 15 per cent refined in Bolivia (most of its coca production), 5 per cent in Peru and 5 per cent elsewhere. Most of this 25 per cent is exported through Central America and the Caribbean or directly across the South Atlantic, sometimes from Brazil and Argentina to Portugal and Spain, which have regular flights and trading links with their former colonies, providing cover for shipment of drugs.

An increasing amount goes via Nigeria, exploiting the fact that many very poor and unsophisticated Nigerians can be persuaded to act as couriers for amounts much lower than other couriers demand, but very large in the context of their living conditions. Many have desperate personal problems arising from poverty or dispersal of their families. They take enormous risks for pathetic sums, and many find themselves in British and other European jails.

The 75 per cent refined in Colombia is distributed and marketed by the big drug cartels, mainly through Central America, Venezuela, Mexico and the Caribbean and sometimes direct to the USA or Europe. This, as described earlier, is mainly organized by large multinational corporations based in Colombia or in the USA, handling other goods as a cover for drug dealing. These other activities flourish because the corporations receive a huge undeclared untaxed income from drug dealing so they can afford to sell their legal products at lower prices and can undercut their straight competitors.[1] This suits them well, because the higher their turnover in legal goods, even making no profit, the better they will be able to conceal their drug transactions and the easier it will be to cover their money laundering.

WORLD DISTRIBUTION

There are many methods of physical distribution of cocaine and these are varied to evade detection. Most often, cocaine is flown out of Colombia in consignments of several hundred kilograms in light aircraft to airstrips in Central America or islands in the Antilles and the Caribbean or direct to Florida. Panama and the Dutch Antilles are particularly favoured distribution points and there are frequent airdrops on to the large island of Aruba as these are harder to detect than aircraft coming in to land; Aruba is also a regular refuelling stop for long-haul flights between Europe and the Andean countries. From the islands, some is transported by speedboat or light aircraft to distribution points in the USA or Canada. Some is shipped or flown concealed in cargo or baggage to distribution points in Europe, of which Spain, Italy and the Netherlands provide the most. Some goes via Nigeria for onward courier distribution. A 5-kg pack of pure cocaine has a potential street value of $500,000 (or $1 million if cut to 50 per cent purity – see Table 8.1). The total world production of cocaine is around 1000 tons in the year – an average of only 600 5-kg packs a day. Such packs can be easily concealed in small consignments of sea or air freight, so it is not hard to see why so much gets through undetected.

Geographically and politically the Caribbean is well suited both for distribution and money laundering. East of the large islands of Cuba, Jamaica, Puerto Rico and Haiti/Dominican Republic is a horseshoe of about 500 miles diameter consisting of small islands, some independent, some autonomous and semi-colonial, and all with established trading links with Europe, especially Britain, France, the Netherlands and Spain, and with the USA. Some have sophisticated banking and commercial infrastructures. They provide good transit points for drugs, with their constant flow of ships, fishing craft, yachts, speedboats and aircraft, large and small; and a plethora of harbours, creeks and airstrips. Here, the small packages of drugs can be distributed and incorporated in a wide range of regularly traded cargoes or in smaller quantities via tourists returning to Europe or the USA. Money to be laundered can be converted into commodities or electronically transferred between independent island banks, often subject to no kind of control.[2]

For local distribution, cocaine is carried by couriers, in the door panels of cars, in personal baggage or, in quantities of a few

Table 8.1   Example of Cocaine Prices, Peru to London

There are no fixed prices. The most consistent are the farmer's selling price of $400 per kg of basic paste containing 70–90 per cent cocaine and the London street dealer's price of $100 per gm of 40–50 per cent cut cocaine. Other prices vary enormously, each trader buying as cheap and selling as dear as he can. Prices for middlemen will depend, for example, on supply and demand and on who pays the courier. The number of middlemen – brokers, importers, distributors, dealers, etc. – also varies.

Seller	Sells to	Price per kg ($)	Typical purity (%)	Price per kg of pure cocaine ($)
Farmer: Peru[a]	*Traquatero*: Peru	400	75	533
Traffic firm: Peru[b]	Cartel: Colombia	4,000	75	5,333
Cartel[c]	Broker, e.g. Caribbean	10,000	100	10,000
Broker[d]	Importer: UK	20,000	100	20,000
Importer[e]	Distributor: UK	40,000	100	40,000
Distributor[f]	Dealer: London	60,000	75	80,000
Dealer[g]	Consumer	100,000	50	200,000
		($100 per gm)		

Notes to Table 8.1 on following page

Notes to Table 8.1
^a Sells washed basic cocaine paste 70–90% pure (see p. 43)
^b e.g. 'El Vaticano'. Pays pilots, terrorists, corrupt army officers, etc. (see pp. 44–5)
^c Cali or Medellin. Provision, refining, marketing, finance
^d e.g. in Caribbean, Venezuela, Florida. Collects from Colombia
^e e.g. Richardson. Pays transport to UK (see pp. 159–61).
^f e.g. Sammy Lewis. Typically cuts to 75% (see pp. 76 and 176–7)
^g Typically cuts to 40–50%. May buy 5 gm for price of 4 gm (see p. 165)

Notes to Table 8.1
ᵃ Sells washed basic cocaine paste 70–90% pure (see p. 43)
ᵇ e.g. 'El Vaticano'. Pays pilots, terrorists, corrupt army officers, etc. (see pp. 44–5)
ᶜ Cali or Medellin. Provision, refining, marketing, finance
ᵈ e.g. in Caribbean, Venezuela, Florida. Collects from Colombia
ᵉ e.g. Richardson. Pays transport to UK (see pp. 159–61).
ᶠ e.g. Sammy Lewis. Typically cuts to 75% (see pp. 76 and 176–7)
ᵍ Typically cuts to 40–50%. May buy 5 gm for price of 4 gm (see p. 165)
Sources: *Wall Street Journal*, 30 June 1986
ISDD, *Drug Misuse in Britain*, London, ISDD, 1992
ISDD, *Drug Update – Cocaine and Crack*, London, ISDD, 1993
Observer Magazine, London, 27 February 1994
Author's visit to Huallaga Valley and Lima, Peru, January 1994

hundred grams, concealed about the person, especially by women in intimate places which they hope will not be searched. Many use capsules such as condoms which they conceal in the rectum or the vagina, or swallow and excrete after going through Customs.

PRICES

Table 8.1 gives a typical example of the price rise from the grower to the street dealer. The apparent rise is 250 to 1 (from 40 cents to $100 per gm) but is in practice nearer 400 to 1, as the average cocaine content will have fallen from about 70–90 per cent to 40–50 per cent on the streets.

The biggest fortunes are made by the Colombian cartel members in their multinational corporations and ranches, some of whom have personal assets worth billions of dollars (see p. 58). High on the list are the Peruvian traffic barons. The individual earnings of British importers range from £100,000 to millions a year. The humblest London street dealer may make £40,000 a year.[3]

The local distribution and street dealing is covered in more detail in Chapters 9, 19 and 20.

9   Crack

THE INSTANT NARCOTIC

Crack is a smokable form of cocaine which gives instant and spectacular results. Pure Cocaine in its usual white powder form is unsuitable for smoking because much of the active drug is destroyed at high temperatures: the powder is usually sniffed – 'snorted' – up the nostrils through a tube; this gives a reaction in about three minutes, which lasts for several hours. Crack gives a much more intense sensation more quickly (in 5 or 10 seconds) but it lasts only for about 15 minutes. When it subsides, the reaction is one of corresponding depression, with an immediate craving for another dose.

Making crack is nearly, but not quite, a reversal of the last stage of the process of making pure cocaine powder. The washed basic cocaine paste, as produced by the farmers in the Andes, is sometimes known as 'freebase cocaine' and is 70–90 per cent pure. It *can* be smoked in that form but is too harsh to be popular. The final purification is done mainly in laboratories in Colombia using ether (see p. 43), and produces the familiar white cocaine powder. The conversion back to freebase cocaine (a name sometimes used for crack) can safely be done in any kitchen in just over an hour by dissolving the powder in water and heating it with an alkaline agent, usually bicarbonate of soda (baking powder), ammonia or caustic soda. It is then dried out and chipped into raisin-sized rocks of crack, with the same degree of purity as the original powder. Cocaine powder sold on the streets is normally cut to 40–50 per cent purity, but it is often used in purer form (70 or even 90 per cent) to make crack, which makes the sensation even more intense. In this form it melts more easily and vaporizes at a lower temperature (98°C compared with 195°C for the powder) and is therefore ideal for smoking.[1] The name 'crack' is believed to be derived from the fact that, when baking powder is used, it leaves an impurity of sodium chloride which crackles when the crack is smoked.[2]

To get the most exciting results, crack is often smoked in an improvised 'pipe' made by fixing tinfoil over a tumbler and cutting a slit through which the smoke can be inhaled. When the crack, shredded with a razor blade, is lit, it burns away in one hit, the smoker inhaling it in a long deep draught.[3]

Crack is believed to have been tried in the Netherlands in the 1970s,[4] and then in the Los Angeles ghetto district of Watts in 1981. The first media reports of it were in the *Los Angeles Times* in November 1984 and in the *New York Times* on 25 November 1985. By 1986 *Newsweek* was calling crack 'the biggest story since Vietnam and Watergate.'[5] In Britain, it was mentioned in the National Drugs Intelligence Unit (NDIU) in 1986. By 1988 it was headline news in the media in both the USA and Britain. 'Crack houses' were appearing in the black ghetto areas of South London, Toxteth (Merseyside) and Moss Side (Manchester); British drug squad officers were visiting the USA to prepare for the anticipated 'crack explosion'. A British newspaper in July 1988 quoted Mother Hale, a saintly octogenarian who ran a clinic in Harlem curing babies born to addicted mothers:

> The heroin and cocaine babies are fighting to live, but the crack babies have no desire to live. They come in today; tomorrow they die. And the mothers don't want them, either. All they want to do is to get out of hospital and get some more crack.[6]

But this view was questioned by Philip Bean, who claims that the babies normally cure themselves if kept in the nursery for two to four weeks.[7]

Since crack is more bulky to transport than pure cocaine, and the rocks are harder to smuggle than powder, the conversion is almost always done by the distributor or dealer in the same country, usually in the same city, in which it will be sold on the street. So the import and distribution up to that point is as cocaine powder, as described in previous chapters. The gangs which make and distribute the crack, both in the USA and the UK, are most often West Indians, known by their Jamaican title as Yardies.

THE YARDIES

The first British 'crack factory' was found in Peckham, South London, which has a large West Indian population. In August 1988, a suspect flat was placed under surveillance and one of the police officers reported that there were forty or fifty callers an hour. When we raided it there were three Jamaicans inside. Two had just arrived from Kingston. The other was from the Bronx in New York. Our view was that this estate, and others with a large black community, had been specially targeted by foreign dealers as places where they could sell crack.

Later, a nineteenth-floor flat in the Milton Court Estate in Deptford, south-east London, was raided. It was protected by a cast steel door with multiple locks and a steel-cased inner door with six steel bolts. Dealing was done through a slit in the outer door, so that the clients never saw their supplier. To get in, the police had to use oxy-acetylene cutters and hydraulic rams. The occupant, who was arrested and convicted, was found in possession of 43 rocks of crack, cocaine powder and cash.[8]

Other raids resulted in the arrest of two West Indian gangsters known to have been leaders of 'posses' in Kingston. These gangs operated in Jamaica on a scale seldom seen outside the USA. They often had links with members of one or other of Jamaica's two main political parties, the People's National Party (PNP) or the Jamaican Labour Party (JLP) which alternated in power. PNP drew support from Fidel Castro so the USA supported JLP. Both parties contained members who were corrupt and, in some cases, were happy to be photographed at the funerals of leaders who were murdered in the gang fights which plagued Kingston.

The footsoldiers of some of these posses in Jamaica and the USA were believed to be numbered in thousands. Their loyalty was based on opportunities for criminal gain and, perhaps more important, protection and collective strength in the their violent environment. Comparisons with the Italian mafias, however, are misleading. There was none of the mysticism and 'honour' on which mafia loyalties are based – just the power and security derived from membership of a violent criminal community able to hold its own with guns and knives. A closer parallel would be with the Medellin cartel in Colombia. The 'dons' of the posses lived a flamboyant lifestyle, flaunting their wealth with flashy cars and heavy jewellery as an assertion of their confidence that no one would dare to touch them.

Like Pablo Escobar in Colombia, they were admired for their success and were regarded as heroes and Robin Hoods by their deprived constituents, using their wealth to distribute food and provide facilities for the children, the poor and the needy. They were community leaders, but their lead was in a dangerous direction.

They saw opportunities for rich pickings in the UK, especially in London, Merseyside and Manchester, working from secure ghetto bases in which they could engender the same fierce loyalty as in Kingston. When the police carried out arrests or investigations, they were often met with violence and always with a wall of silence.

The Yardie gangs in Britain did not operate on the scale of those in Jamaica. They gathered smaller armies, mainly aged between 18 and 24, of which strengths of 30 to 60 at most were typical. (These are discussed further, with examples, in Chapter 19.) They also harnessed the enthusiastic support of the children as messengers and lookouts.

The majority of the crack in Britain, however, has probably been sold by small independent gangs of a dozen or so, by no means all black, and a typical one of these is described later in this chapter (p. 76).

The raids on crack bases in 1988–89 described above were part of 'Operation Lucy', a series of raids by a specially formed Metropolitan Police unit, which made 400 arrests and initiated the deportation of 50 illegal immigrants. The media latched on to these operations because of public concern about the growth of crime and drug trafficking, and the Metropolitan Police gained media confidence through briefings and by facilitating access for reporters and photographers. Politicians, however, became concerned that this was exacerbating racial tension, since most of the pictures showed white policemen, often dressed in armoured and protective clothing, manhandling young blacks. Operation Lucy was therefore discontinued in 1989. By this time, however, a new prophet had emerged to inflame the fires of alarm about crack.

THE 'CRACK EXPLOSION'

On 20 April 1989, the Regional Drug Conference of the Association of Chief Police Officers (ACPO) in Lancashire invited

Special Agent Robert M. Stutman, head of the New York City
office of the Drug Enforcement Administration (DEA) to address
them on 'Crack: Its Effects on a City and Law Enforcement
Response'. He gave a sensational lecture, speaking without notes
and holding his audience spellbound. He described the growth of
crack abuse as the fastest in history, stressing that it captured all
races, black and white, ghettos and suburban, male and female.
He presented alarming figures (some subsequently challenged) of
its effects on violence and especially in child abuse cases, which he
said had quadrupled in New York between 1986 and 1988. He
quoted a survey of 17,000 crack users in the USA of whom 47 per
cent had been involved in fights, 35 per cent with weapons, 1 per
cent committing murders. He described the easy manufacture of
crack and its instant effects. He declared that, of all those who
took crack three times, 75 per cent became physically addicted at
the end of the third time, and that it was a virtually incurable
addiction. It had the reputation of being cheap, but the crack
makers gained a profit of about 300 per cent. Of eight police
officers killed in the previous year in New York City, he said that
seven were killed by crack involvement and in every case the
gunman knew that he was shooting at a policeman; that the
number of police officers allocated full time to drugs rose from 600
to 2700; that all the 3000 DEA agents were armed with
sub-machine-guns; and that 90,000 drug arrests were made in the
city in 1988. He warned that, if Britain did not tackle this problem on a national basis, by law enforcement, education and
treatment,

> I will personally guarantee that two years from now you will
> have a serious crack problem because . . . we are so saturated in
> the United States with cocaine, there ain't enough noses left to
> use the cocaine that's coming in.[9]

The lecture had an electrifying effect. Transcripts of the tape
circulated like wildfire around police forces and to Westminster,
to ministers, officials and Members of Parliament. The Home
Secretary, Douglas Hurd, convened the next month an extr-
ordinary meeting of European ministers in the Pompidou Group
of the Council of Europe. Quoting passages of Stutman's lecture
verbatim, he warned of 'the spectre hanging over Europe'. He
repeated the warnings to the Action on Addiction Conference and

to the Ministerial Group on the Misuse of Drugs. The House of Commons All Party Home Affairs Committee followed with an interim report on crack, highlighting its influence on child abuse. Meanwhile, in June, two senior British police officers spent two weeks in New York, Washington and Boston to seek advice. US police officers told them that the first mistake they had made was not to take crack seriously, and the second mistake had been their failure to set up an intelligence machinery to focus specially on crack.[10]

As a result, a combined police and Customs unit of 24 officers, the Crack Intelligence Coordinating Unit (CICU), was formed in London in October 1989, incorporating some of the disbanded Operation Lucy team and taking over its offices.

Nevertheless, seizures of crack were surprisingly small. In 1989, despite the combined efforts of Operation Lucy and (at the latter end) the CICU, only 0.25 kg of crack was seized, compared with 500 kg of cocaine and 60 tons of cannabis.[11] In August 1990, the decision was taken to run down the CICU.[12] Though cocaine abuse has continued to rise, and the proportion using it in crack form may have reached 20 or 30 per cent, the explosion forecast by Robert Stutman does not seem to have materialized.

The initial popularity of crack probably arose for two reasons: first, the instant and intense gratification it provided; and second, its *apparent* cheapness. A single rock of crack would normally cost £20–25 ($30–40) and would give a wonderful sensation. It might cost much less if the dealer chopped it into very small rocks (e.g. 100 mg instead of the usual 250 mg) or used the first few doses as a loss leader.

Its failure to live up to Stutman's forecasts (though it could still do so) was probably because the instant high was followed by a very deep low, urgently demanding a repeat, so the cost quickly mounted. Those heavily addicted sometimes preferred a series of intense binges, probably at a weekend; this could easily cost £1000 ($1500) and it would take a lot of stealing during the week to keep that up.

An increasingly popular mixture was 'one-plus-one' – a rock of crack followed, as the descent began, by a quarter gram of heroin to provide a deep relaxed sensation for a few hours. This, on average, would cost about £50 ($75) and it was not hard to raise that much by breaking into a car, taking the radio and cashing it in at a car boot sale.

A CRACK DEALER AND CRACK ADDICTS

Jon Silverman, BBC Home Affairs Correspondent, in researching his book, *Crack of Doom*, interviewed a substantial number of dealers and addicts (often consumer-dealers), in prison, as well as police and Customs officers involved in their detection and arrest. Three of these have been selected as best illustrating the patterns of provision and consumption of crack in Britain.

Sammy Lewis was 23 at the time of his arrest in 1991. He was born in England of parents who came from Barbados, and was taken back there for most of his schooling, returning to England at 15. He soon tired of working in a Pizza Hut in Willesden and began dealing in cannabis, later graduating into cocaine. He said that he had a partner in Trinidad who could get cocaine for £2500 ($3750) per kg in Venezuela. Whether or not this was true, its price was ten times more than this by the time it reached Britain. Lewis bought it, usually 2 kg every fortnight, for £30,000 ($45,000) per kg – £30 per gm. He cut it and converted it into rocks of crack and sold it to each of three dealers whom he knew and trusted. They would buy the rocks at about double the price. So everyone in the chain would make about 100 per cent profit in exchange for the risks he took. Lewis reckoned to make £9000–12,000 per week and his crew of dealers about £1500. So Lewis was collecting money at a rate which could have added up to half a million pounds a year if he kept it up.[13] He was eventually arrested in a 'buy bust' operation which will be described in Chapter 20 (see pp. 176–7).

One of the crack addicts interviewed by Jon Silverman was described by him as a 'black beanpole', aged 27, who had financed a crack addiction for six years, partly from earnings and partly from theft. He was initially on cannabis which he financed by stealing car radios and cassettes.

> I was one of the best, you ask anyone. I could remove a radio in 30 seconds or less – even if the car was alarmed. I'd flog them down the pub. A decent machine would fetch £100. It was going very nicely until this guy started undercutting me, selling them for £50.

In 1989, he landed a job on a building site at £500 a week. After a spell in the rave scene, on Ecstasy and Speed, he got into crack, spending £200 to £300 every Friday on rocks. He used these on weekend binges, in the toilet of the hostel where he stayed, and continued work during the week. But soon the £500 was not enough and he turned to crime.[14]

Another addict was Duane, a would-be Yardie, who was financing a crack habit and was only 19 when he was tried at the Old Bailey in December 1993. He was spending over £300 a day for an average intake of 20 rocks of crack, 14 gm of cannabis and two dozen tablets of LSD. He admitted to 600 burglaries, 130 muggings and 220 car break-ins. It was the largest total of offences ever dealt with at the Old Bailey. He got 10 years.[15]

The story of drug abuse and the response to it in Britain will be continued in Chapters 19 and 20.

Part IV

Heroin, Cannabis and Synthetics

10   The Heroin Trail

HEROIN PRODUCTION

World production of heroin in 1993 was less than half that of cocaine. Like cocaine, heroin is normally produced in three stages. The first of these is done by the farmers who grow the opium poppies and the second and third in laboratories. From 10 kg of opium, 1 kg of heroin is produced, with morphine as an intermediate stage. Opium is harvested by scoring the unripe seed pods of the opium poppy. A milky fluid oozes out, similar to latex oozing from the incision on a rubber tree. This 'opium latex' is dried in the sun to produce brown opium gum, which hardens into cakes or bricks. The gum can be powdered and sniffed, or it can be eaten as it has been for centuries in Asia, or it can be smoked.

Opium smoking dates from the development of tobacco smoking in the sixteenth century, after which it spread to Europe. Opium is a relaxant, and its legitimate use as an analgesic is widespread. Opium smoking produces a feeling of drowsiness and contentment, and Samuel Coleridge wrote some of his most inspired poetry under its influence; but it also eventually results in acute depression and mental, physical and moral degeneration, as it did in Coleridge's case. Nevertheless, its use was socially acceptable, like alcohol and tobacco still are, up to the end of the nineteenth century, when the damage done by addiction to opium and to its more concentrated derivatives, morphine and heroin, became clear.

Like coca, opium is a rewarding crop. A hectare of poppies may produce between 5 kg (Uzbekistan) and 12 kg (Myanmar) of opium. Even in Uzbekistan, opium farmers could earn 50 times more than if they grew cotton and nearly 100 times more than if they grew fruit,[1] though this varies in different growing areas.

The opium gum is refined into morphine base with the use of hydrochloric acid. It is then further refined into heroin, which is twice as potent as morphine, using a variety of chemicals, such as acetic anhydride, acetyl chloride, acetone, alcohol and tartaric acid, involving a heating and filtering process. Some of these

81

processes are hazardous, so refining is normally done in laboratories under controlled conditions. It can be refined into No. 3 (purple) heroin, which can be smoked, but for which there is now little demand for export, so it is more commonly precipitated, dried and crushed to make No. 4 (white) heroin, which can be dissolved and injected, as it usually is in Europe and North America. In Mexico, a different process has been developed to produce 'black tar' heroin for export to the USA.

A modern industrial process – the 'poppy straw' process – is used to extract morphine and heroin direct from the dried opium plant, but this is used mainly for commercial production for medical purposes.[2]

Opium comes from two main areas: the 'Golden Triangle' (Myanmar, Laos and Thailand) and the 'Golden Crescent' (Afghanistan, Iran and Pakistan); in each case it is grown in the mountain areas adjacent to the common frontiers of the three countries concerned. A much smaller amount comes from other areas.

To get a fair indication of the proportions produced from each area, the statistics must all come from the same year. The most recent comprehensive figures available (for 1990) are in Table 10.1.

In addition, the three main coca-growing countries, Peru, Colombia and Bolivia, have started growing opium poppies. Their production has not yet become significant in world terms, but the poppy has been found to thrive in some of the soils and environments available in these countries, so it may become significant in the future.

At the rate of 1 kg of heroin from 10 kg of opium, the world production of heroin is about 400 MT (400,000 kg). Like cocaine, heroin is often heavily cut, sometimes down to 10 per cent pure heroin, using inert white powders such as talcum or bleach, so the quality of cut heroin sold on the streets varies a great deal, and its total weight at least twice as much as the 400,000 kg. When there is a glut of heroin or when competition between dealers is intense, the heroin content becomes higher, giving more satisfaction but with greater danger. The average strength of cut heroin sold in London grew from 30 per cent in 1987 to 43 per cent in 1991.[3] In March 1993, seven people died from drug overdoses in nine days in the King's Cross district of London, allegedly due to a dealer supplying 70 per cent pure heroin.[4]

Table 10.1   Opium Production, 1990

Area	Metric tonnes
Golden Triangle	
Myanmar	2780
Laos	300–450
Thailand	40
Total	3120–270
Golden Crescent	
Afghanistan	500–800
Iran	200–400
Pakistan	118–128
Total	818–1328
Other areas	
Lebanon	45
Mexico	6
Guatemala	85
Total	136
Grand total	4074–734

Source: International Narcotics Strategy Control Report (INSCR), cited by Alison Jamieson, *Global Drug Trafficking*, CS 234, London, RISCT, September 1990, p. 14

THE GOLDEN TRIANGLE

Myanmar produces 60 per cent of the world's opium, three or four times as much as any other country. It is grown mainly in the remote areas of the Shan, Kachin and Kayah states, bordering Thailand, China and Laos. Yield averages 12 kg of opium per hectare. The Shan plateau (1000 metres) is ideally suited for opium cultivation, with a mean annual temperature of 27 degrees and 80 inches of rain, 90 per cent of it in the June to October monsoon. Historically the hill tribes have always been hostile to the Burmese in the valleys and the Myanmar government has little control.[5] The Burmese Communist Party, 10,000 strong, held sway over the northern frontier areas bordering China until its disbandment in 1989. Also in the north is the Kachin Independence Army which, with ten other small armies, forms the 17,000 strong National Democratic Front.

The Golden Triangle itself is a mountainous area straddling the borders of the extreme east of Myanmar, the extreme west of Laos and the extreme north of Thailand. This Triangle is dominated by two main insurgency groups operating on the Shan Plateau in Myanmar: the United Wa State Army (UWSA) in the south and the Shan United Army (SUA) in the south. These are controlled by warlords, the principal one being Cheng Chi Fu, normally known as Khun Sa, born in Taiwan, half Chinese and half Shan.

The farmers in the Golden Triangle are from hill tribes such as the Meo, Akha, Lisu and Lahu, in the Shan hills of north-east Myanmar and the high plateaux of Laos. They are poor and rely on the slash and burn method of cultivation, which accelerates top soil erosion. For most of them, cultivation of opium poppies is their sole source of income and enables them to buy only the bare essentials to live. Production increased almost threefold between 1985 and 1990 due to good growing conditions, and because many hill farmers were forced to substitute poppies for food crops to pay off debts to the Haw Chinese traders who live amongst them, lending them money and buying their opium.

The farmers collect the latex from the poppy seeds, dry it in the sun and fashion the gum into lumps of standard size. Some of these have to be handed over as taxes to the village head, exchanged for food and other essentials, sold to the Haw Chinese traders or given to them in settlement of past debts. The village heads in turn pay taxes to warlords such as Khun Sa, and many of the Chinese traders are also Khun Sa's agents. There is no other form of currency but opium in these hills, and there is no government of any kind other than that of the warlords.

The opium gum is carried under armed guard by the tribesmen, on their backs or using mules, to the laboratories, which are mainly situated close to the poppy fields. Here it is converted through the morphine stage and then into No. 4 white heroin, in the same laboratory, still under control of the warlords. Some is refined in Thailand but there are fewer laboratories there now thanks to better law enforcement by the Thai government.[6] The total output from the Golden Triangle is around 3000 MT of opium refined into a little over 300 MT of heroin per year. Typical prices are shown in Table 10.2.

From the laboratories, most of the heroin is bought by Thai-Chinese brokers, usually based in Bangkok. They take a large

Table 10.2   Example of Heroin Prices, Golden Triangle to USA, 1994

Heroin prices vary more than cocaine prices, especially in distribution. These were typical prices for heroin destined for the USA in 1994.

	Selling price per kg ($)
Raw opium from farmer in Shan State, Myanmar	60–75
Morphine base, Myanmar–Thai border	900–1000
Heroin, 70–90 per cent pure, at laboratory	2900–3200
Heroin, 70–90 per cent pure, broker, Bangkok	6000–10,000
Heroin, 70–90 per cent pure, US importer (via Chinese exporter in Bangkok or Hong Kong)	90,000–250,000
* Heroin, 30–40 per cent pure, US distributor	340,000–745,000
* Heroin, 30–40 per cent pure, US street dealer	$940,000–1,400,000

Note

* These final figures show what the distributor and street dealer received per kg of the 70–90 per cent heroin powder which was bought from the importer, to show how this price escalated from the laboratory door to the street – by a factor of about 300–400 times (from $2900–3000 up to $940,000–1,400,000). Everyone in the chain (from broker to street dealer) makes about 100 per cent profit or sometimes much more than that. (The middlemen in transit between the broker and importer vary too much to be included in the table, but they all make this kind of profit.) The white powder sold by the distributor and the street dealer, being only 30–40 per cent pure, has been diluted by large quantities of inert white powder (bleach, talcum, etc.) which costs nothing. The prices they charge for this are about

> distributor $200–400 per gm of the mixed powder
> street dealer $400–600 per gm of the mixed powder

This was considerably more than the average paid for powder containing 40 per cent heroin in London in 1994 ($105–20): see Table 14.1.

Source: Figures compiled from sources in Hong Kong, obtained for the author by Simon Baker

commission and sell it to ethnic Chinese exporters based in Thailand, Hong Kong, China or Taiwan, who may move it by land or sea to Hong Kong and export it from there, or export direct from Bangkok.

The Chinese have traditionally done business with the advantage of strong personal and family relationships, or membership of the same secret society, so that the delivery of the heroin and the passing of money is done with total trust. This has always been their strength in terms of both secrecy and business efficiency. There is little or no paperwork. Khun Sa, half Chinese, heads this network with complete confidence in its discretion and integrity. Contracts, if used at all, are simple and personal. The Chinese captain of a boat from Thailand, for example, will readily hand over heroin worth millions of dollars to the captain of a boat from Hong Kong on the matching of two halves of a torn playing card, provided to them by the broker.

European business people, accustomed to written contracts designed to stand up in court, do not always realize what an enormous advantage their competitors have when they work on a system of trust. Lloyd's of London gathered the lion's share of the world's insurance market because, for three centuries, Lloyd's was a 'club' whose members would make instant verbal commitments with each other without fear of default, providing a speed and efficiency which their competitors could not match. Now that some members have started to distrust and sue each other, like other business people, they might well lose their competitive edge.

The Chinese are not the only people who work by trust where families are involved. So do many Indian traders, whose domination of business in some African countries matches that of the Chinese in East Asia. The Hindu *hawala* ('truth') system, for example, is a great boon to money launderers (see p. 103), being based on trust between members of a family or ethnic group working in continents thousands of miles apart. Again, where identification is needed at all, it is provided by something like an old bus ticket.

Some of the heroin which goes to Thailand may be routed onwards by truck to Malaysia or Vietnam or by various routes elsewhere in South-east Asia. Small amounts are taken out direct from Bangkok by casual air travellers (couriers) to Europe or the USA. Some of these are feckless tourists who see a sudden chance to make a few thousand dollars. Others have just run out of money and are willing to risk the death penalty or life imprisonment by concealing a few hundred grams of heroin in their personal baggage for the price of an air ticket and about $1000. Such people are a boon to drug traffickers.

Most of the heroin, however, is shipped from Thailand in fishing trawlers which keep a sea rendezvous with smaller craft somewhere amongst the islands around Hong Kong. It may be concealed in bales, bundles or bags of rubber or rice, for example, in which case it can be transferred direct to cargo ships lying or loading in Hong Kong harbour. If it is still in loose bags of heroin powder, these will be taken ashore, or perhaps into a houseboat in one of Hong Kong's boat cities, to be concealed in the legs of tables, statuettes, rubber tyres and other popular hiding places for smuggling. These in turn are mixed with other cargoes in huge containers. The problems of searching these containers in Rotterdam are discussed on pp. 150–1.

It may seem surprising that these transshipments are not more often detected. But south Thailand is intersected by a maze of rivers and canals; on the average day, there are some 5000 boats milling around the tortuous coastlines and inlets of Hong Kong and the New Territories. It is a bustling port; quite large cargo ships can be turned round in 12 hours, and there is no way every container or crate could be checked.

The heroin which goes by truck across China direct to Hong Kong crosses into the New Territories through the normal border posts. Again, with 10,000 trucks entering Hong Kong every day, there is no practicable way in which all of these could be searched. The total amounts of heroin are of the order of 1000 kg on a working day, and the smugglers are experienced at varying their methods. Seizures amount to only a small percentage and these are almost always the result of tip-offs.[7]

Hong Kong herself has 10,000 heroin addicts, each consuming about 1 gm per day, so the colony takes about 10 kg a day – 1 per cent of the throughput.

In the distribution to the USA and Europe, both Chinese families and secret societies (triads) again play a part. There are 50 triad societies, totalling 300,000 members, in Hong Kong.[8] It is a fallacy, however, to think that it is these triad societies which organize the operations and gather the profit. Individuals at the two ends of a transaction (e.g. amongst the large Chinese communities in London, Amsterdam, Sydney and California) may well be members of the same triad, which will guarantee their mutual trust, identity and bona fides. But it is the individual business people who handle the money and make the profits, not the triads.[9]

Elsewhere, especially in Italy and East Europe, the Mafia and other organized criminal gangs tend to get more of their heroin from the Golden Crescent, via the Middle East and Balkan routes.

THE GOLDEN CRESCENT

Afghanistan is second only to Myanmar as a producer of opium and produces more than Laos and Thailand put together. Most of the Afghan opium is grown in the northern province of Nangarhar and in the Helmand Valley in southern Afghanistan. The smuggling of the opium gum or morphine paste into Iran and Pakistan is facilitated by the ethnic link between Baluchi tribesmen astride the common borders of the three countries.

Opium production has been a major source of funds for the rival *mujahideen* guerrilla groups in Afghanistan, first in 1978–88 when they were resisting Soviet occupation, and ever since, as they have never stopped fighting each other. The Soviet armies and their puppet Afghan army were largely confined to the towns and the roads between them, so there was no restraint on opium cultivation, and every incentive to increase it. Even if the civil war is resolved, the tribes will still want to control their own territory and to buy arms to do so. A continuing high level of opium production seems inevitable.

Iran has her own problems, including 2 million heroin addicts. They in fact probably consume more heroin than Iran herself produces, but a lot of Afghan and Pakistani opium is refined in Iran and smuggled overland to Turkey, Syria and Lebanon, for onward transmission to Europe and North America. Again, ethnic factors apply. Most of the refining is done in Baluchi areas adjacent to Afghanistan and Pakistan and in Kurdish areas in Turkey.

Pakistan produces opium in the North-west Frontier Province, but less than her neighbours. Pakistan does, however, refine a lot of opium in about 100 small laboratories in the frontier areas. As Colombia does for cocaine in the Andes, so Pakistan produces most of the refined morphine and heroin for the Golden Crescent, most of it as heroin No. 4 suitable for injection. Though much of the finished product goes westwards overland through Iran, some of it is loaded into small boats in the Persian Gulf or the Gulf of Oman and taken to Dubai, a centre for smuggling of all kinds.

FROM TURKEY TO WEST EUROPE

Turkey has largely suppressed her own illicit production since 1971 but Turkish opium is of particularly high quality; it is still grown under strict control for legitimate extraction of heroin and morphine by the poppy straw method, for pharmaceutical use. Turkey remains, however, the key route for most of the distribution of illicit opiates from the Golden Crescent to west Europe. Traditionally, the main route was through Bulgaria and the former Yugoslavia, but this was disrupted by the war in Bosnia, and by restriction of traffic by sanctions against Serbia. So new routes have been developed: through Greece and Albania to Italy; through Istanbul, Bulgaria, Romania, Hungary and the Czech and Slovak Republics to Germany. Some of it is shipped across the Black Sea to Odessa and thence through Ukraine to Poland and west and north from there.[10]

Onward transmission through West Europe is facilitated by the large number of Turkish immigrants, especially in Germany. Fees for couriers escalate as the risk of detection increases to the west. A truck driver from Iran to the Turkish border in 1990 got $150 per kg; from the border across Turkey to Istanbul, $300; and from Istanbul via Bulgaria to Italy, $1500.

THROUGH WEST AFRICA

In the 1990s, an increasing amount of Asian heroin has been routed to West Europe via West Africa, especially through the airports in Benin, Nigeria and Togo and sometimes also Cameroon, Chad, Congo and Zaïre, arriving from both the Golden Triangle and the Golden Crescent. As was described for cocaine (p. 66), desperately poor West Africans are tempted to take risks for much smaller fees than are required to smuggle heroin across Europe; Nigerians, in particular, are perceived to have a better chance of getting into UK.

During 1989 and 1990 there was a big build-up of smuggling by Nigerians. In 1989, 760 West African heroin traffickers were arrested in Europe, of whom 636 were Nigerians. At the end of 1990, 1800 Nigerians were under arrest in Britain alone for drug-trafficking offences.[11]

Seven Nigerian courier organizations were identified in 1990. The drugs were carried on or in the body in special capsules produced by a Nigerian factory. These enabled the capsules to be swallowed and smuggled safely through airport security.[12]

11   Cannabis and Synthetics

CANNABIS PRODUCTION

Cannabis (or hashish) is a plant used to make hemp fibre. Its use as a herbal remedy was recorded in 2700 BC and it has long been prescribed as a sedative and analgesic, though it has now been superseded for medical purposes. It was also used as a stimulant or euphoriant in Syria and Iraq in the eleventh to thirteenth centuries to motivate the first Islamic fundamentalists, the Shia *hashishi* (Arabic for hashish takers); the word corrupted to 'The Assassins'.

Cannabis is taken in three forms: the leaves, rolled and smoked like a cigar, known in the USA as marijuana; hashish resin, which is extracted and dried, to be eaten or smoked; and hashish oil, which is more powerful and is commonly dripped into tobacco and smoked in a pipe or cigarette.

The active hallucinogenic ingredient is tetrahydrocannabinol (THC) which, like cocaine, is carried in varying percentages in the leaves and seeds, ranging from 0.5 per cent in US-grown cannabis, 7 per cent in Jamaican, Colombian and Mexican to 20 per cent in Spanish *sinsemilla* ('without seeds'). Of the treated forms, hashish oil has the highest THC content.

Cannabis is a fairly mild hallucinogenic or euphoriant, but it can cause dangerous hallucinations and behaviour, especially when driving, handling machinery or cooking, for example, and is often taken with alcohol and other stimulants or relaxants, including hard drugs. In itself it does not seem to be physically addictive unless combined with other drugs. Dealers in crack cocaine, for example, have been known to mix ground crack with cannabis so that the smoker quickly experiences the intense and addictive sensation without being aware of having taken crack at all. Cannabis users are generally more likely than others to graduate to the excitement of harder drugs.

Cannabis is very easy to grow and is by far the most widespread drug of abuse, especially in the USA and west Europe. The biggest single producers are Lebanon, Morocco and Colombia, each of which produces about 10,000 MT from 15,000 hectares. Next come Mexico (7000 MT) and the USA (5000 MT).[1] It is grown in many other countries all over the world, including Europe, and total production must exceed 50,000 MT per year, as compared with 900–1200 MT of cocaine and 4000 MT of opium (making 400 MT of heroin). Of 13 million frequent drug users in the USA, cocaine accounts for about 3 million and heroin for under 1 million.[2]

SYNTHETIC DRUGS

There are hundreds of synthetic or semi-synthetic drugs. They are often obtained by misappropriating or adapting legally manufactured pharmaceutical products. Many, however, are relatively easily made in clandestine laboratories, so accurate estimates of quantities are almost unobtainable. Some synthetics are especially made for curing addiction to hard drugs (e.g. methadone, originally synthesized as a substitute for morphine but now largely used in treating heroin addicts). The synthetic drugs most widely abused are barbiturates, amphetamines, LSD and Ecstasy (MDMA).

BARBITURATES

Barbiturates are generally prescribed by doctors and vets for sedation or sleep. There are four main classifications, based on the time to take effect and their duration. Ultrashort barbiturates produce anaesthesia within a minute of injection and are not much taken by abusers. Short and intermediate barbiturates take effect in 15 to 40 minutes; their effect lasts for up to 6 hours after oral administration, and these are the types most sought after by abusers. Long-acting barbiturates take effect after up to an hour and last about 16 hours. All barbiturates build up tolerance and if used without medical supervision can be addictive. Their effects are similar to those of drunkenness and the withdrawal symptoms are anxiety, insomnia and possibly delirium.[3]

AMPHETAMINES (INCLUDING SPEED AND ICE)

Amphetamines are stimulants and, like cocaine, are psychologically addictive. They can be inhaled, taken orally or injected. They are manufactured as powder or as tablets and are normally only 5 per cent pure, cut by glucose, lactose or sucrose, or by caffeine and ephedrine. The effects are similar to those of cocaine; a single 1 gm dose may cost about the same as a quarter-gm dose of cocaine, or considerably less than a quarter-gm rock of crack.[4]

Amphetamine sulphate, also known as Benzedrine, was used quite freely in the 1930s and 1940s, being sold over the counter without prescription. It was popular with students, who took it before examinations, and by others who wanted to keep awake and alert and, as they believed, to make their brains more lively. Before the Battle of Alamein in 1942, one British brigade commander gave Benzedrine to his tank crews when the moment came to advance through the minefield gaps cleared by the infantry and sappers during the first night of the battle, so that they would be 'on a high' as they broke out at dawn into open desert for the decisive battle against the German tanks. Unfortunately the brigadier was unfamiliar with the ways of battles, and it took another full day for the tanks to get through the congestion of narrow minefield gaps and messy fights with pockets of infantry holding out amongst them, so the tank crews spent their 'highs' in the frustration of grinding forward in a gigantic roadblock and were slumped in exhaustion by the time they got the chance to fire their first shots. The brigadier was sacked.

Though inhalers can be bought over the counter, amphetamine tablets are now sold only on prescription, with doses of between 2.5 and 15 mg per day. Drug abusers will use a lot more than this. They have been known to swallow or inject as much as 1000 mg every two or three hours, and their behaviour can become bizarre or violent.[5] This amount (1000 mg or 1 gm) costs about £10.[6] Other common derivatives are biphetamines (containing dextro-amphetamine) and dexedrine (containing dextroamphetamine sulphate).[7]

One of the most dangerous is Desoxyn (methamphetamine hydrochloride, known as 'Ice'). In the USA in 1990 the DEA predicted that Ice would become the next major drug problem, and by 1994 their prediction looked like being fulfilled, as its consumption was beginning to rival that of crack cocaine (see Chapter 9), to which it had many similarities. Like crack, Ice can be smoked, which gives a high within a few seconds but lasts much longer – up to 24 hours.

Ice is easily manufactured in simple laboratories and, unlike crack, can be made without importing any illegal substances, so the enormous hazards, and therefore the expensive bribes and courier fees all along the line in the cocaine trail, do not arise. That is why Ice is cheaper than crack but, by charging £10 per gm, the manufacturers and dealers can make a huge percentage profit with fewer risks than those involved in peddling crack or heroin.

Ice first became fashionable in 1991 in Hawaii, and then spread to become, with Speed and Ecstasy, one of the most popular drugs in the USA and Europe for 'raves' – clandestine mass dance sessions designed to build up into wild euphoria, in which drugs play a major part.[8]

Amphetamines are the most widely consumed synthetic drug. Of the amphetamines used in the Netherlands, Scandinavia, the UK and France, 75–80 per cent are manufactured in the Netherlands and almost all the rest in Poland.[9]

LSD

LSD (or acid) was first synthesized in 1938; it was later found to have effects on the brain similar to psychosis and was used as a tool for research into mental illness. It is no longer used medically. It is taken orally and does not appear to be addictive. Its abuse became very fashionable in the 1960s, especially in the USA, and it is still manufactured there. The chemicals needed are not easy to obtain in the UK, which imports it mainly from the Netherlands. LSD produces hallucinations and can be especially dangerous for drivers, as it also affects judgement of distance. It is usually sold in the form of tablets, thin squares of gelatine ('window panes') or impregnated paper ('blotter acid'), perforated so that the individual tabs, each containing 30–50 mg, can be torn off and placed on the tongue. The effects of larger doses can last for 10–12 hours.[10] A tab can cost as little as £2 ($3).[11]

MDMA (ECSTASY)

Ecstasy (Methylenedioxymethamphetamine – MDMA), as its full name implies, is a variant of amphetamine and is another hallucinogen. First synthesized in 1963, it came on to the drug scene in 1967 in the 'hippie' culture in Haight Ashbury in San Francisco. It is sometimes supplied in white powder form to be 'snorted' up the nose like cocaine, occasionally dissolved in water for injection like heroin, or manufactured, like LSD, in squares of impregnated paper or (most commonly) in tablet form. As it is produced and distributed clandestinely in breach of the law, there is no quality control, so the buyer is often 'ripped off' with a very much diluted product. It costs about the same (£20 or $30) per tablet as a quarter-gm dose of cut cocaine or heroin. Ecstasy is the favourite euphoriant sold in the UK by the organizers of raves.

Though seizures are not a reliable indicator of total traffic, the startling growth in seizures between 1988 and 1989 does indicate a significant growth in the use of Ecstasy. In northern Europe, seizures rose from 6300 dosage units in 1988 to 938,000 in 1989, almost all of it (930,000) in the Netherlands.[12]

Part V
Finance

12 Money Laundering

THE TASK

If the best guess of the world expenditure on illicit drugs is correct ($500 billion a year), this amounts to an astonishing $100 for every one of the world's population. Most of it, however (at least $300 billion), is spent by the tens of millions of regular users on the affluent streets of the West, the typical addict spending $50,000–100,000 a year on the habit, of which 90 per cent is criminally acquired from theft and fraud.

So the core of the money-laundering task begins on western streets, in western shops, bars, betting shops and casinos, and western banks, through which every year at least $300 billion – or $1 billion a day – enter the trail in the form of crumpled notes in local currencies, through the hands of individual street dealers, who mainly work in small gangs. These gangs are the retail outlets of a global network of growers, refiners, traffickers, exporters, importers and distributors which probably amounts to between 1 million and 2 million people.[1]

Well over half this money ends up amongst the assets of large, apparently legitimate corporations, mainly in the form of bank deposits, securities, shares and property. Some of the deposits are in 'fiscal havens', which specialize in running confidential bank accounts with anonymity guaranteed by the government of the haven. Most of the money, however, has become 'legal', that is, its origins have been concealed beyond means of tracing by a series of intermediate transactions. The corporations themselves are also 'legal' in that they carry out some legitimate commercial trading, but are owned by, or are holding the assets on behalf of, the international criminals who control the illicit drug trade. Of the money deposited through the London money market, 10 per cent is believed to be of laundered money. It is deposited in banks which probably have no idea that the apparently reputable individuals or corporations in whose name they hold it have acquired it by criminal means, and that it will be used for further criminal purposes.

The simplest definition of money laundering is that of the Subcommittee on Narcotics and Terrorism of the US Senate Foreign Relations Committee (SFRC):

> Money laundering is the conversion of profits from illegal activities into financial assets which appear to have legitimate origins.

The SFRC identifies three stages: first, *placement*, the physical disposal of the cash; second, *layering*, the process of transferring the funds through various accounts to diguise its origins; and third, *integration*, the movement of laundered funds into legitimate organizations.[2]

FAST MOVING CASH

At the lowest level, a typical dealer who actually sells the drugs on the streets probably handles between $2000 and $5000 a week, of which he pays about half or three-quarters to his supplier and keeps the rest as his profit. These dealers usually work in gangs (see pp. 164–8), which have the collective strength to keep rival gangs out of their territory and organize the safe and undetected disposal of the cash. Their gang leader (who buys their supplies for them) usually controls or makes working arrangements with businesses which are cash intensive and of a kind which makes it easy to conceal illegal activities amongst a large turnover of legitimate activities. Typical examples are betting shops, fast food bars, video or computer spare parts shops; or catering for tourists – cheap hotels or coach tours; or, if it is a larger gang with a lot of cash to launder, casinos, dealers in 'antiques', fine arts, gold and jewellery or second-hand cars. Amongst a large turnover to be banked, cash can be paid in with no evidence of whether the goods or services were supplied or not. No one can prove how many meals or drinks were served, or whether some expensive item 'bought' or 'sold' at a large profit ever existed at all. And if the arrangement is with a casino, it is common for punters to buy or cash in thousands of pounds in chips with no record of what bets they placed.

The money piles up, available when required either for spending or for further laundering to get it out of the country (see next section). Money can be paid out as salaries and wages for people who do not exist or for hundreds of other apparently legitimate purposes.

Another commonly used device is 'cycling', through vending machines or mail order transactions. The goods are 'bought' and 'sold' either in the names of different members of the gang, or by use of aliases so that a person can buy and sell to and from himself, each time at a profit. As a front, a stock of suitable items is available, with enough turnover to conceal the rest, and these items (on paper in the case of mail orders) go round and round, generating a credible profit on paper, which is in fact cash from street sales of drugs.

The growth in popularity of car boot sales has been a boon to criminals. Drug addicts have to steal regularly to fund their weekly expenditure on heroin or crack. What began as an innocent gathering of neighbours to get rid of unwanted junk has now become a prime outlet for stolen goods, often of quite high value, e.g. stolen videos, car radios or hi-fi equipment. Drug dealers, too, can quote non-existent bargains at a car boot sale to explain cash found in their possession from their street sales.

One launderer ran an international art business. On a typical operation, he commissioned a French artist to do some modern paintings at £200 each. He then destroyed the paintings, having forged receipts from 'customers' for £2000 each and paid the 'balance' (in fact the takings from his drug sales) into his art dealing bank account, backed by the real receipts for £200 and the forged receipts for £2000. If there were a query, the French artist would have confirmed that he painted and sold the pictures.[3]

INTERNATIONAL BANKING

Higher up the chain, much of the money is invested in property or shares in the country in which it was acquired. Most of it, however, is laundered through banks and finance companies in a series of countries to make it impossible to trace its source, even if it returns in the end, as thoroughly respectable investments in the country where it started.

It is, however, quite possible for money to be moved in bulk, initially without passing through the banking system. In 1983, an executive aircraft owned by a prosperous businessman was inspected by customs before taking off from Florida for Panama and found to be carrying $5 million in $20 bills in cardboard cartons, all of it the proceeds of drug sales in the USA. It transpired that this aircraft had been doing this weekly for eight months in which it had carried $151 million to Panama, where the bankers (during General Noriega's time) provided a confidential banking and money-laundering service for the Colombian drug cartels, to the considerable profit of Panama. At around the same time, a Colombian launderer in Miami was found to have $3.6 million in stacks of small denomination notes, weighing 700 lbs, in his office and another $5.8 million in his local bank account. He would write a cheque on this account in pesos which could be cashed in Colombia. In the previous eight months, $242 million had passed through this account, for which he had received a commission of 2 per cent – $4.8 million.[4]

The coast of Britain provides natural facilities for importing drugs and exporting either bags of notes or (more often) high value goods saleable anywhere – jewels, watches, and so on. There are 147 regular commercial ports; also 188 yacht marinas with over 40,000 berths, and 150,000 yachts and other pleasure craft around the coast.[5] Sailing to mainland Europe is commonplace and it is very easy for a yacht to make a rendezvous with a cargo vessel at sea or in one of the many harbours and estuaries on both sides of the English Channel. Five easily handled bags each containing 20 kg (100 kg in all) of cocaine may be worth $4 million to a British importer, eventually to be sold for $10 million on the streets. Suitcases full of notes of this value might be four times heavier, but still quite manageable in a small motor cruiser.

Nevertheless, it is now a great deal easier, and probably safer, to switch the money across the world by electronic transfer. Though most western countries have introduced regulations to control this (see Chapter 13) such controls are very difficult to enforce if the launderers have the sense to order its transfer in a large number of small sums from different banks.

One of the easiest ways to transfer money internationally is for a multinational corporation to have a number of subsidiary accounts in different countries. Money can then be paid into the corporate account in one country and drawn out from the corporate account in another. If it becomes necessary to adjust the balance by transfer, this could be concealed in the regular transfers of money or credit to and from subsidiaries. If necessary, false invoices can be arranged, to pay for, say, 'goods provided' to a subsidiary or for raw materials 'bought' from a third country, without any material actually moving at all. The art lies in concealing these transactions amongst a chaff of other transactions in the corporation's ordinary course of business. Again (see p. 66), they can ensure that their legitimate turnover is high because they can undercut their competitors who need to maintain a profit margin.

Fictitious operations or inflated invoicing are common methods of concealing the criminal origins of money. In one case in the early 1980s, the totally fictitious export of fruit from Sicily to an equally fictitious fruit juice manufacturing company in London enabled $46 million from heroin traffic to reach a bank account in Switzerland. In 1985, three brothers in a family jewellery business in Palermo were arrested for using inflated gold and jewellery invoices to a Maltese jeweller to launder drug profits on behalf of *Cosa Nostra*. One of the brothers had also been kidnapped and released on payment of a ransom of $3 million, and it was uncertain whether the ransom was simply extortion from a rich family (as it purported to be) or whether the kidnap never actually took place and the 'ransom' was merely a means of laundering the $3 million.[6] Whether or not it applied in this case, there is strong evidence of fictitious kidnaps and ransoms having been used in other cases as a laundering tool.

In 1985, another typical laundering operation was uncovered in New York and became known as the 'Pizza Connection'. *Cosa Nostra*, who at that time controlled a large part of the heroin traffic and sales in USA, arranged for a number of pizza houses and fast food bars to be bought by New York Italians on whom they could rely to cooperate through to a mixture of incentives and fear of retribution. Dollars from street sales of heroin were delivered to launderers to be banked with the legitimate flow of cash taken across the pizza counters in a trade where bills and receipts are neither asked for nor given. As an extra precaution, they probably made suitable entries in their books to record false purchases of supplies to be reasonably consistent with payments of profits to the launderers.

One of the launderers, Luigi Montalcini (not his real name), had cash delivered to his room in the Waldorf Astoria Hotel in New York. Between 27 April and 2 July 1982, he paid seven cash deposits to a total of $5.2 million into the account of a property and raw materials company, Klatz, owned by a Swiss national. The account was held at a branch of Bank X, and Montalcini took the money there in suitcases, but Bank X became suspicious owing to the large number of small denomination notes involved and his reluctance to enter the bank vaults himself, where he knew that he would be routinely recorded by the security cameras. Bank X made enquiries about Klatz from their Zurich branch and, although the answers seemed reassuring, they asked Montalcini to close his Bank X account. However, he also had access to the account of an Italian development corporation at a New York branch of Bank Y. Between 6 July and 27 September, 11 more deposits totalling $8.5 million were paid by Montalcini into that account; other deposits were on the account of SAK Holdings. Bank Y's legal branch became suspicious and, although the US government urged discretion, Montalcini's Swiss lawyer was informed and the SAK Zurich account was closed in October 1982.[7]

One Mafia launderer who became an informant described how he was brought money in suitcases so heavy that, when they were loaded, the car springs visibly sank. He arranged payment of about $10 million into accounts at a New York bank who transferred it by bank draft or cheque to Nassau or Bermuda. Other banks in Switzerland and Italy were involved through the offices of an iron and steel business which covered the laundering of $20 million within a few years.[8]

If they are spread over a large number of different launderers, covering corporations and international banks, the criminality of these operations is not easy to detect, and the banks themselves were usually unaware that they were being used in this way.

Usury is another activity used to cover money laundering. Companies and individuals often try to avert the threat of bankruptcy by taking out loans with little or no collateral, paying interest of around 40 per cent. Deals of this kind are kept as quiet as possible in order not to prejudice confidence in the liquidity of the borrower, so they can be relatively easily simulated to provide explanations, if demanded, for the transfer of money. In 1991, there were believed to be about 800,000 usurers operating in Italy alone.[9]

The greatest boon to money launderers is the ease of electronic transfer of money to foreign banks; as one writer described it, 'criminal money whizzing around the world at the touch of a computer key'.[10] This was particularly easy in the early 1980s, when the technology had become commonplace but when most banks still regarded client confidentiality – and especially corporate client confidentiality – as sacrosanct in all circumstances. Attempts to modify this were made from the mid-1980s. These are described in Chapter 13, but none has been wholly successful. Since even electronic transfers are usually recorded on the computer and can be investigated, there has been a spread of alternative banking which involves no records and relies on trust. Asian traders have for centuries used the *hawala* system described in Chapter 10 (pp. 85–6) in the context of heroin trafficking. The system is very much alive in Europe because of the large number of Asian immigrants who wish to transfer part of their salaries to their families at home without creating records which could be investigated by the fiscal authorities. There were in 1991 about 1000 *hawala* bankers in Britain, of whom 12 may have been involved in laundering drug money. One was believed to have handled up to $12 million per week, but could not be prosecuted as there was no way of proving that he had handled money 'knowing or suspecting' that it was derived from drug trafficking.[11]

FISCAL HAVENS

There are a number of well-known fiscal havens, (often called 'tax havens' as one of their original functions was to enable individuals and corporations to evade tax liabilities in their home countries). All that is needed is for a business to be incorporated in the haven, often needing no more than a nominal amount of capital and equally nominal registration fees and annual corporation fees (perhaps as little as $100) plus a room with a telephone, fax and computer terminal. It can be incorporated as a holding company free to conduct business all over the world. Large numbers of foreign banks set up branches and the haven will have a national bank of its own. One essential feature is banking secrecy: some of the havens enshrine this in their laws, having a statutory ban on disclosing the names of account holders or information about their accounts – for it is this feature which brings the haven its business.

The havens are in most cases small independent republics or offshore islands which have traditionally enjoyed a degree of autonomy. These provide an ideal environment for setting up 'shell companies' with a façade of legitimate trading to cover their laundering of money for drug traffickers and other criminal organizations. Leon Richardson described one such independent island republic, a former British dependency, now a member of the UN. Its population was about 8000, of whom 5000 were citizens and the remainder were expatriates. It prohibited immigration and seldom issued tourist visas, but had its own airport and airline. Its company laws were remarkably relaxed. Holding companies could be registered as wholly owned subsidiaries, whose books could be kept outside the island's jurisdiction. The subsidiary did not need a board of directors in the country, nor were its accounts required to be audited.[12] Almost any transaction could be routed through the island; any amount of money, for example, could be electronically transferred to an account on the island and, within minutes, electronically transferred out again, without any record of where it had gone. If a launderer transferred money through this account and then through a second and then a third haven, all of which had the same statutory guarantee of bank secrecy, there was no way in which it could be traced. It could in due course emerge as an impeccable investment in shares or property somewhere, or as part of a corporate bank account in which it could be shown to have come from a legitimate source.

In some of these island havens, anyone can register and take out a licence to operate a bank, in one case reportedly for as little as a $60 fee.[13] Fiscal havens of this kind abound in the islands off the coasts of North and South America, especially in the Caribbean and the Antilles, where money laundering can be run in parallel with the role of the islands as transit and distribution points for cocaine (see pp. 67–9). There are also many fiscal havens in Europe, some within the EU. Andorra, the Channel Islands, Liechtenstein, Luxembourg and Monaco all offer incentives to outside investors. Some of their governments continue to protect anonymous bank accounts and to block access for police or fiscal inspection, though most West European governments will now authorize such access if the courts order it on the strength of reasonable grounds for suspecting that an account contains money acquired by criminal means.

13 Countering Money Laundering

INTERNATIONAL MONEY-LAUNDERING LEGISLATION

In the mid-1980s, the US and European governments were becoming increasingly alarmed about the flow of illegal money nationally and internationally acquired by drug trafficking and organized crime, including money from protection rackets and other means of extortion by both terrorists and other criminals.

Attempts to legislate against it were pioneered by the US government, which introduced compulsory Currency Transaction Reports (**CTRs**) to document all financial transactions exceeding $10,000 for domestic and $5000 for international deposits and transfers. The US Drug Enforcement Administration (**DEA**) was established 'to reduce the availability of illicit narcotics and dangerous drugs in the market place and to disrupt the drug traffic through the arrest and prosecution major violators and the removal of their assets'.[1]

The obligation to register CTRs was incorporated in the Money Laundering Control Act 1986 (**MLCA**). Though it produced a snowstorm of data, most of which would never need to be used, the miraculous capacity of computers to pick out specific items from the chaff has made the CTRs valuable both for police investigation and as a hazard and deterrent against money laundering. In 1989 a federal law was added, authorizing the government to track and investigate transactions, to freeze assets if there were grounds for suspicion that they came from laundered drug money, and to confiscate them if that were proved.[2] These measures formed the basis for similar legislation in the UK, Italy and other countries.

In the **Basel Declaration** of December 1988, the heads of the central banks of the 12 leading banking countries – the Group of Seven (G7: Canada, France, Germany, Italy, Japan, UK and USA) plus the Benelux trio, Sweden and Switzerland – committed themselves 'to take steps to identify their clients and the sources of their assets; to report any suspicions to the authorities; and to collaborate with the police and the courts in patrimonial investigation'.[3]

The **UN Vienna Convention** against illicit traffic in drugs was also signed in December 1988. By March 1989, 89 countries had signed it. Some were slow to ratify it, but the Convention came fully into force in November 1990. This committed ratifying nations to introduce the crime of money laundering; to forbid bank secrecy when this offence was suspected; to make provision to freeze suspected assets during investigation and to seize them if the offence were proved; to extradite offenders on drug-trafficking charges; to cooperate internationally in investigation and prosecution and in training and coordination of operations by law enforcement agencies; and to take action to suppress drug trafficking by sea and by air.

The **Council of Europe Convention** on Laundering, Search, Seizure and Confiscation of the Proceeds of Crime also provided for a number of measures for prevention and response including asset restraint, seizure, and their harmonization between contracting parties. This was not confined to members of the Council of Europe; Australia, Canada and the East European and former Soviet republics were also encouraged to ratify it.[4]

In 1989, the G7 countries, again with the Benelux trio, Sweden and Switzerland plus the EC Commission, Australia, Austria and Spain, set up the Financial Action Task Force (**FATF**) to analyse money laundering; to assess national and international measures in force; and to make recommendations. The FATF reported in June 1990 and endorsed 40 recommendations, subsequently extended to 26 countries, including enhancement of action by national financial systems and strengthening of international cooperation.[5]

Also, in 1988, **Interpol** formed a working group to pursue similar cooperation over mechanisms for gathering and sharing financial information connected with drug trafficking. The working group has developed a model law for identification, tracing, seizure and confiscation of assets derived from criminal activity and has published and updated a Financial Assets Encyclopedia.[6] In March 1992, Interpol also established an Automated Search Facility (**ASF**), a system giving access to data held by national systems, but with the proviso that members could specify which countries were to receive their information –

obviously essential in a body the size of Interpol, with 136 members,[7] most of whom distrust at least some of the others.

In parallel with these measures, the heads of state of the European Community set up a European Committee to Combat Drugs (**CELAD**) in December 1989.[8] This aimed to coordinate anti-drug strategies, suppress illicit drug trading and reduce demand. In 1991, the **TREVI** group – a regular committee of EC interior and justice ministers, with associated working groups of their officials, police chiefs, and others – established a European Police Organization, **Europol**, to deal with cross-border crime and, in December 1992, formed a European Drugs Unit (**EDU**).[9]

In 1993, an **EC Directive** came into force, giving a wider definition of money laundering to incorporate other forms of crime as well as drug trafficking:

> The conversion or transfer of property, knowing that such property is derived from criminal activity or from an act of participation in such activity, for the purpose of concealing the illicit origin of the property or of assisting any person who is involved in committing such activity to evade the legal consequences of his action; the concealment or disguise of the true nature, source, location, dispostiion, movement, rights with respect to, or ownership of property knowing that such property . . . (etc. as above); the acquisition of property knowing, at the time of receipt, that such property . . . (etc. as above).[10]

Ponderous, but a reminder of how comprehensive – and almost incomprehensible! – legal wording has to be. The problem lies in the word 'knowing'. It is often not easy to prove the *awareness* of the person accused, who will, of course, have taken every possible precaution to conceal any evidence which might indicate this.

BRITISH LEGISLATION

Britain has been one of the leaders in taking internal measures against the laundering of drug money, partly because such measures often also pay dividends in combating terrorism, to which Britain since 1969 has been subjected in the worst and most persistent degree in Europe. The **Misuse of Drugs Act** was passed in 1972, but the first anti-laundering law was the Drug Trafficking Offences Act 1986 (**DTOA**). This became law on 1

January 1989,[11] and specified that the crime of money laundering was committed when 'retention of control' of the proceeds of drug trafficking was facilitated, 'whether by concealment, removal from the jurisdiction, transfer to nominees or otherwise' or when funds from drug trafficking were placed at the disposal or benefit of another to acquire property by way of investment, and the person who enters into such an engagement knows or suspects that the other person carries on or has carried on drug trafficking or has benefited from drug trafficking.[12] To secure such a conviction it is necessary to show that the launderer 'knew or had reason to suspect' that the money was acquired by drug trafficking.

The Criminal Justice Act 1988 (**CJA**) extended this power to other categories of crime where the defendants could be found to have profited by more than £10,000 ($15,000). It was also incorporated in the Prevention of Terrorism (Temporary Provisions) Act (**PTA**) at its next annual renewal in Parliament.[13]

Under these Acts, the police can apply to the courts for authority to investigate bank and other accounts when they can give 'reasonable grounds for suspicion that they contain money or other assets obtained by criminal means'. Given a court order, the banks are obliged to give police access; if their suspicions prove justified, the assets can be frozen immediately while under investigation and, if appropriate, while charge and trial proceed. If the owner of the assets is found guilty under the DTOA, CJA or PTA, the assets can then be confiscated. In contrast to the normal principles of English law, the onus is on the accused person to prove to the court that the assets concerned were obtained lawfully. (This applies equally to assets obtained from extortion or rackets by terrorist movements or their supporters.)

The DTOA gives immunity from civil or criminal liability to people who disclose suspicions concerning the proceeds of drug trafficking, and makes it an offence for anyone aware of an investigation to tip off the suspect. The police may search for and seize material held by parties not themselves suspected of crime if they have reason to suspect that the materials were originally obtained from drug trafficking. They can also freeze and apply to the courts for confiscation of property from people who were unaware, when they received it, that it was acquired from drug trafficking, for example, if a drug trafficker has given his daughter a car, even if she does not know how he got the money, it can be confiscated.[14]

Under these Acts, the British law regards *all* assets acquired during the six years prior to conviction for drug trafficking offences as proceeds from drug-trafficking unless the accused can prove otherwise. If further suspected assets come to light in the six years after conviction, the prosecution can apply to the courts for their confiscation too, subject to the accused failing to prove that they have a legitimate source. This is to counter concealment of the assets or their removal from British jurisdiction.

In dealing with violent criminal gangs with long arms, the victims or unwilling collaborators may understandably be reluctant to talk. Exactly the same procedure has applied to extortion by the 'loyalist' and republican terrorist movements in Northern Ireland – the UVF, UFF, IRA and INLA.

The effective use of anti-laundering laws depend a great deal on intelligence. People are much more willing to corroborate evidence which has been presented to them by the police from other sources, than they are to initiate presentation of the evidence. The handling of informants is discussed in Chapter 20.

In 1992, the British National Criminal Intelligence Service (**NCIS**) was formed, incorporating most of the other police intelligence units, including the National Drugs Intelligence Unit (**NDIU**) which had been formed in 1985. For political reasons, Britain has always been reluctant to allow the formation of a national police force, and has therefore jealously preserved the independence of her 48 county or regional police forces, which are controlled by police authorities made up of elected local councillors and magistrates. The Home Office does retain a strong influence on efficiency, but not on operational control, by virtue of paying half the cost of the force out of general taxation. London is the exception, the Metropolitan Police in New Scotland Yard being wholly funded by the Home Office. The Metropolitan Police have always maintained intelligence resources available to back up local forces with the loan of officers from Special Branch (**SB**) and from the Criminal Investigation Department (**CID**) – but it is up to the local forces when and whether they 'call in Scotland Yard'. The power and complexity of modern police computers, however, have necessitated the formation of NCIS, 450 strong , working with the Police National Computer (**PNC**), with links to its German equivalent at Wiesbaden (the first and best in Europe) and PNCs of other friendly countries. The intelligence arms of the regional crime squads (**RCSs**),[15] which had been established in 1964, were also reorganized into five regional crime intelligence offices (**RCIOs**), also computerized and part of the NCIS system. (This is further discussed in Chapter 20.)

The success of almost any intelligence system, whether it is dealing with terrorism, drug trafficking or other crimes, lies in getting *specific* information. The best informants, obviously, are people involved in or on the fringes of the criminal organization itself. When such people give information, they will realize that they are taking dangerous risks; some will give it in the hope of leniency in punishment for their own crimes; most, however, will need two kinds of incentives, a generous reward and a guarantee of security for themselves and their families, perhaps with a new identity in a new country. This may be expensive, but an informant with inside knowledge is the most cost effective of all measures against terrorism and crime. The recruiting and handling of informants in UK is discussed in Chapter 20. The Italians also developed this, both against right- and left-wing terrorists and against the Mafia, with their *pentitismo* techniques (see pp. 135–7) and they can teach the rest of the world a lot.

ITALIAN LEGISLATION

In Italy, the links between organized crime and drug trafficking have always been closer than in other west European countries, so it is not surprising that their drug addiction, extortion and money laundering are also the highest in west Europe. They have been slow in passing the necessary laws, perhaps due to corrupt links between politicians and the Mafia. The laws, when passed, have been good ones, but the Italians, criminals or otherwise, are adept at finding ways round them.

Italian law 55 of 1990 predicates certain types of crimes to which the money-laundering provisions apply, that is, to any person who 'substitutes money, goods or property derived from aggravated robbery, aggravated extortion, kidnapping for the purpose of extortion or crimes concerning the production or trafficking of narcotic or psychotropic drugs'; or who obstructs the identification of the source of such property; who invests money, goods or property from the above-mentioned crimes in 'economic or financial activities'. Thus money laundering is defined as a synthesis of three elements: the predicated crime which precedes the laundering; the conduct of the launderer (concealment, removal, obstruction, etc.); and the degree of awareness – knowledge or suspicion – of the criminal origin of the funds. This aspect – awareness – is implicit in the Italian criminal code, unlike the British, so does not need to be spelled out in law 55.[16]

Italian law 197 of 1991 forbids all transactions in cash, in foreign currency or in transferable instruments over the value of 20 million lire ($15,000) except in traceable form and carried out by authorized intermediaries. The intermediaries are obliged to register all such transactions with details of the persons by and for whom the transaction was performed, including name, date of birth, place of residence, profession, tax reference number and the reason for the transaction. Each bank branch register of such transactions must be integrated into a computerized archive in the bank's head office. There will be no national database but the Italian Exchange Bureau (**UIC**) may perform arbitrary checks to ensure proper functioning of the system and carry out statistical analyses of the aggregate data provided by each intermediary. If anomalies emerge, the UIC must inform the Treasury Ministry which will then order an investigation. At the same time, the banks themselves have an obligation under the UN Vienna Convention (which Italy has ratified) to disclose any suspicious circumstances.[17]

WAYS ROUND THE MONEY-LAUNDERING LAWS

Reputable banks may have no reason to 'know or suspect' that sums deposited or transferred are the proceeds of criminal activities. Philipp Bros in London were exonerated from all blame for recycling $250 million of cocaine profits for the Medellin cartel by gold sales and purchases in 1987–9.[18] But the most notorious case of crooked international banking was that of the Bank of Credit and Commerce International (BCCI). This bank's head office was in Luxembourg, but it was mainly owned by one of the Arab Gulf states, and had branches all over the world, including major activities in London and Tampa, Florida. Suspicion that it might be involved in drug money laundering was first announced early in 1986. After more than two years of investigation in six countries, forty-three of BCCI's staff were arrested in October 1988, including nine senior managers. The laundering of cash from drug sales in USA was described in a newspaper at the time:

> After collecting up to $1 million in cash, the [undercover] agents would have a local bank transfer the money to the BCCI branch in Tampa. BCCI then wired the money via a New York bank, first to its head office in Luxembourg and then to BCCI in London. There it was converted into a certificate of deposit which was used as security for a loan made by BCCI in the Bahamas to a bogus corporation. Now the money was ready to be returned to the original account at BCCI in Tampa. From there it would be wired to its final BCCI destination, a branch in Uruguay. It was taken in cash to Colombia. The difference between the original amount of the certificate of deposit and the loan represented the bank's profit, according to the investigators.[19]

Sadly, a large number of BCCI's individual account holders, mainly Arabs and Pakistanis, had innocently invested their savings in it and lost heavily, though the government of Abu Dhabi (a major stakeholder) attempted to compensate some of them. The Bank of England was blamed for listing BCCI as a reputable bank for investment long after the investigations had begun in 1986, and it was suggested (but denied) that this was because the intelligence services were getting valuable information and did not want to disrupt the bank's operations.[20]

In January 1990, BCCI admitted that $32 million had been laundered through its branches, especially the Tampa branch, and that it had also acted as banker to General Noriega.[21] It was said to have moved at least $28 million for Noriega and continued to move his money out of US jurisdiction even after he had been indicted.

BCCI was charged as a corporation with money laundering in the US courts and, under a plea bargaining agreement in 1990, pleaded guilty and paid $14 million in drug money forfeiture, in exchange for which the US Attorney-General dropped all charges against the corporation. This was criticized by the Subcommittee on Narcotics and Terrorism of the US Senate Foreign Relations Committee:

The result [is] that the bank ended its criminal liability by paying no fine, but merely turning over the profits of drug trafficking to the federal government. . . . The sole remaining defendants in this major money laundering case are individuals. Instead of eliciting information from these officials in order to fully examine the operations, structure and practices of the bank itself, the Justice Department can only probe the behaviour and motives of the individuals.[22]

There was also a trial in the UK, but there was not sufficient evidence to prove *corporate* knowledge or approval of the criminal actions undertaken in BCCI's name.[23] The launderers had clearly covered their tracks well.

At the lower end of the money-laundering process is the placement of cash. Faced with the obligation of the banks to register transactions above a threshold of $10,000–15,000, the launderer's response is 'smurfing' – splitting the cash into smaller deposits below that limit. The problem is that, with large amounts to place, the dealers will either have to pay many visits to different banks, arousing suspicion if they are spotted, or employ accomplices holding other accounts with the risk of them being careless or becoming informers. It may be easier to take suitcases full of notes overseas, but this can be risky in Britain because, under Section 25 of the **Criminal Justice (International Cooperation) Act 1990**, customs officers have the power to seize cash being carried out of UK in excess of £10,000 ($15,000) if there are 'reasonable grounds' to suspect that the cash represents the proceeds from drug trafficking. A person carrying that amount might find it hard to explain. To get it back, the launderer would have the onus of proving a legitimate source to the courts. The safest way is for the dealers' gang itself to be part of a cash-intensive business which legitimately takes very large amounts of money every day – casinos, betting shops, and so on.

Many banks are reluctant to report transactions of $10,000–15,000 because of the cost. Banks in the USA make some 6 million CTRs a year and each one costs $17. In Britain, there are 17,000 bank branches with 70 million bank accounts and there are 6000 building society branches. There is an even greater problem in Italy, where the black market is recognized as an indispensable part of the economy. In many countries, there is a great deal of tax evasion and corruption. If clients fear that their bank may give way to government orders to breach confidentiality, they will move to one which they are sure will not. So it is not only the banks in fiscal havens but also many others, in countries which have ratified the Vienna Convention, which will tacitly try to avoid making CTRs or disclosing suspicious transactions.

Another factor is that, although there is legal protection for breach of professional secrecy, there is no guarantee of anonymity. In a country with a high level of violence in crime, the cashier who has grounds for suspicion, or the bank's lawyer through whom it would be reported, may be tempted to keep their suspicions to themselves. In Italy, criminal vendettas account for a high proportion of the 1500 murders a year by organized criminal gangs.

Very few disclosures do in fact result in successful prosecutions because of the necessity to prove 'beyond reasonable doubt' that the accused person 'knew or had strong reason to suspect' that the funds deposited or transferred were derived from drug trafficking. In Britain, there were nearly 4000 suspicious disclosures under the DTOA in its first year of operation, but there were only 17 money-laundering convictions resulting in £27.2 million ($40 million) being confiscated.[24]

The percentage of convictions for most types of crime in Britain is depressingly low, but particularly so for money laundering. Despite the power of judges to order assets to be frozen 'if there are reasonable grounds for suspicion', and the onus lying on the accused to prove the legitimacy of the source, their confiscation requires a criminal standard of proof, 'beyond all reasonable doubt', not only of guilt of the drug-trafficking offence but also of the amount by which the accused has benefited from it. Though this is a proper principle regarding guilt for the offence itself, there is a strong case for directing juries to accept a civil standard of proof 'on the balance of probabilities' in deciding on the assets to be confiscated.

Another problem in Britain is that, if the defendant absconds before the case comes to trial, confiscation cannot be ordered without the presence of a guilty party. This can sometimes be got over by convicting a number of defendants for conspiracy. It would be better, however, if Britain followed the continental procedure for 'trial in absentia' so that frozen assets can be confiscated if the accused fails to appear in court to prove their legitimacy.

A further difficulty in Britain lies in realizing the amount of the confiscation order. There are many ways in which professional criminals and their lawyers can obstruct realization of their assets. In 1989, of confiscation orders to the value of £7.9 million ($12 million), only £1.1 million ($1.7 million) were realized.[25] If it is accepted that half the $4 billion spent on drugs in Britain (at least $2000 million) is profit, the amount confiscated is less than 1 per cent of that profit. Justice is failing.

The world is also failing to realize the assets which convicted launderers have contrived to transfer to foreign countries. Sometimes this is covered by bilateral agreements between EU states. Many countries have ratified the European Convention on Laundering, but court procedures, definition of offences and standards of proof differ between countries. Italy, for example, is alone in having the offence of 'Mafia association' but applies the offence of money laundering only to certain predicated crimes (see pp. 111 and 131). The concept of corporate criminal liability is in some countries vague and in others non-existent (e.g. in Italy).[26] Sadly, as with the experience of extradition, some governments will find ways of evading their obligations if they feel that doing this will serve their national interest or avoid embarrassment. Finally, whenever any legislation begins to take effect, sophisticated drug traffickers and other organized criminals, with their legal and financial advisers, adapt their methods to avoid it.

CONCLUSION

The mass of anti-laundering legislation passed since 1986 has forced the drug traffickers to change their methods, but it does not seem to have reduced the amount of drug trafficking. If the example quoted for Britain in 1989 is typical, the judiciary has succeeded in proving the criminality of about 5 per cent of the rewards identified as having been received by drug traffickers in the form of laundered assets, and is actually confiscating less than 1 per cent of them. So long as drug trafficking and laundering remain so profitable and carry such a low risk of paying the penalties if caught, more and more organized criminals will be attracted to the trade. The campaign against laundering must be directed – as mostly it is – at all organized crime and not just drug trafficking, because they are intertwined. Trafficking drugs and laundering the profits are international, so international machinery for countering and detecting it must be better geared to match this. Success will depend on the twin pillars of recording transactions and intelligence.

Computer science makes it possible to deposit or transfer money in a few seconds, and for all such transactions to be recorded with a minimum of labour and therefore of cost. Given the right criteria to look for, it should be possible to programme the computers to trawl through the maze and identify connected or suspicious items equally cheaply. This, combined with PNCs, should rapidly improve domestic detection of money laundering. The linking of PNCs within the EU and other countries of goodwill should enable this to be extended internationally.

The traffickers and other criminals will, however, continue to evade this system so long as there are banks and governments – especially in fiscal havens – which refuse to cooperate against them. The only effective response to this is for the governments and banks of the countries which do cooperate, which handle between them well over 90 per cent of all transactions worldwide, to boycott, collectively, the banks of countries which do not. We should take heart from the 1978 Bonn Convention, when the mere threat of a G7 boycott of any countries which failed to cooperate in combating air piracy has forced the offenders into line over hijacking. There are many loopholes between international judicial systems but the answer will lie, not in trying to stand-ardize, but in harmonization and cooperation. The judicial systems and traditions differ too deeply to be standardized (e.g. the adversarial system of the UK and USA and the inquisitorial system of mainland Europe). But all sides should accept the principle that persons accused of committing offences against the laws of another country should be liable for trial in that country in accordance with its laws and judicial procedures. This is a prospect already accepted by all tourists and business people whilst on another country's soil.

For serious offences, including any with an international dimension such as money laundering, provided that there is prima facie evidence that the accused individuals were in the country or otherwise personally involved, they should be liable for extradition without recourse to any claim that it was a 'political offence', to face trial in that country; all other countries involved should cooperate in providing evidence and enforcing subpoenas for any witnesses required. The pursuit of harmonization should aim to convince political and public opinion that such trials will be fair and to provide a right to appeal to an international court if there are grounds for doing so. To achieve this will need a great deal of work and of goodwill. The incentive must be the desire to check the alarming growth of international organized crime, while the coercion must be the threat of exclusion from other benefits of cooperating with the main stream.

Other international measures which should be pursued, through the EU, Europol and the Council of Europe and, on a wider front, through the UN and Interpol, include:

To agree procedures for dealing with corporations or individuals who have accounts in more than one country.

To establish procedures for international judicial and police cooperation in over-riding bank secrecy where fiscal as well as criminal irregularities are suspected and to introduce sanctions to enforce this as described in this chapter.

To encourage all countries, including Italy, to introduce the concept of corporate criminal responsibility.

To agree procedures for sharing the proceeds of confiscated assets between countries which have cooperated in the investigation.

To encourage incentives for giving information on the lines of those successfully applied in Italy – e.g. leniency, generous rewards, confidentiality and short and long term security for informants.

To establish international data bases for transactions concerning items whose value is above an agreed level, such as works of art, antiques, jewellery and precious metals.[27]

The international campaign to achieve this in the UN and other international institutions must be based on the hard facts that drug trafficking finances crime by a sum greater than the turnover of every industry in the world other than the defence industry, causes half the murders in the USA and half the thefts and burglaries in UK and, above all, ruins millions of lives.

The ways to defeat the traffickers are to prevent them from enjoying the financial fruits of their crimes and to achieve a high rate of conviction. We are failing in both of these at present. A high prospect of getting caught is the best of all deterrents, and good intelligence – to identify targets and gather evidence to make convictions stick – is the best weapon to bring this about.

Part VI

The USA and Continental Europe

14 What is on Offer?

DRUGS AND ORGANIZED CRIME IN THE CONSUMER COUNTRIES

The first half of this book has looked at the production and distribution of cocaine, crack, heroin, cannabis and synthetic drugs. It has shown how these activities generate and finance terrorism, crime and corruption, at their worst in Peru and Colombia, but also in many other countries involved in production and distribution. The rival guerrillas fighting the civil war in Afghanistan, for example, are almost entirely funded by opium production. All of these evils are financed by the money paid by drug addicts, mainly on the streets of the USA and Europe.

The second half of the book therefore examines how the import and sale of drugs in these consumer countries are organized; and how, as well as the damage they do to the Third World, drugs generate crime and violence in their own countries, not only by drug users to fund their addiction, but also by the trafficking gangs to secure their markets. Drug trafficking is inextricably linked with organized crime in the USA and in East and West Europe.

The USA is the biggest consumer and will be examined first; then the Italian mafias, which are the model for organized criminal gangs worldwide, and also in many cases lead and fund them. The role of mafia expertise is nowhere more in evidence than in Russia and East Europe, where the post-revolutionary strains are giving a boost to organized crime and drug trafficking which are overflowing into West Europe. Finally, there is a case study of drug trafficking and crime in the UK, weighing up the alternatives for tackling the drug problem in consumer countries as a whole.

THE SHOPPING LIST

Table 14.1 summarizes the drugs available on the streets of the USA and Europe, with rough estimates of their street prices. As

Table 14.1   Approximate Street Prices of Drugs, 1994

Cocaine	50% pure	per gm	£60	$100
Crack	60–80% pure	per gm	£80–100	$120–150
Heroin	40% pure	per gm	£70–80	$105–120
Cannabis		per 4 gm dose	£16–20	$25–30
Cannabis resin		per 4 gm dose	£12–16	$20–25
MDMA (Ecstasy)		per tablet	£15–20	$25–30
Amphetamine sulphate (Speed)	dose		£10	$15
Methyl amphetamine (Ice)	dose		£10	$15
LSD		per 50 gm tablet	£2–5	$3–8

Sources: ISDD, *National Audit of Drug Misuse in Britain*, London, ISDD, 1993; *Observer Magazine*, 27 February 1994, quoting from NCIS, Police Press Office, HM Customs & Excise and Release

with most of the figures in this book, they are only a best guess from the wildly differing figures available. In this vast clandestine, criminal, multinational trade, there are no annual reports or accounts, and all concerned have an interest in concealing the facts. Many buyers are ripped off without knowing it and, since exporters, importers and dealers make huge profits, they can afford to sell at any time they choose at half price or less, to lure new buyers.

Single quarter-gram doses of cocaine, crack or heroin usually fall between £15 ($25) and £25 ($40); so do single doses of cannabis and Ecstasy. Amphetamines (£10 or $15) and LSD (£2 or $3) are the cheapest. But all are cheap enough for anyone to try a dose or two.

Once hooked, the dependence is likely to grow and become more insistent, especially on heroin and crack, so that new consumers will soon be willing to steal whatever is necessary to fund the habit until they are typically stealing 90 per cent of what they spend on it. Unless they become consumer-dealers themselves, buying 5 grams for the price of 4 to get their own free, they will remain as hooked on stealing as they are on drugs.

15 The USA

THE US DRUG WAR

The USA is central to the global drug problem in every field, being by far the largest consumer, thereby generating the lion's share of the world's $500 billion drug turnover. There are believed to be 3 million regular cocaine users, of whom half may take crack, and between 600,000 and 800,000 heroin addicts.[1]

The trouble begins with solvent abuse by quite young children. One survey recorded that 44 per cent of high school seniors (aged 17) had taken drugs at least once and that 12.6 per cent were frequent users.

The social effects are horrific. Every year 15,000 Americans die from the effects of illicit drugs. It is estimated that there are 1 million people infected with the HIV virus, of whom a quarter have AIDS. One-third of these were infected by needles used for intravenous (IV) drug injection. By 1989, the number of IV drug users with AIDS was doubling every 15 months.[2]

ORGANIZED CRIME IN THE USA

The USA has been plagued by organized crime since the years of Prohibition (1919–33), when crime was heavily financed by 'bootleggers' of alcohol. Illicit drugs now finance an enormous proportion of the crime. US criminal syndicates have links with the Italian mafias, the Japanese Yakusi, the Chinese Triads, the Jamaican Yardies and, increasingly, with the new mafias emerging in Russia and eastern Europe. These are discussed in context in succeeding chapters.

Since US dollars are the prime currency in drug trading, much of the money laundering is done through US banks or through foreign banks with branches in the USA. (see Chapters 12 and 13).

The DEA has estimated that 50 per cent of all US cocaine is distributed through Los Angeles and most of the rest via Mexico and Florida. When carrying drugs overland from Mexico, couriers can expect about $1000 per journey, which is a great deal more than they could earn in any other way. A pilot flying an unregistered aircraft from Colombia into the USA by night without lights or radar may earn between $250,000 and $500,000.[3]

There were 90,000 murders in the USA in the years 1990–3.[4] It was estimated that 50 per cent of the homicides in the USA were drug related. Most of these were by drug dealers trying to drive rivals out of their territory. The Cali cartel, with some 10,000 Americans working for it, had the biggest share of the US cocaine market even before the Medellin cartel began to fall apart in 1991. During 1990, the Cali cartel controlled the market in New York (sharing it with the Sicilian Mafia), in Los Angeles (with Jamaicans and Haitians) and in San Diego (with the Mexicans). The Medellin cartel was dominant in New Orleans while both Cali and Medellin operated in Miami alongside Cubans and Puerto Ricans: there was plenty of scope for gang warfare. Crack in the USA was largely processed and distributed by Jamaican gangs, especially in the east and midwest. Dominicans and Haitians also operated in the east and black criminals from Los Angeles in north California.[5]

ATTACKING THE SUPPLY SIDE

The alarm about the growth of drug addiction in the 1960s and 1970s, both in the USA and West Europe, led initially to a concentration on the demand side – on trying to suppress domestic drug trafficking and addiction. Consumption and addiction continued to grow, however, to a great extent due to it being fashionable amongst pop stars and other youth heroes. The individual quantities, measured in grams or fractions of a gram, were so small that detection seemed a hopeless task. The addicts were ready to pay high prices and, since they had to steal in any case to find the money, they stole whatever was necessary. And, of course, the dealers became more sophisticated and more ruthless in cashing in on this demand.

In 1986, the UN General Assembly resolved to 'mobilize the international community in an unprecedented global counter-offensive against the international drug menace'.[6] In the same year, President Reagan called for a national crusade, increasing the funding for law enforcement and stiffening the penalties against convicted drug traffickers.

At the same time, Reagan proposed economic sanctions against drug-producing countries and in 1988 enhanced the role of the military in anti-drug operations.[7] Frustrated by the failure of demand reduction, the USA switched her priority to the supply side and in 1989 President Bush announced a trebling of economic and military aid to drug-producing countries ($2 billion over five years).[8] In the event, US federal funds for supply reduction increased fivefold, reaching $8.6 billion by 1993.[9]

One prejudicial factor, however, has disappeared from US supply-side strategies since the late 1980s – the obsession of US governments, notably that of President Reagan, with the Cold War. There had been a great reluctance to take any measure which might weaken the ability of Third World governments, especially those in Latin America, to resist Communism. If drug measures were judged likely to have the effect of strengthening subversive movements, they were supported only half heartedly or not at all. Action which might have increased popular support for SL in Peru or for FARC in Colombia were avoided, and some repressive leaders were helped to stay in power because they were regarded as bulwarks against Communism. The classic example was General Noriega in Panama, a pivot country for transit of cocaine and for laundering of drug money. Noriega's relations with some of the drug barons and with the laundering banks meant that he was in possession of a great deal of information. He skilfully fed selected information into the CIA. He was seen as one of their star collaborators and was publicly praised for his contribution to the drug war, while large amounts of money were going into banks in Panama. There will always be conjecture about how much US officials knew about his activities. This is a dilemma which arises in many delicate intelligence operations. By definition, double agents have a foot in both camps. Both sides are usually aware that this is so and accept it as part of the risk, in the belief that the balance of advantage of access to information is in their favour.

There were always some people who doubted the effectiveness of concentrating on the supply side of drug trafficking. In an interesting article in 1991, David Whynes argued that there were four approaches to this policy with regard to drug production but that none had succeeded, nor were any likely to do so.[10]

'First, governments might agree to pre-emptive purchasing of the growers' output at or above the market rate. Whynes calculated that, in the case of coca, this would cost $1.05 billion per year, about 1.7 per cent of the combined GDPs of Colombia, Peru and Bolivia. The lure of a guaranteed higher price would also encourage the *campesinos* to grow more coca, not less.

His second alternative would be to make coca production illegal, imposing fines, imprisonment and crop destruction. This, however, would arouse bitter and probably violent protest amongst the *campesinos* and, in Peru, would lead them to turn to the SL terrorists to safeguard their livelihood. The governments of the producing countries would be half hearted in enforcing these measures, not only because of the unrest they would cause, but also because of the foreign exchange (albeit illegal) which would be lost. The drug cartels had in any case sufficient power and financial muscle to circumvent attempts to enforce these laws.

The third alternative posed by Whynes would be to offer bounties to *campesinos* who grew substitute crops. Whynes argued, however, that such a bounty would have to be very large to make the substitutes more profitable than coca – he estimated about $150 million year, 150 times the amount currently allocated for this purpose by the UN Fund for Drug Abuse Control (UNFDAC). It must be added that, since the actual payments to *campesinos* for their cocaine paste is so small a percentage of the market price of cocaine, the drug cartels could happily double or treble it without any significant effect on their profits (see p. 68).

The fourth alternative would be to impose a tax on coca production to raise the market price and depress demand. Once again, however, the cartels could without difficulty add enough to the *campesinos*' price to cover the tax. As will be argued later, if a tax were to be effective at all, it would have to be collected at the demand end, from the importers, dealers and consumers, not from the producers (see pp. 195–8).

Whynes also examined the prospects of supply-side meaures against opium and heroin. These had some success in the 1970s in Turkey and Mexico, with the result that the quantity of heroin entering the USA fell by one-third between 1976 and 1978.[11] Turkey, by strict repressive measures, has succeeded in keeping her own production of opium down, but remains a regular supply route for heroin from the Golden Crescent (see pp. 88–9).

Production of a new and highly potent form of heroin – black tar – in the 1980s restored Mexico's place as the largest single supplier of heroin to the USA in 1987.[12]

The biggest opium-producing countries, Myanmar in the Golden Triangle and Afghanistan in the Golden Crescent (see pp. 84 and 88), are two of the poorest countries in the world, and the areas in which they cultivate the opium are remote and inaccessible, so supply-reduction measures there have little hope of success.[13]

ATTACKING THE DEMAND SIDE

Nearly all the measures for drug supply reduction considered in the previous section have been tried by the USA or by the UN under US leadership and (as pointed out) the US government spent $8.6 billion on them in 1993. Attempts continue, but to little avail, so US governments have increasingly been turning back to trying to reduce the demand There is still strong resistance to decriminalization or legalization of drugs, so the measures have been mainly focussed on suppression.

There have, since 1988 been fairly severe maximum and minimum sentences for federal drug trafficking (i.e. across state boundaries). These are set out in Table 15.1.

The US philosophy of repression of domestic drug trafficking is 'zero tolerance'. President Clinton in 1993 declared that legalization or decriminalization would 'foster America's self-destruction as a nation'. Determined attempts have been made to harness the media and influential members of the entertainment industry to depict drug use as 'destructive, vile and weak'.[14] A concerted campaign on this basis in 1985–9 did reduce the number of yuppie drug addicts by creating a social stigma, but had no overall effect. New York police made 90,000 drug arrests in 1988, but the total number of heroin users in the USA increased by 100 per cent from 600,000 in 1985 to 1.2 million in 1989, and it was estimated that, if drugs other than cocaine and heroin were also included, 6 per cent of all US citizens were drug addicts.[15]

The USA has, however, pioneered some effective legislation to curb money laundering; this was described in Chapter 13.

Table 15.1   Examples of US Federal Drug-Trafficking Penalties, 1988

FOR SMALL QUANTITIES

Cut cocaine mixture	500–4999 gms
Cut heroin mixture	100–999 gms
Amphetamine mixture	100–999 gms
LSD mixture	1–10 gms

Sentences for a first offence

Minimum 5 years, maximum 40 years, plus fine $2 million
or, if the offence results in death or serious injury,
minimum 20 years, maximum life, plus fine $5 million

and for a second offence

Minimum 10 years, maximum life, plus fine $4 million
or, if the offence results in death or serious injury,
minimum life, plus fine $8 million

FOR LARGER QUANTITIES

Cut cocaine mixture	5 kg or more
Cut heroin mixture	1 kg or more
Amphetamine mixture	1 kg or more
LSD mixture	10 kg or more

Sentences for a first offence

Minimum 10 years, maximum life, plus fine $4 million
or, if the offence results in death or serious injury,
minimum 20 years, maximum life, plus fine $4 million

and for a second offence

Minimum 20 years, maximum life, plus fine $8 million
or, if the offence results in death or serious injury
minimum life, plus fine $8 million

Source: DEA, *Drugs of Abuse*, Washington, DC, DEA, 1989, p. 9

AN ARMED SOCIETY

A major cause of the high incidence of violent crime in the USA is
the nation's gun law, and particularly the dogged insistence on
retaining the Second Amendment to the Constitution, enshrining
the right of every US citizen to bear arms.

This right is deeply ingrained in US culture: its roots stretch back to colonial days when, in the seventeenth and eighteenth centuries, the individual British settlers had to defend themselves both against hostile Indians and against rival French settlers competing for the same land. Except for occasional seaborne expeditionary forces, such as Wolfe's army which captured Quebec in 1759, the British government always made it clear that the settlers had to organize their own defence – just as the East India Company in the same period had to provide its own army in India. This led to the culture of the Minutemen, who kept their muskets in their homes, in readiness to turn out instantly to defend their villages in the event of a French or Indian attack. It was these same Minutemen who in 1775 ran circles round the ponderous Hessian redcoats marching in close order as if on a parade ground, and the culture became a hallowed one.

The actual wording of the Second Amendment, adopted by Congress in 1791, clearly indicates its original purpose:

A well regulated Militia being necessary to the security of a free state, the right of the people to bear arms shall not be infringed.

The retention of this right has no longer anything to do with a militia. It was kept alive through the nineteenth century by the tales of how the West was won, and currently by the argument that criminals are armed, so that if the citizens are barred from carrying arms, the only people with guns will be the criminals. This view is promoted by a professional public relations campaign by the rich and influential National Rifle Association (NRA).

The result is that, in a population of 250 million, there are estimated to be 216 million guns at large,[16] and the USA has one of the highest homicide rates in the world. A selection of the highest and lowest amongst large countries in 1992 is given in Table 15.2.

This is going to be very hard to cure. Against powerful opposition, President Clinton pushed a $30 billion Crime Bill through Congress in August 1994. Among its provisions were to ban 19 'assault weapons' (automatic and semi-automatic) favoured by street gangs; to employ 100,000 more police officers; to spend $6 billion on building more prisons, and nearly $9 billion on reducing the causes of crime by providing job training, after school activities and drug treatment. The Bill also

Table 15.2   Murder Rates, 1992

Country	Murders	Population	Murders per million
Colombia	30,000	33 million	910
Russia	23,250	150 million	155
USA[a]	22,500	250 million	90
Germany	3,200	80 million	40
Britain[b]	1,250	50 million	25
Japan	1,500	125 million	12

[a] About half the murders in the USA are drug related.
[b] England and Wales. Northern Ireland, with a population of 1.5 million, had 85 murders in 1992, i.e. 57 per million.
Sources: *The Economist*, 19 July 1994; Control Risks Briefing Book, 1993

added 60 more crimes to the list of federal offences incurring the death penalty.

On 11 August 1994, Congress rejected the Bill by 225 votes to 210. The 210 included an unlikely alliance between 48 hardline Southern Democrats (who supported the NRA gun lobby and objected to money being spent on 'young layabouts') and 10 black Congressmen who objected to the widening of capital offences and the exclusion of a clause enabling judges to prevent executions on the grounds that there was a disproportionate number of black convicts condemned. The Bill was eventually passed, with most of the social measures reduced, saving $3 billion, but the ban on the 19 assault weapons and the increased expenditure on police and prisons approved.

American presidents attempting to combat the gun lobby face the evidence of a survey by *US News* which shows 86 per cent of men and 63 per cent of women supporting the right to keep guns in American homes.[17]

16   The Italian Mafia

THE ORIGINS OF *COSA NOSTRA*

All large-scale criminal organizations, domestic or international, model themselves as far as they can on the Italian mafias, especially on *Cosa Nostra* ('our affair') in Sicily, but also on *Camorra* centred on Naples, *'Ndrangheta* in Calabria and *Sacra Corona Unita* in Apulia. 'Mafia' is an Italian generic term for organized crime but it also has a legal definition in Italy, that is, an association consisting of three or more members 'of a mafia kind' when

> those who form it make use of the power of intimidation provided by the associative bond and of the state of subjugation and of criminal silence (*omerta*) which derives from it to commit crimes, to acquire directly or indirectly the running or control of economic activities, of concessions, grants, contracts and public services in order to realize illicit profits or advantages for themselves or for others.[1]

The Sicilian Mafia can trace its origins from the thirteenth century, as an organization of secret societies amongst the rural population to mediate between the peasants and their feudal landlords, and to protect them from domination by corrupt officials working for the foreign governments which occupied the island until the middle of the nineteenth century. The mafia was organized in 'families' under strict disciplinary control of their leaders, who enforced their own systems of law and justice. Members of the 'family', who became known as 'men of honour', took an oath of silence (*omerta*), accepting that the penalty for breach of it was death. When Italy became an independent country in 1860, and Bourbon rule was ousted from Sicily, the new government attempted to root out the mafia, but with only limited success.[2]

Prohibition of alcohol in the USA from 1919 to 1933 led to the formation of criminal gangs organized amongst the large number of Italians who had emigrated to America during the nineteeth and early twentieth centuries, some of whom had been members of the mafia. These gangs thrived on the massive flow of money which people were prepared to pay for illicit liquor – just as present-day organized criminal gangs thrive on drug trafficking. These beginnings have played a dominant part in the development and structure of organized international criminal gangs worldwide, and the links between gangs in Italy and North and South America have remained particularly strong.

Cosa Nostra was severely eroded by Mussolini in the 1920s and 1930s, but much of the leadership was still intact in Sicily in 1943 when the USA was planning to invade the island. Thanks to their links with Italian Americans, *Cosa Nostra* were able to play a valuable part in the reconnaissance and planning of the invasion. US officers, sometimes guided by mafiosi released from prison in the USA, were parachuted into Sicily and established a network of contacts with Sicilian Mafia bosses, as a result of which the US invasion and the initial occupation of large areas of Sicily were completed almost without bloodshed.

One of the leading American mafiosi was Salvatore Luciano ('Lucky Luciano') who had close contacts with the head of the Sicilian Mafia, Don Calo, in the town of Villalba. US tanks heading for Villalba carried Luciano's insignia, a yellow handkerchief marked with the letter L fluttering from their radio aerials. The Americans thereafter appointed Don Calo as Mayor of Villalba and authorized him to reinstate his armed bodyguard; they acted on Don Calo's suggestions in appointing mayors and other officials throughout western Sicily, and gun licences were granted freely to their 'men of honour', entrusted with the task of subduing banditry and Communist guerrilla activity. At the same time, the mafiosi opened up a profitable black market, particularly in American cigarettes. All criminal charges against Don Calo and his friends were removed from police records and within a few years the whole of western Sicily was governed by a network of criminals whose political power had been legitimized and institutionalized.[3] This set in train the sinister pattern of linkage between the mafia and the highest in the land – political and commercial – throughout Italy, which was to be spectacularly revealed to the world in 1993.

Lucky Luciano, his slate wiped clean of murder and other charges on condition that he left the USA, established a lucrative criminal organization based in Naples.

MAFIA STRUCTURE AND ORGANIZATION

The building blocks of the mafia are the families. Typically, a family contains about 50 men of honour or soldiers, but they are sometimes as big as 200. Each is normally based in a single town or locality over which it has absolute jurisdiction.

Cosa Nostra in Sicily has about 180 families (also referred to as 'clans' or 'factions') with a total of around 5000 men of honour. 'Family' is a confusing title in that they are based on territorial rather than blood ties. Families are autonomous so that intelligence about one family does not necessarily give leads to another, but *Cosa Nostra* does have a superimposed pyramid structure. For every province except Messina and Syracuse there is a *cupola* which includes all the families in that province under a *capo commissione* (chief). The *capi commissione* form a *supercommissione* at the head of which is a *capo di capi* (chief of chiefs) who is normally known to very few people.[4] Salvatore 'Toto' Riina, head of the Corleonese family, gained this post in the early 1980s after a series of bloody internal mafia wars.

There is no such hierarchy in the other two main mafias. *Camorra* (Naples) in 1993 had about 7000 members in 130 'clans'. *'Ndrangheta* had 6700 members in 126 *n'drini*, mainly based on blood ties, which are even more independent, with consequently more internal clashes and murders; in 1991, for example, there were 142 allegedly mafia-related murders in Calabria compared with 32 in Palermo.[5]

All these three, and other Italian mafias – and the criminal networks in East Europe which have copied them – rely on rigorous control of their members, based on loyalty and the vow of silence, in exchange for which they promise not only wealth but also protection as members of a closely knit team. This begins with their probation and highly charged initiation rituals and their insistence that no one is a proven man of honour until he has committed himself by a serious crime, usually murder.

THE PURSUIT OF POWER

The mafias and their imitators, though they acquire enormous wealth, seek that wealth as a means of securing institutional power, through corruption of senior politicians (national and regional) and control of key sectors of industry, finance and public services. They have therefore varied the focus of their activities and the administrative and commercial sectors and commodities on which they concentrate to achieve their financial and political control.

In the 1950s, with the rapid urbanization and technological development in Italy, they switched their focus from the agricultural areas to urban building licences, construction and public service contracts. They had virtually total control of the construction industry in Sicily. They also built up a lucrative market in smuggled cigarettes. In 1963, however, *Cosa Nostra* enraged the Sicilian public by a car bomb massacre in Palermo, provoking the deployment of 10,000 police and *carabinieri*, who made 1200 arrests. This was followed by the first two major mafia trials and a number of important leaders fled to escape arrest.[6] This, however, had an unintended by-product in that they spread their families to other parts of Italy.

By the end of 1969 they had recovered but, as tobacco traffic declined with growing availability, they increasingly switched to heroin. They found that 1 kg of morphine base bought in Afghanistan for $2000 would reach six times that value in changing hands through Turkey and Greece to Milan and more than a hundred times its value when sold in the USA. This completely transformed the mafia's financial strength. They also moved heavily into cocaine but, by the late 1980s, they found their monopolies eroded by rival traffickers on new routes (as described earlier in the book) and, taking advantage of changing practices in banking and international money transfer due to the microelectronics revolution, they concentrated on extending their power in banking and international financial institutions.

All the while, as they had done from the days of Lucky Luciano and Don Calo in 1943–5, they continued to penetrate the political establishment, particularly the Christian Democratic Party (DC) which they ensured had a permanent majority in every coalition government from 1948 to 1963. Suitable politicians were targeted, initially lured by the promise of campaign funds and, even more effectively, by an offer to deliver the votes of all who dared not disobey them in areas controlled by each mafia family – or threatening to divert those votes from the DC politicians if they did not cooperate. In the mid-1980s, *Cosa Nostra* controlled 180,000 votes in one city whose total population was only 700,000.[7] On the average, each man of honour would be in a position to deliver 40 to 50 votes from amongst his friends and relations.[8] Once hooked, politicians dared not defect for fear of exposure or possibly murder.

As with the 1963 bomb, however, *Cosa Nostra* overstepped themselves in 1982 and again in 1992. On 3 September 1982 they assassinated the *Carabinieri* General Carlo Alberto Dalla Chiesa, who had only six months previously been appointed Prefect of Palermo. His appointment had clearly alarmed some of the Sicilian politicians, as Dalla Chiesa had been spectacularly successful against both left- and right-wing terrorism on the mainland in 1981–2. His murder aroused great public outrage and induced Parliament to pass the 'Rognone La Torre Law'. This made 'association of a mafia kind' (as defined on p. 131) a crime in itself, and gave greatly widened investigative powers to public prosecutors. It placed the onus of proof of a legitimate source of assets on the owner and provided draconian powers of punishment, including a lifetime ban from professional or public service against anyone found guilty under this law. This had a devastating effect on the mafia.

In 1992, *Cosa Nostra* murdered two very popular judges, Giovanni Falcone and Paolo Borsellino, who had been fearlessly investigating and exposing mafia activities and people in public life associated with them. This paved the way for the dramatic political revolution which drove the DC from power in 1993, and resulted in the investigation of corruption charges against large numbers of the politicians in both the DC and the other traditional parties – especially the second largest, the Socialists, who had shared power with them.

THE MAFIA *PENTITI*

General Dalla Chiesa's success against the right- and left-wing terrorists (especially the Red Brigades) had resulted from his brilliant handling of 'repentant terrorists' (*pentiti*), whom he persuaded to give information in exchange for leniency in sentencing, sometimes amounting to a pardon. As a result of this, the Italian police were able to arrest about 700 terrorists (500 left wing and 200 right wing), virtually ridding Italy of the scourge of terrorism ever since. It was expected that, as Prefect of Palermo, with the police under his control, he would apply the same *pentitismo* technique against *Cosa Nostra* and this was presumably why they murdered him. Allegations were rife that politicians who feared that he might unearth their corrupt links with the mafia set up the murder plot or, at least, turned a blind eye to it. Be that as it may, the outcry over his murder led to a public demand that his successors should apply *pentitismo* to the mafia. It was, however, slow in getting into its stride because the mafia instilled far greater terror of reprisals than any of the Red Brigades or right-wing terrorists had done. But the first breakthrough came in 1984 and it gathered momentum with the appointment of Judges Falcone and Borsellino.

In September 1984, Tommaso Buscetta was extradited from Brazil. He was an old-style *Cosa Nostra* chief who had fled to New York and then to Brazil in the 1970s; he broke with the movement after he had backed the losing side in a bloody bout of internecine mafia war in 1981–3, in which about 1000 mafiosi and their families were killed, 600 of their bodies never being found. Seven of Buscetta's close relatives had been killed in order to punish him, since he himself was out of reach in Brazil. For Buscetta, this savage murder of his relatives was such a betrayal of the tradition of 'men of honour' that he felt himself no longer tied by any moral obligation to his vow of *omerta*. He gave information and evidence leading to arrest warrants for 366 mafiosi.

Another *pentito* at this same time was Salvatore Contorno, a footsoldier who had also been on the wrong side in 1981–3; no fewer than 35 of his relatives had been murdered. Contorno sought Buscetta's approval before becoming an informant, and his information resulted in 127 more arrest warrants being issued. In all, at the first 'mafia maxi trial' in 1986–7, there were 475 defendants. There were life sentences on 19 of them and 342 other convictions, though some were modified on appeal.[9]

Cosa Nostra's response was the murder of Judges Falcone and Borsellino on 23 May and 19 July 1992. Both had become national heroes before they were murdered and *pentitismo* spread fast. By the end of 1992 there were some 200 collaborators under protection.[10] In the mid-1990s there seems to be every prospect of more mafia trials and, no doubt, of mafia reprisals.

SURVIVAL OF THE MAFIA

Cosa Nostra are certainly not dead and are unlikely to die, though they have been severely weakened and the magic of their hold on their men of honour has been irrevocably eroded. Their response has been dispersal. They are spreading more widely across Italy and increasing their cooperation with other mafias – *Camorra*, *'Ndrangheta* and *Sacra Corona Unita*.

Time will tell whether they are able to recreate the links they had in the 1980s with senior politicians, judges, police officers, bankers, and so on, often using membership of secret masonic lodges such as P2. So much has been revealed of these links, however, that the Italian public, a new generation of politicians, and more courageous investigative journalists, may be able to reveal such links before they take deep root. Ultimately this will depend on how effectively the mafia can use corruption and intimidation to rebuild the screen of venality and terror around themselves, powerfully enough to deter detection or betrayal.

Meanwhile, the mafias still have enormous resources and, under pressure in Italy, they are exploiting the opportunities for crime, investment and money laundering in the former Soviet Union and East Europe. They are especially applying their expertise to organizing the emerging Russian mafias on similar lines, with such success that there is a possibility that these will in turn spread their activities and begin to compete with the Italian mafias themselves.[11] The same is happening on a smaller scale in other East European countries. This is further discussed in Chapter 17.

17 Russia and East Europe

TWENTY-SEVEN NEW DEMOCRACIES

The East European revolutions of 1989–92, and the second Russian revolution initiated by President Gorbachev in 1985 and completed in 1992, dwarfed all previous European revolutions (e.g. 1789, 1848 and 1917) in their international significance. The disappearance of the Warsaw Pact and the sudden ending of the Cold War were widely hailed as the outbreak of peace, but they have left a world which is probably more unstable than it has ever been since Stalin died in 1953.

The disintegration of the Soviet Union and Yugoslavia and the collapse of Communist governments throughout East Europe created, within three years, twenty-seven new democratic republics dedicated to becoming market economies. All had deeply rooted instabilities built in. Their former command economies, distorted by subsidies, disintegrated, with in most cases a partial collapse of distribution of food and other essential supplies. There were no alternative systems in being to fill the gap – which was avidly filled by black marketeers and criminal gangs. There were no political or administrative infrastructures other than the then discredited and demoralized *nomenklatura,* and no pluralist institutions in being to act on their own initiative. The police and intelligence agencies – KGB, *Stasi, Securitate,* etc. – were in name disbanded almost overnight. Their successors, such as they were, lacked organization and experience, and their anxiety not to appear as repressive as their predecessors made them hesitant and ineffective. Arms galore became available from some of the Warsaw Pact armouries whose security and control fell apart, and demobilizing soldiers were sometimes tempted to sell their own weapons and to steal others and sell them too. People were desperate for money and often for food too, so they bought from black marketeers and turned to whatever crime was needed to pay them. Governments, realizing that the alternative might be starvation and rioting, often turned a blind eye. Currencies inflated alarmingly. By 1993, at least six of the new republics had voted back to power a government of former Communists under a new name, and the old *nomenklatura*, in default of any other experienced public officials, were reappearing as bureaucrats.

ETHNIC AND RELIGIOUS MINORITIES

Every one of the twenty-seven new republics contained inextricably mixed ethnic or religious minorities within its frontiers, some left over from the peace settlements of 1919 and 1945, and others from centuries of tsarist and Stalinist empires. The Russian Federation itself contained twenty autonomous republics (Tartarstan, North Ossetia, Checheno-Ingushetia, and so on) in at least five of which ethnic Russians were in a minority compared with such titular communities as Chechens and North Ossetians.

Then, in every one of the other fourteen former Soviet republics, which became new independent republics after 1992, there were ethnic Russian minorities, varying from 41 per cent in Kazakhstan and 33 per cent in Latvia to 7 per cent in Georgia and 2 per cent in Armenia. These are shown in Table 17.1. They caused considerable internal tensions. In Moldova, a predominantly Russian area declared itself independent from the new state, and part of the Red Army garrison remained in occupation. The predominantly Russian Crimean peninsular in Ukraine wanted to rejoin Russia, an especially sensitive problem as the Soviet Black Sea Fleet, now split, was based in Crimean ports. In some of the Baltic states the new government imposed conditions for Russians to qualify for citizenship rights, including an obligation to speak the language of the ethnic majority in the state.

In addition to the Russian minorities, many of the new states also contained other ethnic minorities, often with racial and emotional ties to neighbouring states, such as Armenians, Azeris and Uzbeks. Some potentially explosive mixtures are shown in Table 17.1.

Many of the former Warsaw Pact countries in East Europe were potentially just as explosive. Yugoslavia did explode in 1991, and one of her former constituent republics, Bosnia, was thrown into a vicious civil war from 1992 onwards. Other dangerous minorities included Albanians in Serbia, Serbs in Croatia, Turks in Bulgaria and Hungarians in Serbia, Slovakia and Romania.[1]

Table 17.1   Ethnic Minorities in Former Soviet States

Russian Minorities in Former Soviet Republics (%)			
Kazakhstan	41	Belorus	12
Latvia	33	Uzbekistan	11
Estonia	28	Tajikistan	10
Kirghizia	26	Lithuania	9
Ukraine	21	Azerbaijan	8
Moldova	13	Georgia	7
Turkmenistan	13	Armenia	2

Other potentially explosive mixtures in former Soviet republics	
Armenia	Azeris (5%)
Azerbaijan	Armenians (8%) concentrated in Nagorno Karabakh
Georgia	Armenians, Azeris, Abkhazians, South Ossetians
Kazakhstan	Ukranians (6%)
Kirghizia	Uzbeks (12%)
Lithuania	Poles (7%)
Moldova	Romanians (64%), Ukranians (14%), Gazauz (4%)
Russia	Bashkirians, Chechens, Cossacks, Ingushetians, North Ossetians, Ruthenians, Tartars. (There are many autonomous republics, regions and areas, some of which contain more non-Russians than Russians.)
Tajikistan	Uzbeks (23%)
Turkmenistan	Uzbeks (9%)

Source: *The Economist*, 14 March 1992

These mixtures have resulted, not only in civil strife, but also in providing the basis for thousands of criminal organizations engaged in cross-border crime throughout Europe.[2]

ORGANIZED CRIME IN RUSSIA

The growth of organized crime in Russia is perhaps the most alarming in the world. It began as soon as Gorbachev introduced *glasnost* (the start of free speech) and *perestroika* (restructuring the administration), thereby loosening the cork in the bottle in which the Russian people had been confined during centuries of tsarist and Communist discipline. He still retained the Communist Party and kept the *nomenklatura* in post, including the KGB, realizing that, in the absence of any other trained officials, the alternative would be a collapse of the administration of government and of law and order. Gorbachev also kept the massive subsidies of food and other necessities, and a wage scale based on an artificial currency exchange rate. This meant that, apart from the *nomenklatura*, black marketeers and international businessmen with access to dollars and other hard currencies, few people could afford to buy anything but these essentials. By 1990, the street exchange rate of the rouble for hard currency was 30 times its official rate. The shelves of shops became emptier as black marketeers (often moonlighting *nomenklatura*) bought up the supplies at source and sold them on the side to those able to pay. The KGB, trying to cultivate a new image, switched their priority from counter-subversion to counter-racketeering, but there was no way in which they could stem the flood. Inevitably, more and more people took to petty crime to pay black market prices, and the black marketeers developed into organized criminal gangs.[3]

When Yeltsin came to power in 1992, the KGB was officially disbanded (or renamed), but the flood was by then more or less out of control. The Italian mafias, scenting a lucrative hunting ground, moved in to assist in the organization of crime. By 1993 it was estimated that there were some 4000 organized criminal gangs in Russia, 200 of them operating across the borders into other republics in the Commonwealth of Independent States (CIS) – a loose association of former Soviet republics formed by Yeltsin. The strength of these gangs varied between 10 and 100.[4]

Behind the Russian criminal structure there had for many years been a body of 'godfathers', each of whom guided and coordinated a number of gangs and looked after their money. These godfathers had been a feature of Russian society since tsarist times. They were known as 'thieves in law' (*vory v zakone*), and 289 were listed in 1994.[5] They masterminded the development of the criminal gangs but their control and influence declined as the more professional mafia-style organizations extended their domination and exacted 'licences to operate' from the smaller gangs.

At the bottom of the structure were the shopkeepers and street traders. These were free to sell from kiosks in the streets without any requirement for accounting. They opened channels to the West in order to acquire goods which were hard to get and therefore commanded high prices, but they could operate only if they paid protection money. In January 1994 an investigation into organized crime commissioned by President Yeltsin recorded that 'every, repeat, every owner of a shop or kiosk pays a racketeer'; that no one trusted the police; and that few believed that laws passed by Parliament would ever be enforced.[6] The chief of the Moscow police was himself reported as saying that 95 per cent of his rank-and-file police and 20 per cent of their officers were corrupt. Russian police were dismally paid, with a colonel allegedly getting as little as $100 a month. Virtually all did other part-time jobs, some two or three and, as in Peru (see Chapter 5), some corruption was inevitable. A senior official at the Ministry of the Interior told *The Economist* that the opportunity for receiving bribes was the main reason for recruits going into the police; and that the same judges who had once been responsible to local party officials were still sitting and that many were also corrupt.[7]

The racketeers who collected the protection money were the rank-and-file of the criminal gangs, 'common criminals' who operated on the streets, also selling drugs and weapons and acting as pimps for the prostitutes. The racketeers were employed by the next level up, the 'businessmen' who, like the Colombian drug barons, ran apparently legitimate businesses as a cover for more lucrative criminal activities. They, in turn, paid bribes to corrupt officials, mainly of city or local governments, who, it was estimated, received 30–50 per cent of the proceeds of crime.[8] This was merely a continuation of the established practice of paying Communist Party officials – the *nomenklatura* – in the Soviet Union. Present-day officials, however, often themselves former *nomenklatura*, now faced the familiar mafia or Latin American style alternatives – a body full of lead if they refused to take the silver, or if they failed to do as they were told.

So, like *Cosa Nostra* in Palermo, the leaders of the criminal gangs used their money to extend their power, and used that power to make more money. Viktor Ilyukhin, chairman of the Security Committee of the Duma (Parliament), claimed in 1994 that 81 per cent of the voting shares in privatized companies were controlled by criminals.[9]

The range of crimes now extends far beyond racketeering, into theft, robbery, swindling, fraud, counterfeiting, gambling, prostitution and trafficking in drugs and arms.[10] The arms traffic is facilitated by former soldiers who, on demobilization, have chosen to remain in the areas where they were posted,[11] whether in Russia or other republics, having established thriving networks to acquire and dispose of weapons.

Disposal of nuclear material, especially from Russia, Ukraine and Kazakhstan, is another dangerous development. As with drugs, small quantities, easy to smuggle, carry a high value. There are plenty of countries whose agents are ready to buy. It is not only the ex-soldiers and criminal gangs who take part in this. Corrupt officials, struggling to keep their empires intact in times of economic chaos, may square their consciences into taking money to enable them to provide the public services expected of them as well as lining their own pockets. It is conceivable that, faced with national bankruptcy (as in Ukraine), unscrupulous politicians might in the future make secret deals with their opposite numbers in countries like Libya or Iran.

In the first quarter of 1994, there were an average of 84 murders a day in Russia. Most of these were by rival criminal gangs or were contract killings arising from commercial and financial competition.[12] In 1992, the murder rate in Russia exceeded that in the USA and was second only to Colombia amongst large countries (see Table 15.2 on p. 130). Crime of all kinds reached a peak in 1993, though there is a guarded hope that it may be levelling off (see Table 17.2).

Table 17.2   Reported Crimes in Russia per Million of Population

	1992	1993	1994[a]
Murders	155	197	184
Rapes	92	97	83
Aggravated assault	204	270	208
Robbery	1,109	1,241	868
Bribery	22	30	35
Embezzlement	268	251	248

* Annual rate based on extrapolation of first six months of 1994
Source: *The Economist*, 9 July 1994

DRUGS

Narcotics – production, trafficking and consumption – are another fast-growing problem in Russia and in the other 26 new republics, and its effects are spreading into West Europe including Finland. In Russia, Interpol estimates that there are at least 1.5 million regular drug users, 500,000 of whom are heavily addicted. This, in proportion to the population, puts Russian consumption as high as in Italy and higher than in any other West European country. Two-thirds of the addicts are aged under 30, which suggests that the total numbers will rise.[13]

Russia has 1 million hectares under cannabis cultivation,[14] and street prices are extremely low by world standards – about $50 per kg of cannabis resin in Moscow.[15] This is about one-hundredth of the street price in London ($5 per gm or $5000 per kg), and is one more indication of the enormous percentage of the street price which goes to the traffickers between the sources of drugs and the addicts on Western streets.

Opium and heroin are, however, the main drugs of abuse in Russia and in the other new republics, right through to the Baltic states. Most of it comes from Afghanistan via the land route across the Central Asian republics, Tajikistan, Uzbekistan and Turkmenistan. Tashkent is the focal point on the railway, and new international airline connections have opened in Samarkand, Boukhara and Termez (on the Afghan border). Another factor here was the addiction of large numbers of Soviet soldiers to heroin during their war in Afghanistan in the 1980s. Just as the North Vietnamese distributed heroin to weaken and corrupt the US army in the 1960s, there is good reason to believe that the Afghan *mujahideen* aimed to do the same to the Soviet army, with some success. As a result, there is a hard core of maturing ex-army addicts in Russia and other former Soviet republics; many of these are now heavily embroiled in heroin trafficking.[16]

Considerable quantities of opium are also grown in Uzbekistan. As elsewhere, it is very profitable for the farmers. As noted in Chapter 10 (p. 81) growing opium earns about 50 times as much as growing cotton or 100 times as much as growing fruit.[17] The heroin traffic routes go west through Turkmenistan, the Caucasus and Turkey; or north through Ukraine to East Europe and the Baltic states. There are believed to be 30,000 addicts in Lithuania, Latvia and Estonia. Russian criminal gangs have begun to operate increasingly in Finland, trafficking in drugs and the other commodities of organized crime and, as an indication of growth, 745 Soviet citizens were arrested in Finland in 1991 and 1992 compared to 32 in 1989.[18]

Latvia also has a well-developed pharmaceutical industry and a joint German and Latvian police raid in 1993 seized over 3 tonnes of Ecstasy disguised as influenza pills. Of the amphetamines seized in the EU, 15 per cent had been manufactured in Poland.[19]

OTHER ORGANIZED CRIME IN NORTH AND EAST EUROPE

Since 1991, smuggling in the Baltic has burgeoned. The principal transport is via the ferry traffic between St Petersburg and Latvia and Estonia; by individual sailors in Russian freighters; and by freighters specializing in smuggling. This is organized by professional criminal gangs, again mainly Russian. As well as drugs, they smuggle many other commodities, including copper nickel and cobalt; illegal immigrants, including prostitutes from as far away as Southeast Asia; hard currency; arms; and radioactive materials. Kidnapping for ransom by the Russian mafias has become increasingly professional and this has recently spread across the Baltic states and Scandinavia.[20]

Illegal immigration into West Europe received a big boost in 1991 and 1992 from four causes: the relaxation of border controls, especially within the EU; the unification of West and East Germany; the economic chaos in East Europe following the 1989 revolutions; and, most of all, the disintegration of Yugoslavia leading to civil war in Croatia and Bosnia.

The prime destination for refugees was West Germany, because of a reputation for the greatest prosperity and for a tolerant attitude towards asylum seekers. West Germany had always welcomed German-born refugees from East Europe and especially from East Germany, and accepted many tens of thousands each year from Asia and the Middle East, but the flow became a flood by 1992. From 102,675 in 1988, the total entering Germany rose to 255,675 in 1991,[21] and to about 440,000 in 1992.[22] Thereafter the number began to decline as Germany tightened her immigration laws – to 323,000 in 1993 and probably under 150,000 in 1994. This compared with 25,000 each year since 1992 to Britain.[23]

The majority of illegal immigrants to Germany came through Poland and the Czech and Slovak Republics, where international criminal gangs provided a facilitation service for a comprehensive fee of $500 to $2000 (normally around $1000 or DM 1500). Their procedure was to gather the intending immigrants near a suitable frontier on the Czech or Polish side. They provided the immigrants with forged papers, collected the fee, and took them up to the frontier – either on a quiet stretch of the River Oder or by a wooded 'green frontier'. Those on the banks of the Oder were given directions and a rubber dinghy to be handed to an agent on the German side of the river. Those on the green frontiers would be launched to make their own way through the woods with directions on where to go on the German side to meet a guide. If they were caught and turned back or arrested and deported, their fee would cover a second attempt. Assuming that all went well, however, the agent might well arrange accommodation and help in finding a means of livelihood (possibly legal but more likely illegal) either in Germany or in another EU country. Under the Single European Act 1986, they could move quite easily across internal EU frontiers. Some, of course, from both South-east Asia and East Europe, would already be destined for employment as prostitutes.

Illegal trading between Germany and East Europe is another lucrative activity for professional criminal gangs. Expensive cars are stolen in the West and smuggled out for sale in East European countries where they have a high scarcity value. This is very highly organized, with different people specializing in different jobs, not knowing each other, so that detection of one does not lead to the others. One common method is to buy a smashed-up car cheaply and then steal another of identical model and colour. The number plates, with engine and chassis numbers, are transferred, with the documents, to the stolen car. This can then be sold at a good price with everything apparently in good order to accord with the records of the smashed car in the vehicle registration system. This is made easier if the stolen car was originally registered in a different country from that of the wreck whose identity it has acquired.[24] Quite often, the gang takes an order through a dealer for a particular model and colour of used car, and then finds one to steal and smuggle to fill the order.

Prague has in recent years become a focus for the European headquarters of a wide range of organized criminal gangs aiming to exploit the rich pickings available from the West. These include groups from Ukraine, Russia, the Caucasus and Central and East Asia including China and Vietnam.[25]

THE THREAT TO WEST EUROPE

Criminal activities and ethnic tensions in the East now pose a threat to West Europe which may prove greater than any it has faced since NATO contained Soviet expansion in 1949. The great majority of the heroin, most of the cannabis and many of the synthetic drugs come from or through the CIS and East Europe. The Western currencies and economies are destabilized by vast amounts of illegal money (like seawater sloshing about in the bilges of a ship), including counterfeit currency, laundered drug money and the smuggling of arms and nuclear materials. There is an increased prospect of maverick governments acquiring nuclear weapons. The governments of Libya, Iran and others would pay a lot for the means to make them and there are people ready to take their money to get them what they want.

The implications of illegal immigration are amongst the most serious. Illegal immigrants, often without realizing it in advance, form a natural pool of captive labour for criminal gangs, including drug traffickers. The papers which their facilitators have provided may pass a casual police check, but they are seldom adequate to survive the more detailed examination that would arise in applying for a job or for social security benefits. They would soon be found out and deported. Some, therefore, have little option but to turn to crime or prostitution to keep alive. Once beholden to criminal gangs, they have to do what they are told or face exposure or worse. They are likely to be recruited for high-risk tasks such as acting as couriers for arms smuggling or drug distribution. Prostitution is historically a refuge from despair, but crime and drug smuggling may in the end lead to an even worse fate.

The biggest generator of organized crime in the West, and the subjugation and suffering that goes with it, is the money fed daily into the drug trade on the streets.

18 Italy, Germany and the Dutch Experiment

ITALY

Organized crime in Italy was discussed first, in Chapter 16, because the new CIS and other East European criminal gangs all model themselves on the Italian mafias. *Cosa Nostra*, especially the dominant Corleonesi family, are known to have sent experienced mafiosi to organize these gangs, no doubt hoping to extend their profits and their power in new areas where there will be less police pressure than in Italy, especially in the light of the successful application of *pentitismo* against the mafia in their homeland. *Cosa Nostra*, *Camorra* and *'Ndrangheta* have already been dispersing their activities in new areas of Italy and elsewhere in Europe for some years.[1]

Within Italy herself, the total profits from organized crime are believed to amount to $120 billion per year. The total profits from drug trafficking are estimated at between $4.8 billion and $9 billion, including $3.72 billion from heroin, $0.72 billion to $2.88 billion from cocaine and $1.55 billion from cannabis, plus a proportion from synthetic drugs for which the estimates vary too much to be worth quoting. Italy's total of $4.8 billion to $9 billion compares with $4 billion to $4.5 billion in UK and $1.2 billion to $2.4 billion in Germany.[2] The estimated number of regular drug users in Italy varies from 300,000 to 500,000; the government now provides drugs for about 80,000 registered addicts for treatment in 'therapeutic communities'.[3]

Apart from drug trafficking, other activities of organized crime in Italy include public works contracts (a traditional mafia field), protection money and other forms of extortion, arms trafficking and, to a lesser extent, gambling, prostitution (including illegal immigration), loan sharking (gaining a hold on victims by trapping them into debts they cannot repay), and trafficking in counterfeit money, precious metals, works of art and antiques. All these activities involve money laundering, which was discussed in Chapters 12 and 13.

GERMANY

The involvement of criminal gangs from East Europe in Germany was discussed in Chapter 17. A leaked report from the *Bundeskriminalamt* (BKA: police intelligence service) estimated that, by the end of 1991, Italian organized crime had invested about $50 billion in the former East German states.[4] On the night that the Berlin wall came down (9 November 1989) the Italian state police Economic Crime Unit noted that a well-known *Camorra* member telephoned his brother in Berlin, urging him to go at once into East Berlin to buy up all available property he could find, for pizzerias, restaurants and other business purposes.[5] *Der Spiegel* magazine in January 1992 quoted a *Bundesnachrichterdiest* (BND: foreign intelligence service) report that the drug cartels had also penetrated the German economy with apparently legal investments, including public and private enterprises, newspapers and television stations. Like the Italian mafias, they were clearly seeking power as well as money in a country which is increasingly dominant in the EU.

Drug sales in Germany ($1.2 billion to $2.4 billion) are less than in most EU countries in proportion to the population. Generally, the Germans deal firmly with drug trafficking but policy varies between states (*Länder*), which have more autonomy than the states in most other EU countries. Bavaria (Catholic and conservative) aims, like the Americans, at zero tolerance. In some Northern *Länder* the approach is more liberal. In October 1994, for example, the court in Lubeck ruled that possession of 4 kg of cannabis resin was within the legal limit.[6] Taking a cannabis resin dose as 4 gm, 4 kg is a thousand doses – around three years' supply for one person, which in practice means that most of it would be intended for sale to others. If this were to become a normal attitude in Germany (which to date has not been so), this could indicate a liberal trend towards cannabis on the lines adopted by the Dutch.

THE NETHERLANDS

The Netherlands has the reputation of being the most lax country in the EU in dealing with drugs. This causes considerable resentment amongst her neighbours, particularly as more hard drugs are imported via Rotterdam than through any other port in Europe. Dutch tolerance, however, has not led to the explosion of addiction or of drug-related crime that many expected, and the experience provides valuable evidence in the debate on how best to deal with the problem. The USA is at one end of the spectrum, committing huge sums of money to both reducing supply and suppressing the import, trading and consumption of drugs on the streets; the Netherlands is at the other end.

The Netherlands is one of the few European countries which have not ratified the 1988 UN Convention against Illicit Traffic in Narcotic Drugs and Psychotic Substances, whose signatories made drug trafficking illegal in their countries. Nevertheless, her so-called Opium Act does prohibit drug trafficking; the government simply chooses not to enforce its law; it presumably feels that, if it were to decide in the future to legalize drugs, hard and soft, altogether, it could not do so if it had ratified the UN Convention.

In 1976, the government revised the Opium Act to make *possession* of 30 gm or less of cannabis leaves or resin a misdemeanour and not a criminal offence (30 gm is roughly a week's supply for a regular cannabis user). In practice, the police do not usually bother to seek out and confiscate quantities of less than 50 kg.

Much Dutch cannabis is home grown, and this keeps the price low – about $1.50 per gm compared with $4–5 in the UK. At this price, Dutch users seldom need to steal to buy it. There are 300–400 open 'hash cafés' on the streets of Amsterdam, all well known to the police, and there is at least one in every sizeable town.

Heroin and cocaine are also sold freely on many street corners. The police retain strong powers against hard drugs but were instructed by the Ministry of Justice in 1985 not to use them. Hard drugs are more easily obtained in the Netherlands than in most EU countries because of the massive transit traffic through Rotterdam from which Dutch drug importers make prior arrangements to extract what they have paid for.

As was described for heroin in Hong Kong (see pp. 86–7) it is virtually impossible to spot a few kg of heroin amongst the transit cargo in the busiest port in Europe. The port handles about 280 million tonnes of cargo per year, including 2.5 million containers. Only 10 per cent of the containers are destined for the Netherlands, the other 90 per cent being transshipped elsewhere in Europe. Of the 6000 containers arriving on an average day, only 7 or 8 are searched; these are selected from the 10 per cent destined for the Netherlands, because it is not unreasonable for the Dutch to expect the recipients of transshipped containers to inspect them themselves.

Despite the relative ease of smuggling them in, hard drugs are still expensive because most of the price has already gone to the drug barons and international traffickers before they reach Rotterdam. The street price of both heroin and cocaine is around $75 per gm in Amsterdam, compared with $100 in London or New York – the saving resulting from the open and largely risk-free distribution and sale at the street corners and alleys where the addicts know they can get what they want.

The police know where most of these are, but prefer to keep them under discreet surveillance rather than drive the traffic underground. Their aim is to spot the consumers, encourage them to apply for treatment and prevent them from doing harm, for example, by driving under the influence of drugs or other anti-social behaviour – a Harm Reduction Policy (HRP). Intravenous heroin injectors can get clean needles free, so only 8 per cent of the Netherlands' AIDS victims are 'junkies', compared with 26 per cent of those in the USA. The Dutch police estimate that they have guided about 75 per cent of heroin addicts to undergo treatment, usually with methadone substitution.

By watching the street sales of hard drugs, the police are also able to spot many of the dealers and put them under surveillance if they wish. This can lead them to the big importers with overseas contacts, whom it is more important to catch.

There is relatively little drug-related crime in the Netherlands. There is less incentive for the dealers to bribe the police or to fight each other for territorial rights, especially as they know that the police could probably identify them if they did. Also, because addicts are usually spotted early, there are few drug-related deaths. In 1987, two years after the 'non-enforcement' policy was introduced, there were 18,000 deaths ascribed to tobacco, 2000 to alcohol but only 64 to heroin and virtually none to cocaine or other drugs. These figures come from authorities with an interest in justifying their policy but they are none the less impressive. The percentage of addicts is less than in the USA, Italy or the UK, which is certainly not what their critics would have predicted in the mid-1980s. One estimate puts the number of registered addicts as low as 20,000 out of a population of 15 million.[7]

As a senior Dutch policeman put it: 'The Americans offer us big money to fight the war on drugs their way. We do not say our way is right for them, but we are sure it is right for us. We don't want their help'.[8]

There are snags. Amsterdam attracts large numbers of 'drug tourists'. Of Amsterdam's drug addicts in 1990, 2000 were foreign; if they become sick or anti-social, the police try to spot them and send them home but many come back. Others simply come to buy hard drugs for less than their own street price and take them home to make a tidy profit.[9] This annoys the Netherlands' neighbours and so does the fact that up to 80 per cent of the EU's amphetamines are of Dutch manufacture.

To sum up: Dutch policy is usually described as decriminalization. Drugs are not legalized; possession for personal consumption is tolerated; selling hard drugs is still illegal, so the police have the power to prosecute if it gets out of hand, but generally they prefer to let it happen in the open, guide the addicts to treatment, spot the dealers and use them to get leads to the importers. Drug addiction, drug-related deaths and drug-related crime are low in proportion to the population.

The availability of hard drugs at 75 per cent of the EU average is due to the relatively unimpeded distribution within the Netherlands. The drug barons and international traffickers still get their full price, so the Dutch contribute as much as anyone else to financing international crime. On the other hand, if they were to legalize drugs, that is, allow importers to buy cocaine and heroin direct from the growers, they would be available on Dutch streets at a fraction – perhaps only 5 or 10 per cent – of the $100 per gm paid by other European addicts, so there would probably be a massive flow of Dutch drugs into the rest of Europe.

The pros and cons of suppression, decriminalization, licensing and legalization are discussed in Chapters 21 and 22.

Part VII
The United Kingdom

19 Drug Trafficking in the UK

PATTERN OF DRUG ABUSE IN THE UK

In Western Europe, Britain is second only to Italy in drug abuse in proportion to the population. Attempts were made to control it in the Pharmacy Act 1868. Generally, however, it remained socially acceptable (as illustrated by the Sherlock Holmes stories at the turn of the century) until 1914, when there was a scare about cocaine being passed on to soldiers by prostitutes, reflected in the Defence of the Realm Act 1920. Drug abuse was not a serious problem until the 1960s, when cannabis, LSD and other synthetics became part of the hippie culture spreading in the USA.[1]

When drug abusers sought treatment from their general medical practitioners or from a clinic, they were recorded in a national register, and the number of registered addicts rose rapidly from 333 in 1958 to over 1500 in the 1970s and 25,000 in 1994.[2] The numbers registered, however (like those of seizures of illicit drugs), do not give a reliable indication of the total number of abusers. In 1994, there were probably between 200,000 and 300,000 regular abusers. But ongoing research by the Institute for the Study of Drug Dependence (ISDD) suggested that in 1993 between 2.5 million and 5 million people had taken drugs at some time in their lives. In October 1994 the British government's Consultation Paper, *Tackling Drugs Together*, estimated that 6 per cent of the population (3 million people) take at least one illegal drug in any one year.[3] Most of those were users of cannabis (which accounted for 80 per cent of the arrests) and almost all of them were under 35. Release, the organization dedicated to treatment of addicts, estimated that nearly 85 per cent of drug users in Britain were taking only cannabis.[4]

Under the Misuse of Drugs Act 1971, drugs of abuse are categorized into classes indicating their propensity for addiction and the seriousness of their other effects. Class A includes heroin, cocaine (including crack), LSD and Ecstasy (MDMA). Class B includes cannabis, amphetamines and barbiturates. Cannabis has always predominated and there has been a steep rise in the use of amphetamines (Speed and Ice) and of Ecstasy. Heroin and cocaine have never accounted for more than a small percentage of the totals in UK.

The most disturbing figures are those for children and young people. ISDD estimated in 1993 that 6 per cent had tried drugs or solvent sniffing by the age of 11, 11 per cent by 14, 19 per cent by 15 and 22 per cent by 16. By the age of 20, one-third of young men and one-fifth of young women had abused drugs.[5] The other worrying development has been the growth of the 'rave' craze – uninhibited mass dances, usually in barns or warehouses, in which LSD, Ice, Speed and Ecstasy are a fundamental part of the culture. Of the £3 billion ($4.5 billion) spent each year on drugs of abuse, it is estimated that over £700 million ($1 billion) is spent on Ecstasy and that a million young people attend raves each week.[6] As stated earlier, about half the total value of thefts and burglaries in Britain are carried out to buy drugs and only 10 per cent of the money spent on drugs is legally earned.

Surveys of small samples can be misleading, but one does seem to be consistent with other data, and has the merit of being comprehensive. It was carried out by interviews in some depth with 80 young offenders aged 15–24 in West Yorkshire in 1994. Of the 80, 93 per cent had tried drugs in their mid-teens and had become regular users by the time of the interviews. More than 80 per cent admitted to 'a lot of crimes'. More than 60 per cent were unemployed, saying that they found crime more lucrative than work and that social security benefits were not worth claiming. Of the 80

70 had tried cannabis and 65 were now regular users
46 had tried acid/LSD and 17 were now regular users
23 had tried heroin and 11 were now regular users
19 had tried crack and 11 were now regular users

The first step was usually cannabis, and the commonest starting age was 13–16. Drug abuse was invariably linked with truancy. Most of those beginning at these ages became drug-using criminals at 17–21. The survey noted that anti-drug education began too late, and concluded that it should begin at 10–11 and that more effective measures should be taken to prevent truancy.

Of the 80, 26 (about 33 per cent) admitted having sold drugs, mostly cannabis, Ecstasy, amphetamines and LSD. They believed this to be more lucrative than other forms of crime and carried a lower risk, but that the snags were high capital outlay and severe penalties if caught. Drug taking caused unpredictable violence, particularly when 'coming down', and was at its most dangerous when combined with joy riding. Expenditure by the 80 ranged from £60 to £300 during a weekend or £130 to £600 in a week.[7]

Moving on from this survey to drug users in Britain as a whole, other records suggest that the heaviest individual expenditure of all is likely to be by an addicted crack user. A weekend binge of 50 rocks (each lasting only 15 minutes, leading to intense craving for another within an hour) would cost £20 ($30) per rock – £1000 for the weekend; a heavy daily user might consume 100 rocks – £2000 ($3000) every week. That would amount to £100,000 ($150,000) in a year – inevitably financed by crime.[8] An example of crack marketing, from manufacturer to user, was given on p. 76.

ORGANIZATION

The concept of a 'Mr Big' in much journalistic treatment of drug trafficking in Britain is a misleading one. It is applicable to the source countries – for example, Pablo Escobar in Colombia, El Vaticano in Peru and Khun Sa in Myanmar – but is not typical in Britain at all. Though the mafia have on occasions tried to establish agents in Britain (e.g. Di Carlo: see next section) they have seldom succeeded. Cocaine and heroin importers in the UK are normally individuals or groups of two or three criminals operating with a team of casual couriers and runners, typically a total of fifteen or twenty people. These importers buy overseas, not directly from the Colombian cartels or Khun Sa, but from brokers in, say, Bogotá, Venezuela, Jamaica, Los Angeles or Miami for cocaine or in Bangkok, Hong Kong, Karachi or Lebanon for heroin. Quantities handled are small compared with the money involved. A major importer might, for example, bring in 200 kg in a cargo container or a yacht, and for this he would probably pay the broker between $3 million and $5 million. More commonly, however, he will get his couriers to import it in 10 kg or 20 kg consignments. Even 1 kg smuggled in by a Nigerian or

Jamaican courier in her handbag (they are mostly women) may
have cost the importer $25,000–50,000 and have a final street
value of $100,000 – or $200,000 if the distributors and dealers cut
it to less than 50 per cent purity, for example with cornflour, as
they usually do.

The importer will typically sell it in lots of about 2 kg to a local
distributor operating in, say, a housing estate in London,
Liverpool or Manchester. This distributor will break it up into
smaller packages suitable for street dealers or sometimes small
gangs of dealers – especially in areas like Moss Side in Manchester
where there are rival gangs competing to hold their territories.
But, like the importer, the distributor will probably operate with a
small team of runners and lookouts. When cocaine is converted to
crack, this is normally done by the distributor or the dealer. A
distributor usually prefers to sell to a limited number of street
dealers whom he knows well, aiming to keep the total number he
deals with, in his team and those who buy from him, down to
about 20. When drug dealers are caught, either by the police or
by rival gangs, it is almost always the result of one of their trusted
circle accepting an attractive incentive to betray them, so they
like to keep this circle small.

The street dealers themselves may also try to minimize the
security risk by using runners to clinch the deals in the street.
They prefer not to hand drugs over on the street for fear of police
surveillance, and the runners may lead buyers to an alley where
the drugs are handed over more discreetly. The wise dealer aims
off for any one of his clients being a police plant. Various means of
avoiding the trap are illustrated in the case studies which follow.

The importers and distributors are usually people already
established in criminal activities, because they would otherwise
not be able to raise the capital for their initial purchases. The
price of even a week's supply for a small distributor will run into
several thousand pounds. Terms are usually cash.

The cannabis pattern is fairly similar. The synthetics, though
larger in volume of sales than heroin or cocaine, are usually
handled in smaller lots by a larger number of dealers. Consisting
mainly of small packets of pills manufactured in UK or in
mainland Europe, or of sheets of impregnated paper in the case of
LSD, they are much less risky to smuggle.

Occasionally, business people without a criminal record move
into drug distribution or importing as a sideline, either because

their current business is not making a profit or because they think that the pattern of it is suitable for concealing diversification. The majority of distributors and dealers, however, have graduated from other forms of crime. A successful criminal may find himself with a lot of money and decide that the quickest way to double it is in drugs.

There is also diversification within the drug trade. The majority of drug abusers take a variety of drugs so the dealers cater for them and switch where the market beckons. As the trade is criminal and clandestine, there are no controls and no way of enforcing agreements other than by threats. Since at each level they hope to make about 100 per cent profit, exporters, importers, distributors and dealers can afford to cut prices when there is a glut or when they want to lure a buyer. If they sense a security threat, they will cut their losses and switch to new ground.

IMPORTERS

Direct mafia involvement in Britain is rare but does occur. A Sicilian *Cosa Nostra* family, based in Venezuela with links in Canada, set up a highly lucrative business in London in the 1980s under Francisco Di Carlo, owning a hotel, a wine bar, an antique business and a travel agency. These provided comprehensive cover for importing cannabis from Kashmir and heroin from Thailand, usually concealed in furniture consigned by sea to Southampton or Felixstowe. Some was unloaded for the UK market and the rest sent on to Montreal. Di Carlo was arrested in 1985 in possession of 35 kg of heroin, probably bought for around $750,000 with an anticipated street value of $3.5 million.[9] In January 1987, David Medin, financed by the Detroit Mafia, was arrested in London with two suitcases containing 36 kg of pure cocaine with a street value of $3.6 million – or up to double that if heavily cut. He had smuggled it from Bolivia via Buenos Aires or Rio di Janeiro, whence the procedure was to conceal it in heavy machinery and send it by air freight to London. Companies trading in computer parts in London and Jersey were geared to launder anticipated profits of these operations up to $3 billion per month.[10]

But more typical of Britain was an operation begun by Eddie Richardson on his release from prison in the 1980s. He had been imprisoned in the 1960s as a leader, with his brother, of a violent criminal gang. On his release, as cover, he ran a scrap yard and was detected by Customs as being in contact with Donald Tredwen, a south London car dealer with a record of smuggling, who was also found to be in contact with a baggage supervisor for a cargo handling company at Gatwick Airport. All three were placed under surveillance. Tredwen made frequent visits to Bangkok and on one of these, in January 1987, a check of hotel records showed a telephone call to Richardson's scrap yard. During 1987, Richardson arranged 14 transfers from the Thai Bank in London to its Bangkok branch. Two large consignments of cannabis from Bangkok were seized in June and September 1988, one of 300 kg by air freight, the other of 4500 kg in a sea cargo of plastic flowers, with a total street value of over $20 million.

The police felt that the evidence was not yet certain to secure convictions, so surveillance was intensified. Richardson and Tredwen were seen meeting three Latin Americans, named Teixeira, Alarcon and Garcia, with Colombian and Venezuelan passports. Teixeira, who was a stranger to London, sent a fax from a Fleet Street print office to Quito, Ecuador, giving details of money received from 'Ed', 'Don' and 'Edon' totalling about $750,000. The fax also mentioned flights for an unknown couple to Quito. These were identified from a meeting with Teixeira and were tailed to Gatwick. They were seen to have no baggage, but airline records revealed that they had had suitcases when they arrived in the country. They were clearly couriers and, from the weight of the cases, had presumably brought in some 44 kg of cocaine which, it was calculated, would have cost about $40,000 per kg ($1.75 million in all), with a street value of $4.4 million. This cocaine was never recovered but the route had been revealed.

In January 1989, Alarcon returned to London, still under surveillance. Police searched his room and found a bill of lading (cargo) for a consignment of balsa wood from Ecuador to Le Havre, where it was to be transferred to a ferry for Portsmouth. British Customs asked their French colleagues to let it through and a British Customs officer accompanied it to Portsmouth and thence by road to Southampton, where it was searched. There were 2000 kg of cannabis and 153.8 kg of cocaine – some of it marked in a way indicating its source to be the Cali cartel in Colombia. Within 24 hours, Richardson, Tredwen, Teixeira and six others were arrested with ample evidence for conviction.[11] It is a fair guess that fewer than a dozen people, including the Latin American couriers, need ever have been involved at the UK end, and nine of them went to prison, Richardson for 25 years, but the potential profits for the gang, for the last consignment alone, could have been around $10 million.

Not all importers work on that scale but they can still become very rich. With the aid of an informant, the Metropolitan Police arrested Wendell Daniels in December 1991. He was a Jamaican who had been involved in cannabis importing for some years but turned to crack in the 1980s. In his safe houses were found 717 gms of cocaine, 480 gms of crack of 90–7 per cent purity, and 675 gms of cannabis. As a middleman, he would probably have made £30,000 ($45,000) profit from that – which was just what he had in stock that day. His assets included eleven properties in UK and Jamaica but, apart from owning a BMW, he did not lead a lavish lifestyle. In preparation for his trial, these properties and other assets he had acquired in the previous six years were assessed to be worth £1,021,152 ($1.5 million), during which time he had declared a total income of £58,980.[12]

COURIERS

The couriers run by Richardson and Teixeira were described in the previous section. Those involved in the big cargo consignments were no doubt paid a great deal to ensure that they kept quiet – and would have continued to earn that kind of money. It is not known what the two Latin Americans with the suitcases containing an assumed 44 kg of cocaine were paid.

More often, however, couriers are ripped off. Many do a one-off assignment because they are pressed for money, and are too frightened of the consequences to give information. Amongst the saddest cases are some of the Nigerians. Nigeria, as has been described earlier in the book, is now a main staging point on both the cocaine and the heroin routes, partly, no doubt, because of the availability of cheap and gullible couriers with a good chance of getting into Britain; also because Nigeria's Commonwealth trade links provide plenty of cargoes to be exported without very efficient control or documentation.

Most Nigerian couriers are women, often carrying babies, which gets them sympathetic treatment. Many carry the drugs sealed in condoms, which they swallow, and excrete after passing through Customs. Some have been known to swallow more than 100 condoms and they often take pills to block their bowel movements. For smuggling possibly tens of thousands of pounds worth of cocaine, the average fee for a Nigerian courier is £1000 ($1500), which seems to them inconceivable wealth. If they are caught, their average sentence is six years, based on the amount they are smuggling.[13] Once in prison in England, they are bewildered, thousands of miles from their families, with no understanding of the processes of English law.[14]

Jamaican women born in Britain are often also used as couriers to smuggle cocaine into Britain, sometimes for no more than the fare and a few hundred dollars for a holiday in Jamaica. The traffickers select people who are vulnerable, short of money and easy to persuade – for example, with relatives they want to see or, best of all, with a baby whom they want to show to their family in Jamaica.

In British courts, sentences are calculated on the police estimate of the street value of the drugs. Based on a 1987 Appeal Court judgment, guidelines are

£1 million 'many kg of heroin'	14 years minimum
£100,000 'a few kg'	10 years minimum
'An appreciable amount – fractions of kg'	4 years

with sentences reduced for pleading guilty or for cooperating, for example by giving information, or continuing with arrangements for smuggling under police observation to trap other members of the gang.[15]

In one example, a female British-born Jamaican courier, taking her first chance to visit her grandparents and half-siblings in Kingston, was given her air ticket, holiday expenses and £500. She was caught on her return to Gatwick with 250 gm of 90 per cent pure cocaine. Assuming that, after dilution, this would be sold as 400 gm of cut cocaine at £60 ($90) per gm, the initial street price valuation was £24,000. In court, however, the street value was given as £57,000 and she got a four-year sentence. Another female Jamaican courier was caught with 200 gm of cocaine in a condom concealed in her vagina, and was sentenced to six and a half years. Both suspected that they had been set up as 'sacrificial lambs'. It is customary for sniffer dogs to check incoming flights from Jamaica and, if they pick up the scent of drugs, Customs will intensify their search. The gang leaders may give a tip-off (untraceable) so that Customs catch a courier with a small consignment, the hope being that Customs will be satisfied with that, and miss out on a much larger consignment on the same aircraft.[16]

A rather more complicated procedure was spotted by Customs in 1986. A pair of brightly dressed black women were in transit at Gatwick from Jamaica to Brussels. One was seen behaving suspiciously with a body belt; they were found to be carrying drugs and arrested. Brussels Airport was at this time particularly insecure because departing passengers, after X-ray checks at the 'passengers only barrier', had access to a large duty free shopping area in which arriving passengers could also shop before going out through Customs. Arriving passengers could therefore hand over guns, bombs, drugs or money, to departing passengers who had already been searched. In this case, the arriving Jamaican couriers had a rendezvous in the shopping area with two smart, white young ladies in business clothes on their way to embark for London Heathrow. The drugs would have been handed over and possibly bank notes for laundering passed back in exchange. This would have been done by, say, exchanging shopping bags or the body belts themselves in the shopping centre ladies' cloakroom. The two white 'business women' would have attracted no particular attention at Heathrow on a flight arriving from Brussels and would have probably passed unchecked through the green channel with the drugs.[17]

If they can, traffickers will employ couriers to Britain with British passports. If not, it is easy to substitute a new photograph in a stolen passport with the aid of a heat gun. Alternatively, there is the method, first described by Frederick Forsyth in *The Day of the Jackal*, in which the forger picked out the grave of a dead child born on a suitable date with a common name and applied for a passport in that name. This technique has been successfully copied in real life.

Criminals sometimes apply for a passport in the name of a person still alive with a suitable name and age, and get away with it unless they are arrested for some other reason. The Gwent Passport Office handles 10,000–15,000 passport applications per week and those completed before 1990 (valid for 10 years) were not computerized. The parents of Susan Cole, a blonde girl in

Kent, were astonished when the police notified them that their daughter had been arrested for drug smuggling, and even more astonished to be told that she was a black Nigerian with two children![18]

The new machine-readable British passports should make detection of this kind of thing easier, but there will be many old ones in circulation until 1999. Even the new ones will still be vulnerable to forgery until they contain biometric data unique to the authorized holder, as is recommended on pp. 186–7.

Drug traffickers, with their eyes on making huge profits and avoiding imprisonment, emulate the mafia in the ruthlessness of their intimidation, torture and murder to enforce their will on their foot soldiers and to eliminate their rivals. Couriers may be lured to agree to a low-risk smuggle of a small amount of a Class B drug, only to find, on reporting to pick it up in Kingston or Lagos, that they are instead required to carry a large consignment of cocaine or heroin – albeit for a higher fee. There is no escape, because by then they know too much, so they are terrified that defection would lead to retribution against themselves or their families. The bosses like a courier with a child, not only to beguile the Customs officers, but also because it gives them a stranglehold on the mother.

It can be argued that couriers generally know very well what they are doing; that they are consciously smuggling for personal gain; and that, in most cases, they know that the drugs they are smuggling will damage other people's lives. Nevertheless, when people are desperate, faced with intolerable situations from which they see no other way out – stranded far from home without the price of an air ticket, or with starving children deserted by their father – this kind of reasoning is far from their minds. They are usually the most vulnerable of footsoldiers. Hanging these footsoldiers as they do in Malaysia and Thailand has little effect on their employers, to whom they are low-cost expendable labour, usually on one-off assignments.

DISTRIBUTORS AND RETAILERS

A typical crack distributor – Sammy Lewis – was introduced in Chapter 9 (p. 76) and his detection and arrest will be described in Chapter 20. Distribution and retailing often overlap but, as one successful trafficker remarked, 'good dealers do not handle the stuff themselves',[19] a view shared by the police. He bought cocaine and heroin in London and marketed it in a north-western city. He insulated himself from the street retailers through three inter-mediaries – two being his nephews and the third an old friend. Their patch was a cul-de-sac, in which they had ten or fifteen sellers working, about five from their own houses and the rest from the street, each street dealer having his own patch, usually designated by a particular corner, café or lamppost. A seller would be given a pack of 7 gm of heroin for a day, or he could get two packs if he thought he could sell them. Cocaine and crack sales were higher. There was a lot of competition from other dealers but the leader and his team were probably turning over more than 1 kg a week, taking at least £60,000 ($90,000) on the streets.

A smaller team of three in their twenties, all with criminal records, was led by 'Ian', operating from his parents' flat on a London council estate. The parents were not involved, apart from receiving £200 a night for use of the flat. Ian took care never to meet the buyers, who got to know that his 'office hours' were 6–10 pm. By 6 pm a queue would form in the street and the team would supply between 20 and 30 people a night. The 'donkey' of the team would collect their money at the door and the heroin would be dropped from a first-floor window. Sometimes another member of the team would deal direct in an alley way. This was not a very sophisticated operation and was soon put under surveillance by the police.[20]

Sometimes selling is a convenient sideline to another activity. Nicholas Dorn interviewed a taxi driver and a prostitute who did this. The taxi driver initially provided other taxi drivers with amphetamines (Speed) to keep them going through the night shifts. He usually sold about 7 gm a day. Dealing was easy because the other drivers would call him up on the radio net and the cabs would meet. Later, news that he was a dealer got around the customers and when they telephoned for a cab they would specify his number. He was making about £500 ($750) a week profit on amphetamines as well as his cab earnings but he dropped out of it after six months as he realized that in time someone was bound to talk.[21]

The prostitute, 'Jill', worked on a much larger scale. She was a single mother with four children. She used a pager system for her prostitution and also for buying and selling drugs. The police traced her through surveillance of others she worked with. She was charged with nine others with conspiracy to supply heroin. She was found with only 28 gm of heroin in her possession but there was damaging evidence on the pager of dealings over a long period. She had £18,000 in the bank and £12,300 in other assets (stocks and shares, car, and so on). On the morning of her trial her lawyer received an offer from the prosecution – five years and confiscation of £18,000 if she pleaded guilty. She declined and got fifteen years (reduced on appeal to nine) with £30,000 asset confiscation. The other nine defendants nearly all pleaded guilty, but they had no bank accounts so they got off more lightly.[22]

Contrary to popular mythology, most of the biggest drug importers and criminal gangs in Britain are led, not by blacks, but by white businessmen or criminals who have the necessary capital. Though they will normally operate in small groups, their turnover (as in the Richardson-Tredwen gang mentioned earlier in this chapter) may be enormous. There are, however, also some black ghetto areas plagued by continuous gang warfare comparable to that between the 'Crips' and 'Bloods' in Los Angeles.

One such area is Moss Side in Manchester, with neighbouring gangs in Cheetham Hill and Salford. The gangs there may be 30 to 60 strong and are often linked to the far bigger gangs (the 'posses') operating in Jamaica (see pp. 72–3). The main ones operating in 1993 were

Gooch Close (Moss Side)	About 30 strong	Average age 20
Dodington (Moss Side)	About 30 strong	Average age 18
Cheetham Hill (to the north)	About 60 strong	Average age 26
Salford (to the west)	About 40 strong	Average age 26

The Cheetham Hill gang were the most sophisticated. They wore uniforms of boiler suits and balaclavas and operated on military lines. The Gooch Close and Dodington gangs in Moss Side were bitter rivals and wore different coloured bandanas. All of these trafficked on a large scale in heroin, cocaine and crack. The Salford gang supplied Ecstasy, Speed and other 'clean' drugs to raves in the city centre.[23]

There was an increasing tendency to carry guns. The gang leaders established 'respect' through fear, and paraded it by wearing heavy jewellery, etc. The style of hero worship and discipline was fascist. The henchmen were loyal to their leader not only for fear of what he would do to them if they were not, but also for fear of what others might do to them in retribution if they were left unprotected in the event of the death or arrest of their leader.

Starting with cannabis in the 1960s, heroin supply became prominent with the gangs in Moss Side in 1987. Initially this was not run by the big gangs but was a far more dispersed and widespread activity. Individual leaders built up enough capital to employ teams of black teenagers who operated freely in open spaces like shoppping centres where, in 1987–9, anything up to 40 sellers at a time could be seen hawking their wares.[24] In the car parks, they bargained through the half-opened windows of the cars. At this time, a successful leader could buy 1 kg of heroin for £25,000 ($37,500), dilute it and package it into thousands of 100 mg or 250 mg doses, hand his army of teenagers a plastic bag apiece, with as many of these doses as they thought they might hope to sell in the day, and get three times his capital outlay back from the streets.[25]

The police watched and recorded these bustling market-places on video cameras but were cautious about intervening as there had been some very ugly anti-police riots in Moss Side in the 1980s. In 1989, however, they mounted Operation Corkscrew, based on this video coverage, resulting in twelve successful prosecutions including two of the principal dealers. Sentences ranged from seven to ten years.[26]

From 1989, therefore, the dealers' operations had to be more discreet and efficiently organized. The big gangs took over, especially the Gooch Close gang, though they were violently challenged by the Peppermill Mob, which was later absorbed into the Dodington gang. In one five-week period, ten were wounded by shooting, stabbing, slashing and burning before a Gooch Close man was killed in April 1991.

Selling was organized by mobile phone networks. Thirteen of these networks were monitored by the police in 1992–3, three for heroin, one for crack and nine selling both. 'One plus one' was becoming a popular buy – a quick high from a rock of crack followed by a quarter-gram injection of heroin on the rebound. Potential buyers would get the mobile phone number from another user and call it from a public phone box. (As an indication of gangland discipline, no phone boxes were vandalized in Moss Side!) If the supplier had any suspicion of a trap, he would either refuse the deal or set a trap himself by staking out the delivery point before the sale. Sale points were *ad hoc*, not fixed, and were often several miles from the place from which the call had been made. Cutouts were used, so that the person actually delivering the drugs often did not know whom he was working for.[27] School children were widely employed as lookouts, speeding to and fro on their bikes.

The demand was such that dealers needed to operate round the clock to meet it. To cover the night hours, some would allow regular users to get into debt, and then proposition them to wipe the slate clean if they agreed to run the mobile phone from their own homes during the night and arrange deliveries without the dealer being personally involved.[28]

Police investigations revealed links between Moss Side gang members and Jamaican criminals in London and Kingston. Jamaican criminals regularly visited Britain and there was a flow of cash to Jamaica.[29] There was a very real fear that the gang warfare might escalate as it had in Los Angeles so, in 1991-3, the Greater Manchester Police mounted two more operations, which are described in Chapter 20.

20 Anti-Drug Enforcement in the UK

INTELLIGENCE ORGANIZATION

In most forms of crime the victim (e.g. of a robbery) or the family in the case of a murder or disappearance, will tell the police, who start their investigation from there. In the case of drug trafficking, the victim, the user of the drugs, tries to conceal it, so the police have to start by identifying a gang member, usually by surveillance, and turning him into an informant. This may involve working upwards through several levels of dealers and distributors unless couriers can be spotted, leading direct to a big importer, as in the Richardson case (see pp. 159–61).

Police intelligence in the UK, up till 1993, operated on three layers. There were nine regional crime squads (RCSs) incorporating 20 drugs wings, plus the Metropolitan Police Central Drugs Squad – a total of some 110 officers in London and 330 in the regions.[1] For the reason given above, they targeted the couriers where possible, in cooperation with Customs.

At the next level down were the local drugs squads run by the 43 county and city police forces in England and Wales and the area drugs squads in London. Their targets were the distributors and dealers and they worked in plain clothes, conducting surveillance, recruiting informants and themselves carrying out 'sell busts' and 'buy busts' to obtain evidence for convictions. The uniformed police, who sometimes spotted dealers on the streets, either arrested them or notified the drugs squads for undercover action.[2]

At national level, the Central Drugs and Illegal Immigration Intelligence Unit was redesignated in 1985 as the National Drugs Intelligence Unit (NDIU), splitting drugs and immigration intelligence (briefly linked again in Operation Lucy and the Crack Intelligence Coordinating Unit – see Chapter 9). In 1993, the NDIU was incorporated in the National Criminal Intelligence Service (NCIS), initially with a total strength of 450 (on all kinds of criminal intelligence in England and Wales, not just drugs).[3] By 1994, 1300 police officers were engaged solely on drugs.[4]

INFORMANTS, INFORMERS AND WITNESSES

The most cost effective of all intelligence operations is to recruit, encourage, reward and protect a good informant. An 'informant' is one who works within or has contact with the target organization and agrees to give information (usually in the course of continuing those contacts), as distinct from an 'informer' who gives information about things which have already happened. An informant can give information about future plans. Informants were the decisive factor in winning the war in Malaya, and techniques developed there have been used successfully in Italy, Northern Ireland and Peru.

Good informants can cost a lot. In addition to leniency regarding their own crimes (usually the initial incentive) they must be generously rewarded on results, protected and if necessary relocated, with their families. Even if this costs the equivalent of ten years' pay (roughly what it cost in Malaya), it is still more cost effective than paying ten more police officers or buying surveillance equipment or helicopters.

The police use four codes for grading sources of information:

A   Where there is no doubt about the integrity of the source, or if he has in the past invariably been reliable.
B   Where the source has proved reliable in most cases.
C   Where the source has in most cases proved unreliable.
D   Where the source is previously untried.

The information itself is coded 1 to 4:

1   Known to be true without reservation.
2   Known personally to the source but not to the handler.
3   Not known personally to the source but corroborated by other information received.
4   Not known personally to the source and cannot be corroborated.[5]

An informant using inside knowledge of a criminal, terrorist or drug-trafficking organization takes great risks. Once he has betrayed information for which the organization would kill him if they knew, he becomes totally dependent on the support and discretion of his handler, and their relationship may become very close. Persuading the informant to cooperate has little to do with morality or ideology and all to do with self-interest or the fate of his family or friends. The best informant is usually someone who has or has been taking part in the illegal activities being targeted, in which case his strongest motivation will be to evade or reduce the consequences of the crimes he has already committed. The second strongest is the hope of future security, physical and economic, including the security of his family. Occasionally there may be a motive of revenge against the gang which got him into this predicament or simply to get them locked up before they discover what he has done and take retribution. Some informants may have other, more devious aims, for example, to get the police to break up a rival gang on their patch.

'Ninety-nine per cent of informants come from arrests', according to one police drugs squad officer.[6] When arrested, the person may deny the charge, refuse to cooperate, plead not guilty and take the full sentence. He may make a plea bargain, for example by giving the police the identity of the importer, distributor or dealer or the location of the drugs. He may even testify against them in court, though the police will try to avoid this. Alternatively, he may agree to continue to take part in operations with the gang and keep the police informed – potentially the most productive of all, but also the most dangerous.

His assistance may be a one-off operation, such as visiting a dealer under discreet police surveillance and, as he emerges, signalling by a prearranged gesture that the wanted person is inside with drugs in his possession so that the police can go in and catch him red handed. Or it may be a continuing operation over several months, after which the informant may be relocated and rewarded with all charges dropped.[7]

The payment or alleged payment of rewards gives great opportunities for corruption, which may be difficult to prove. This is an inevitable hazard, because it is essential to keep the identities of informants, their links with specific information, and transactions with them, highly confidential. They should be recorded, if at all, only in a coded form known to a minimum number of people. If this were otherwise, other potential informants would get wind of it and not take the risk.[8]

There is inevitably a moral dilemma in rewarding criminals and allowing them to enjoy a prosperous retirement, but this has to be balanced against other crimes prevented and lives saved by their information.

Though not comparable with an informants, good informers can also be of great value, especially if they guide the police to other sources of corroboration and new evidence, so that they do not have to appear as witnesses at all.

There are, however, many hazards in handling informants, informers and potential witnesses for the prosecution. If the circumstances were such that torture, threats or inducements could have been used, it will certainly be alleged by defence lawyers that they were, to secure an acquittal or, more effectively, to bide their time and get convictions quashed on Appeal. If the defence succeed in convincing the court that an informant has been involved, but the police will not release his identity, the judge may dismiss the case or the Appeal Court may quash the conviction.[9] If the judge demands that the informant be called as a witness, the police will probably drop the case. If an informant does agree to give evidence in court as part of a plea bargain, his sentence may amount to protective custody, but the police will thereafter have an open-ended commitment for his protection.

The BBC and ITV cooperate with the police in encouraging members of the public to give information in programmes such as 'Crimewatch'. A private security company, ADT, also founded the Community Action Trust (CAT) in 1988 to raise funds from the London business community to reward informants and informers, and extended this to drugs in 1990. The *Guardian* in 1990 estimated that this has enabled rewards of up to £100,000 ($150,000) to be paid,[10] but it has also been said of the supergrass system, long used by the CID against criminal gangs, that 'while it put many of the robbers in prison, it also guaranteed freedom to some of the worst offenders'.[11]

This dilemma was well illustrated in Italy in 1980-2. A particularly unscrupuluos *pentito*, believed to be guilty of nine murders, was released and relocated after a brief period in prison, while many who had committed less serious crimes served long sentences because of him. But, thanks to *pentitismo*, it is estimated that 400 people who would otherwise be dead are still alive.[12]

TYPES OF OPERATIONS

The commonest types of police operations arising from information are raids, sweeps, street policing, 'buy busts' and (more rarely) 'sell busts'.

Raids and sweeps have been a regular tactic in areas such as Moss Side and Brixton where there was evidence of widespread drug trafficking. Sometimes these were 'fishing trips' in which it was hoped that evidence would be turned up and information acquired from people questioned. Police stop and search powers were enhanced by the Misuse of Drugs Act 1971 and further by the Police and Criminal Evidence Act 1986 (PACE), and used where there was a pattern of serious crime in the district, including drug dealing.[13] The 'acid house craze' – raves in barns, warehouses and in the open air, with use of Ecstasy, Speed, Ice and LSD – led to raids being extended to include these events in 1989; a 1990 Amendment to the Criminal Justice Act 1988 gave the courts the right to confiscate their profits. A person was also liable to a ten-year sentence for conspiracy to manage premises knowing that drugs would be supplied there.[14]

An intensification of normal street policing and surveillance has often been used to gain information for raids in areas in which drug dealing is believed to be rife but where the police have little specific evidence.

This was done in the Moss Side area of Manchester and led to raids and arrests which broke up the open pattern of drug dealing in 1989, as was previously described in Chapter 19. Two operations of this kind in the Notting Hill area are described later in this chapter.

The arrest of Sammy Lewis (see pp. 76 and 176–7) was an example of the 'buy bust'. 'Sell bust' operations are ethically and legally more questionable. An undercover officer sells drugs to a distributor or dealer. This may confirm that the dealer is in business and enable his activities to be monitored but, if he comes to trial, the defence will argue that the 'sell bust' amounted to incitement to commit a crime.

PUNISHMENT AND CIVIL LIBERTIES

The maximum penalty for drug trafficking in Britain is life imprisonment. In addition, the financial penalties for money laundering, which were described in Chapters 13 and 19, can result in additional terms of imprisonment if the assets attributed by the court are placed out of reach and not handed over. This imprisonment ranges from 12 months for £10,000 to 10 years for

£1 million unpaid. A person ordered to hand over assets will presumably have been found guilty of either a drug-trafficking or money-laundering offence 'beyond reasonable doubt'. The additional imprisonment would be based on his failure to meet the onus of proof of their legitimacy and his failure to produce them, rather than on proof that they were criminally acquired 'beyond reasonable doubt'.[15]

Under the DTOA, it is also an offence for anyone aware of an investigation into money laundering to tip off the suspect. This would apply especially to a bank employee or financial adviser who, when compelled under the DTOA to provide what would normally be confidential information, informed the client. The Act, however, also gives bankers and financial advisers immunity against civil or criminal liability for disclosing any suspicions that they may have about their client's affairs to the authorities.

If the defendant is shown to have given some of his illegal proceeds to someone else not connected with the crime, such as a member of his family, this could be seized even if the recipient was unaware of the source of the money.[16] This seems harsh but, if it were not so, it would be an obvious tactic for anyone fearing arrest on such charges to use this means of placing his assets beyond reach with his family or trusted friends.

Since 1986 the police, under PACE, have had power to defer access to legal assistance for up to 36 hours when investigating serious offences such as drug trafficking. They can also delay informing relatives if there are grounds for believing that recovery of the suspect's drug-trafficking proceeds would be hindered.[17]

EXAMPLES

Operation Trident in June 1987 was an example of breaking into a criminal organization by intensified policing. Mass drug trafficking was taking place openly in the area of All Saints Road, in London's Notting Hill, similar to that described in Moss Side in Chapter 19. Police raids on the streets would have resulted in riots, as they had in Brixton in 1981 (Operation Swamp). Trident began with four covert observation posts, from which the movements of dealers and buyers were logged. A dossier was built up on each dealer. At the end of June, 17 dealers and 144 buyers were arrested. Following that, uniformed police appeared in greater numbers and, working with local authorities and other agencies, they launched renovation work to lay bare the hidey-holes – alleys, doorways, etc. – in which drug deals could be done unobserved. The police were surprised to find that 95 per cent of the people welcomed this action, saying that they had been waiting for years for something to be done to curb the drug traffic.[18]

Operation Mint followed in October and November 1989, on similar lines. Two covert observation posts were established, initially as a pilot scheme for a week, in which no arrests were made. Then, as in Trident, police started taking detailed notes of the deals. In three weeks they recorded 123 deals, mainly of cannabis and cocaine (including 12 of crack) but only one of heroin. They followed 64 buyers and arrested them outside the area. All the sales were by 16 dealers, who were arrested – all simultaneously early one morning in their residences – and remanded in custody for 6 months, during which drug dealing virtually ceased in All Saints Road.[19] Most of the dealers were convicted and their money confiscated; for the next few years at least, drug trafficking ceased to be significant in the area.

Operation Dalehouse concentrated on crack-related crime in Brixton from August 1991 to November 1992, during which a database of dealers and buyers, to a total of 3500, was built up. These included a number of leading gangsters from the posses in Kingston visiting Britain, and the data revealed that substantial numbers of Jamaican illegal immigrants were returning regularly to Britain. One had been deported eight times in the year, each time returning with a different forged passport. In all, 247 arrests were made; all except about 20 refused to answer any police questions. Even those who did cooperate, for example, by recognizing someone from a photograph, would know him only by a street name. By cross-checking with information from other sources, for example about cars or girl friends, their identity could usually be established. The perpetrators of fifteen serious crimes (four murders, ten attempted murders, four of which were against policemen, and one kidnap) were identified. In many cases, however, they were never caught because of the ease with which they moved in and out of the country, and because of the reluctance of others to give evidence.[20] It would be hard to find a stronger argument for the issue of ID cards carrying biometric data (see pp. 186–7).

The next two examples are taken from Moss Side in Manchester again, where the pattern of operation of larger gangs, also with links to Jamaica, was described on pp. 166–8. After Operation Corkscrew (on similar lines to Trident and Mint), drug dealing in Moss Side was largely arranged on mobile phone networks which buyers contacted from local phone boxes. This trade was tackled in two major operations in 1991–3.

The first of these, Operation China, began with video cameras in a concealed observation post, which recorded 37 deals over a five week period in 1991 (36 for heroin and one for crack). One early morning in August 1991, 200 police officers in 40 unmarked vehicles converged and arrested 23 dealers, mostly aged between 18 and 24, with the paraphernalia of drugs, mobile phones and, in many cases, weapons. Some were earning up to £3000 ($4500) a week. They received sentences of between three and seven years. Many buyers were also arrested and were usually dismissed with a caution, but their diaries were very valuable in piecing together the numbers of the mobile phone networks and the street names of the dealers.

Operation Miracle, in 1992–3, was based on monitoring these mobile phone networks. This revealed the diversification from heroin, which up till 1991 had dominated the market, into the combined use – 'one plus one' – of crack and heroin.[21]

Operation Howitzer was a 'buy bust' which resulted in the arrest of Sammy Lewis, a crack distributor whose *modus operandi* was described in Chapter 9 (p. 76). Lewis was buying about 2 kg of cocaine every two weeks from an importer and was making £9000–12,000 ($14,000–18,000) a week by converting it into crack and selling it to three trusted dealers in north London.

In March 1991 Lewis was approached by 'Ricky', an old friend who had moved from London to Nottingham, which Lewis knew was a strong crack market. Ricky said that he had a friend called 'Andy' who was looking for a source of supplies of crack to sell in Handsworth, Birmingham. Lewis unwisely agreed to a meeting, not suspecting that 'Andy' was an undercover policeman. Ricky took Andy to meet Lewis on the Church End Estate near Harlesden, where Andy bought a quarter of an ounce (7 gm) of crack for £320 ($480). He said he would like 4–5 ounces a week and they agreed to meet again. Lewis tapped in a telephone number on the memory of Andy's mobile phone. Three days later, Andy bought another quarter of an ounce in two small slabs. They then arranged a third meeting, on 14 March, to pick up the first of what were to be regular consignments of 4 ounces (113 gm) for £7000 ($10,500).

At 6 pm on 14 March 1991, Andy called on his mobile phone and confirmed the meeting. At 9.25 pm he drove to the agreed rendezvous in Taylors Lane, NW 10, in a new Daimler Jaguar, fitting the image of a prosperous drug dealer. There were quite a few vehicles and pedestrians around. No particular attention had been attracted when a white Transit van had parked a few minutes earlier and the driver got out and walked towards the main road. A plain clothes policeman sat in front while four others – an unarmed snatch squad – lay out of sight in the back of the van.

Andy called Lewis on his mobile phone and was told to wait in the car. Two other men wandered up, clearly Lewis's minders, and sat on a nearby street bench. Ten minutes later, Lewis came to the car and Andy lowered the electric window. Andy confirmed that he had the money in the boot of the car. Lewis went down a small side street and returned to hand over a package containing some slabs of crack. Andy declined Lewis's offer to let him weigh it and this may have aroused Lewis's suspicions. A car with headlights came by and he walked away to sit on some steps at the entrance to a block of flats nearby. Two of the plain clothes policemen were approaching, pretending to be a pair of rowdies returning from a pub and, by arrangement, they split, one diverting, phone card in hand, saying he must make a call from a nearby phone box. He had been trained in judo and jumped on Lewis, who drew a gun, shot and nearly killed the second policeman and broke away. He threw away the gun as the third and fourth back-up policemen gave chase and eventually caught him hiding under a van in a cul-de-sac.[22]

This was a fairly typical buy bust operation, but it is surprising that none of the policemen was armed. Lewis pleaded guilty to possession of drugs but pleaded self-defence for the shooting, saying that he assumed that he was being attacked by a rival gang who he knew carried guns. He was sentenced to five years for supply and possession of Class A drugs and seventeen years for attempted murder.[23]

DRUGS IN PRISONS

Drug abuse in prisons has caused serious concern. Estimates of numbers vary enormously but one of the most authoritative (in 1992) suggested that between 35 and 50 per cent had used drugs before arrest – 35 per cent cannabis, 9 per cent heroin, 9 per cent amphetamines and 5 per cent cocaine (including 1 per cent crack). Only 10 per cent of men and, surprisingly, 25 per cent of women were dependent (i.e. addicted) on entering prison, mainly those injecting heroin or amphetamines.[24]

Apart from drugs such as methadone issued under medical supervision for treatment of addicted prisoners, large quantities of drugs are smuggled into the prisons. Drugs have become the prime unofficial currency and thereby the prime source of power (like that of the traditional 'tobacco barons') within the prison community. These are smuggled in capsules by family visitors, either in the mouth or in the anus or vagina – 'orally or anally' as the prison service describes it.

One way to prevent this would be to conduct intimate body searches of every visitor on arrival. This would certainly arouse resentment. So would intimate body searches of the prisoners themselves at the end of each visit. Another alternative would be to have a daily search of the prison, including the cells, by sniffer dogs. This could lead to detection and confiscation of most of the drugs but would again arouse resentment amongst the prisoners.

There is, however, a serious risk that prisoners who have not used drugs before may acquire the habit in prison if abuse is not checked; also that the spread of AIDS – already a serious problem in the prisons – will be increased by intravenous injection. This risk is particularly severe in women's prisons as many inmates are prostitutes, already HIV positive, and their profession will make them the likeliest to spread the infection in the community after their release.

In 1990, official estimates put the number of serious drug users in prisons at 1800 but the National Association of Probationers put it at between 9000 and 18,000, which is about 30 per cent of the prison population.[25]

Some members of the prison service may prefer to take a tolerant attitude towards drug abuse in their prisons. They might think that, provided it does not get out of hand, it is better to turn a blind eye in the interest of maintaining the constructive working relationship on which the rehabilitation of prisoners (as distinct from punishment and deterrence) depends. Success in rehabilitating a fair proportion of their prisoners is an essential part of the motivation and job satisfaction of most prison officers. Also, many of the prisoners who take drugs (especially cannabis) do themselves no harm and are more contented than they would be if denied this solace. The risk of AIDS would also be greater if the exchange of needles were driven wholly underground. But the arguments against tolerating drugs in prisons, except for medical treatment, are far stronger.

The pros and cons of stricter suppression in general are further discussed in Chapter 21.

THE OPTIONS

The world is losing the war against drugs and Britain is no exception. Home Office figures published in June 1994 clearly indicate this. The number of registered addicts has nearly trebled in six years, from 11,000 in 1987, to 22,000 in 1991, to 25,000 in 1992 and 28,000 in 1993. Figures for registered addicts are not a reliable guide to the total, because they are those who are referred by their doctors or who volunteer for treatment, most often for fear of AIDS. But within these figures there are some more convincing and worrying trends. The 1993 figure included 11,600 *new* addicts, an increase of 21 per cent on the new addicts in 1992. The largest increase was among those under 21. More convincing still was the increase in the number of deaths. Deaths of registered addicts rose 27 per cent to 510 and the total number of drug-related deaths by 4 per cent to 14,000.[26]

Commander John Grieve, Director of Intelligence at New Scotland Yard, presented a disturbing report on 18 March 1994 to the Drug Policy Forum attended by representatives of all agencies involved in combating drugs in London.[27] He said that London had had double its share of drug abuse in proportion to its population. Heroin consumption had risen steadily. Abuse of amphetamines and Ecstasy had risen sharply with the growing popularity of raves. Consumption of cocaine had greatly increased, with a corresponding increase in crime and especially in violent crime. The violence was of three kinds: by those under the influence of drugs or of withdrawal symptoms; gang fights; and in the course of robberies, etc. to fund drug addiction.

In this study, it was estimated that on average hard drug addicts needed about £33,000 a year to finance their addiction. One drug addicted thief had committed 959 crimes to support his habit, including 600 burglaries, 130 street robberies and 220 thefts from cars: at one stage before he was caught he was committing 100 burglaries a month – 3 a day. Some victims refer to 'our burglar', the same one having burgled them eight or nine times and been arrested by the police as many times. (This reflects badly on the judicial system, which will be discussed in Chapter 21.) A large number of the victims were old, vulnerable people living alone.

John Grieve confirmed that a large number of the new addicts were young and had usually been introduced to drugs by members of their family or close friends. He suggested that one of the reasons why the legislation against money laundering was not achieving more was that so much of the money was both stolen and spent at the bottom end of the market.

He had earlier chaired a workshop on drugs at the ACPO conference in 1993 and said that all the police could do at present was to sit on the lid and try to keep the problem from getting too much worse until all agencies – police, intelligence, social, educational and the media – were mobilized to take effective joint action. Since the present measures were failing, he advocated an open mind, if necessary 'thinking the unthinkable'.[28]

There are four possible approaches to solving this problem: suppression, with more drastic measures than at present; decriminalization on Dutch lines; wider licensing under government supervision to cut out the criminal traffickers, who would continue to be pursued and prosecuted; or licensed legalization, like the repeal of Prohibition in the USA in 1933. These alternatives will be examined in Chapters 21 and 22.

21 Could Suppression be Made to Work?

THE RECORD OF SUPPRESSION

Suppression of drug trafficking has been made to work in Turkey, but only by using methods which would probably not be accepted in the more liberal democracies of the USA and West Europe. Japan has succeeded in developing a climate of public opinion which rejects and despises drug addicts. This is the best approach of all in countries in which there is a tradition of discipline and obedience. Of the West European countries, only the German people have historically shown this capacity but it has probably been bred out of them for a generation by what Hitler did with it. There little likelihood of any other Western democracies developing this attitude. Even if the 'silent majority' were to accept it, the criminals and the kind of people who become drug addicts certainly would not.

The use of the death penalty to deter drug traffickers, as in Malaya, Singapore and Thailand, has generally succeeded only in capturing the 'minnows' – the small-scale couriers – and has had very little impact on the big fish in the drug trade. Capital punishment is most unlikely to be accepted by Parliament in Britain and, for reasons which will be explained (see p. 184), would probably be counter-productive. The attempts at suppression, with or without a liberal policy of harm reduction, does not seem to have been effective in any Western country. The greatest suppression effort has been by the US government, both inside the USA and in the producing and transiting countries. The 'war on drugs' was first proclaimed by President Nixon in 1972 but it was not until George Bush became President that it began in earnest. Bush allocated a budget of $40 billion to attack traffickers abroad and dealers in the USA. President Clinton cont-inued the same policy and allocated the same budget. The effects were minimal; cocaine consumption declined but there was no perceptible effect on the hard core of cocaine users who accounted for four-fifths of the cocaine consumption. Heroin consumption soared. Arresting and convicting drug users merely diverted police effort from the importers and dealers and overcrowded the prisons with users whose addiction probably became worse with exposure to the professional criminals and drug traffickers in jail.[1] All the same, the majority of mainstream American public opinion supported being 'tough with junkies and tough with pushers' with the same gut reaction which led them to want guns in their homes (see pp. 127–30).

SHOULD BRITAIN'S PENAL POLICY BE CHANGED?

Is suppression working in Britain? If not, should we move to one of the alternatives ('thinking the unthinkable') broached at the end of the Chapter 20: decriminalization, licensing or legalization? An increasing number of judges, senior police officers, and of those involved in treating addiction and at least one of Britain's most influential journals – *The Economist* – have come round to the idea of radical change.[2]

Relaxing the pressure would be hazardous. The Dutch think that what they are doing is working. The Spanish have tried something similar and had second thoughts.[3] If Britain tried it and failed, could the authorities ever restore their grip? Or if relaxation were to prove politically unacceptable, what would the government need to do to make suppression work?

Britain would have to be much tougher on the importers and dealers. The US government in its Controlled Substances Act 1970 (CSA) imposes stringent penalties on first offences: for handling 5 kg of cocaine, the statutory penalty is a minimum of 10 years (or 20 years if it leads to death or serious injury) up to a maximum of life, plus a fine (see Table 15.1 on p. 128). But everyone knows, especially the criminals, that 'life' does not mean life. Is there a case for a more steeply rising increase for second and third offences?

There was in 1994 a wave of enthusiasm in US public opinion polls for applying the baseball rule to crime – 'three strikes and you're out'. If people are convicted of a serious offence three times, should they ever be allowed to make the community suffer again? Is there a point at which forgiveness and the hope of redemption should give way to the protection of potential victims of crime?

The question could be applied to other serious (and serial) crimes as well as drug trafficking, such as child abuse, violent rape, murder, attempted murder or grievous bodily harm in pursuit of criminal intent. For some of these, perhaps two rather than three offences should mean prison for 'life meaning life'. For others, for example, murder in the course of a serious crime, one may be enough; and that might be justified also for a professional importer, for criminal gain, of enough hard drugs to ruin a substantial number of people's lives. It is arguable that individuals who have knowingly and repeatedly brought death, disablement and ruin to other people's lives have no moral right ever to be free in the community again, and that they should know the penalty in advance. For some, that prospect might be more of a deterrent than the death penalty.

'Ruin' is the right word for the life of someone who becomes heavily addicted to heroin, also probably to crack. Though treatment may succeed with the addict's cooperation in breaking the addiction, if former addicts are later faced with a crisis which they lack the character to handle – the breakdown of a vital personal relationship, the spectre of bankruptcy or imprisonment – there is every likelihood that they will turn back to drugs to escape from reality.

Four quarter-gram doses of heroin in a day, every day (or the equivalent concentrated in a weekend binge) amounts to 7 grams a week, or a little over one-third of a kilogram a year. Certainly in the case of heroin, a year at this rate would result in heavy addiction. A year of crack at this rate, while less physically addictive, might in practice be *more* subject to relapse in the event of a severe personal crisis, as the intensity of the psychological craving for crack may remain in the former addict's mind for ever.

It is fair to assume that a person in possession of 1 kg of heroin or cocaine, enough for three years' supply for a heavy user, does not intend it to be solely for his own use and that he is knowingly causing at least three other people to become or remain heavily addicted. For this, the baseball 'three strike' rule would apply. The defendant would be told that a second conviction would carry a four times heavier sentence; and a third, perpetual imprisonment. For example, for a first offence, three years; second offence, twelve years; third offence, life meaning life.

The same principles could well be applied, not only to other serious crimes but also, at a lower level, to dealing with the persistent offender – a quadrupling of the minimum sentence for each repetition. For example, a sentence of one year for an unlicensed joyrider taking and driving away a car and driving dangerously would rise to four years for a second offence, sixteen for a third and life meaning life for a fourth. At present the joyrider is able to repeat it indefinitely, each time putting other people's lives seriously at risk.

Possession, trafficking in or laundering profits from 5 kg of a hard drug (presumptively addicting at least 15 other people for personal gain) might carry a minimum sentence of 10 years, accompanied by a warning that another conviction for any of a number of listed offences of similar gravity would incur a penalty of life meaning life.

An importer or dealer who distributes 10 kg of a hard drug in a year can be assumed to have ruined 30 people's lives, some irrevocably. He could not conceivably intend that quantity for his own use. The majority of the public would support the view that such a person should never be free again; life meaning life with no remission; and that he should know this before he commits the offence.

The majority of the British public also favour restoration of the death penalty but Parliament has consistently voted against it – and rightly so. It would be counter-productive, both for murder and for even the most extreme drug offences. Apart from the moral dilemma of taking life in cold blood, the death penalty is irreversible if new evidence comes to light, which has occurred in some tragic cases. And it would probably result in fewer convictions: first, because people would be less willing to give tip-offs, which are most often the start of a successful police operation; second, because witnesses might be inhibited in giving evidence, both from reluctance to have blood on their hands and out of fear for their own lives; and third, because juries would be less likely to convict. Penal history suggests that it is the fear of conviction, not the scale of punishment, which is the greatest deterrent to criminals.

Perpetual imprisonment would, however, arouse strong objections amongst prison officers who need to be able to offer incentives (hopes of parole or remission) and threats (forfeiture thereof) to exercise authority; also, a man in for life meaning life may feel that he has nothing to lose by total non-cooperation, violence or even murder of a prison officer.

But every top security prison has, under various names, a Control Wing, including solitary confinement, for violent or recalcitrant prisoners, and to protect 'Rule 43' prisoners under threat from those in the normal cell blocks. Some prisons also have a third regime, a Special Security Unit for selected long term prisoners in what is intended to be an escape-proof 'prison within a prison' within which they have relatively free association with each other and good facilities for recreation, exercise, study and more frequent visits. These can be abused, as they were in Whitemoor Prison in 1994, where several IRA prisoners were able to escape after acquiring guns and explosives and constructing rope ladders within the unit, due to astonishingly lax security and failure to control and search visitors. Other prisons, however, have run such units successfully for 20 years or more. This three-regime system would offer a strong incentive for lifers to graduate from the cell blocks to the Special Security Unit, with warning that abuse of privileges would result in return to the cell blocks, or in serious cases to the harsher regime in the Control Wing.

Once 'lifers-for-life' had come to terms with the certainty of spending the rest of their days in prison, the majority of them would settle for a tolerable existence with especially the opportunity to associate with friends.

The essential advantage of life meaning life sentences, however, would be the deterrent effect on others contemplating an offence – so long as prisoners were in no doubt at all that the sentence was going to be enforced.

CONVICTING MORE OF THE GUILTY

'It is better that ten guilty people go free than that one innocent person is convicted'; and 'a person is legally innocent unless proved guilty beyond reasonable doubt'. These are two cardinal principles of English law and, though it would also be worth adopting the Scottish intermediate verdict of 'not proven', these principles must remain. There are, however, strong reasons to believe that, of those who plead not guilty, are tried and acquitted, at least half did in fact commit the offences as charged.[4] These, predictably, are the most expert criminals and those assisted by the most unscrupulous lawyers. It is urgently necessary to find ways of convicting more of the guilty, and many of the measures needed to do this would in fact also reduce the risk of wrongful arrest and conviction of the innocent.

The first of these is to facilitate identification. The majority of citizens in Europe and the USA already carry more than one card in their pockets to prove their identity, including electronic or magnetic data and in some cases photographs. They carry these from choice to enable them, for example, to get money from their bank accounts by safe means which prevent imposters from doing so, to gain admission to a place of work or club, or to obtain concessionary bus or rail fares. They have also accepted for many generations the need to carry passports. All but three (Denmark, Ireland and the UK) of the twelve EU countries in 1995 require their citizens to possess identification (ID) cards. In some countries such as Germany these ID cards and passports are machine readable, that is, they contain data which the holder can read – full name, date of birth, and national insurance number or passport number with date of issue. These are printed on the card in characters which can be read by the card holder and also by a computer using Optical Character Reading (OCR).

The machine-readable card or passport can confirm, almost instantly, that there is no police bar against entry of the authorized holder. Many also contain a photograph, but experiments are in progress in Germany and the Netherlands to substitute (or add) biometric data unique to the card holder, such as digital hand geometry or fingerprint characteristics. This is a quantum leap from the photograph.

It is often suggested that the ID card should be a general card containing medical data, social security entitlements and police records of certain specified convictions such as for child abuse or drug offences. That would be a great mistake. The public would justifiably suspect that this information would be accessible to officials of all kinds who had no reason to have it, and would prejudice their chances of getting jobs or being given financial credit. Any data of this kind must be recorded only on the computers of the organizations which deal with it, for example, the PNC for criminal records and the National Health Service (NHS) for medical data. The OCR data on the card (name, date of birth, national insurance number, etc.) would simply enable the police, social security or other official to check whether the computer of *their* organization had any records concerning the holder of *that* card. That kind of information would be confidential to them and subject to the Data Protection Act 1984. For certain purposes, other organizations could be given the right to refer the case of someone applying for a job; for example, a school or children's home could check with the police that an applicant had no entries on child abuse. The biometric data on the card would have a quite separate purpose, to enable those possessing a simple machine to screen the finger or hand and match it to the digital data on the card to ensure that the person presenting it was the authorized holder.

Such a machine would have no civil liberties implications, and could be used, not only by police, immigration and social security officers, but also by banks and building societies to confirm that they were paying out money to the person entitled to it. In fact, it would make sense for banks and then financial organizations to give their clients the option of having their biometric data on their bank or credit cards as well, to ensure that no imposter could get their money. Produced in bulk the machine does not cost much.

In a democratic society, there should be no civil right for a citizen to conceal his or her identity and certainly no civil right, by forgery or theft of a credit card, to impersonate anyone else.

Matching a person's DNA molecules to body fluids is another very reliable form of biometric data, but analysis of the sample takes too long for on-the-spot identity checks. The proposed DNA databank of people convicted for certain crimes, including violence, sex crimes and child abuse, would both help to convict the guilty and enable innocent people to prove their innocence much more conclusively than by an alibi. People convicted of supplying illicit drugs should also have their DNA recorded on the databank.

The right to silence must be preserved but juries should also have the right to interpret silence. All interrogation in police stations should be taped, in serious cases on video. The caution should read:

> You are not obliged to say anything but my questions and your answers or failure to answer will be recorded on this tape of which you will receive a copy. You and the prosecution will be free to present any part of this tape in evidence at your trial.

This is shorter and clearer than the 66-word version proposed by the Home Office in August 1994, which warned that 'if you do not mention something which you later use in your defence, the court may decide that your failure to mention it now strengthens the case against you'.

There is nothing new about interpreting silence. A 5-year-old child caught at the jam cupboard quickly licks his lips to remove the forensic evidence; his mother asks 'What are you doing?' He folds his arms and exercises his right to silence; his mother has no difficulty in drawing her own conclusions.

Given a video recording, the jury could see the face of accused persons as they refused to answer. But the accused or their counsel could also select bits of tape to show the police bullying, harassing, offering inducements, and so on. So the tape and the right to use it would be fairer to the accused; also to the victims and potential victims in convicting more criminals.

There is one other technique for perverting the course of justice which has been growing since the 1960s – the intimidation or corruption of juries and witnesses by other members of criminal and terrorist gangs still at large. If a judge considers that the threat – or a perceived threat – of this could influence jurors, the judge should have the power to order that the jury's anonymity should be preserved by sitting them in a separate room, or if necessary in a separate building, with five video screens showing permanent close-ups of the judge, the accused, the witness and the prosecuting and defence counsel. Television is now sufficiently familiar for speakers to persuade viewers without seeing them and for the viewers to judge their sincerity. Politicians persuade and are judged by this means almost entirely now, more effectively than at pre-television hustings.

If this were done, *selection* of jurors would need to be done *in camera* by the judge, best aided by an ombudsman, taking account of criteria discussed with prosecution and defence counsel to avoid risk of prejudice.

If a judge believed that certain witnesses should also be protected from identification, the judge should be empowered to order that they too should be concealed from the accused and from the public and their voices electronically disguised (as again is regularly done on television). Only the anonymous jury and the judge (through a desk monitor and headphones) would see the witness on the screen and hear the voice undisguised.

The use of a video jury would not prejudice a fair trial; concealing the witnesses, however, should be done only when the judge thought it to be essential. It has already had to be done in some terrorist trials, especially in Northern Ireland, and in criminal trials too where the identity of undercover police officers or informants needs to be safeguarded. This is sometimes an inevitable price to pay in the quality of a public process of law in dealing with criminal organizations which calculatedly set out to make an open judicial process unworkable by corruption or intimidation.

TREATMENT OF ADDICTS

Consuming illicit drugs should not be a criminal offence, though some of its consequences should. For example, driving a car under the influence of drugs must remain a criminal offence as it is with alcohol. So must theft, violence, intimidation and malicious damage in pursuit of or in consequence of drug abuse. Unauthorized selling of illicit drugs, or possession of amounts more than is credibly for personal use must also remain a crime.

Addiction, whilst not a crime in itself, should be treated as a contagious disease unless there are changes in the attitude towards distribution, as discussed in Chapter 22. So long as street prices continue at their present levels, very few heavy users of addictive drugs can fund their addiction from their lawful income. Almost all turn to crime or to selling drugs to others. The second of these has generally the more damaging effect. It is one of the main reasons why drug abuse in Europe and the USA constantly increases. So, if we continue to rely on suppression to overcome the drug problem, no known addicts should ever be free without supervision to pass on their addiction in the community.

As soon as consumers of illicit drugs are identified, whether by police, doctors, social workers or teachers, they should be compulsorily registered and thereafter monitored. This monitoring should include regular urine or blood tests. Even if one of the other policy alternatives is adopted (see Chapter 22), the addict should be encouraged to cooperate in treatment to end the addiction. If the tackling of drug abuse is to rely on stricter suppression, as discussed in this chapter, then the treatment would need to be compulsory. The issue of controlled supplies of drugs under medical supervision should be conditional on the addict reporting regularly for treatment and cooperating in overcoming the addiction. If addicts cannot or will not make progress, they should be warned of the consequences and, if they still fail to progress, they should continue treatment compulsorily, if necessary in custody, until the DDU doctor judges it safe for them to be released to resume voluntary treatment. Thereafter, they should still be registered and tested, at longer intervals according to medical judgement. Means of financing such treatment are discussed in Chapter 22.

THE BRITISH GOVERNMENT'S STRATEGY REVIEW, 1995–8

In October 1994, the British government's Central Drugs Coordination Unit (CDCU) issued a Consultation Paper on strategy for England in 1995–8 entitled *Tackling Drugs Together*.[5] This aimed

> To take action by vigorous law enforcement and a new emphasis on education and prevention to increase the safety of communities from drug related crime, reduce the acceptability and availability of drugs to young people and reduce the health risks and other damage caused by drug misuse.

The government invited comments by 12 January 1995 with a view to publishing a strategy in spring 1995. Targets were set out for each of the next three years, 1995–6, 1996–7 and 1997–8, for the Departments of Education and Health, the Home Office, the police, the probation service, the prison service and HM Customs and Excise. The Consultation Paper reviewed existing strategy and summarized statistics which, though admittedly not precise in view of the clandestine nature of drug abuse, clearly indicated that it had increased, year by year, from 1990 to 1994.

The paper proposed lines of action through 1995–8 to see that the law against supply and trafficking in illegal drugs is enforced, to reduce drug-related crime and the public's fear of such crime, and to reduce the level of drug misuse in prisons. It invited the police, Customs, probation and prison services to propose changes in their operational strategies by June 1995 and then, in consultation with each other and with local authorities and other agencies, implement them from 1996 onwards. The government proposed to allocate additional resources to schools from April 1995 to enable them to offer effective programmes for drug education to give pupils the facts and warning of the risks; also to raise the awareness of the issues among school staff, governors and parents. Interdepartmental publicity campaigns would incorporate role models to motivate young people to resist drug abuse. These campaigns would be coordinated by the Department of Health, who would also develop policies for treatment of drug abusers and measures to reduce the spread of HIV and other diseases by drug abuse.

Great stress was laid on multi-agency action and involvement of the media, on the lines proposed by John Grieve (pp. 179–80). Local authorities would be asked to establish drug action teams with representatives of their education, NHS, police, probation and prison services. These teams would be advised by drug reference groups with a broad membership from voluntary organizations, social services, environment and health departments, schools, local businesses, housing organizations, general medical practitioners, pharmacists, youth services and other community organizations. *Tackling Drugs Together* included case studies of a successful Drug Advisory Council on these lines established by East Sussex County Council in 1986 and of a Community Task Force set up under police chairmanship in Newmarket, West Suffolk, in 1993. This also involved local media and sports personalities.[6]

Tackling Drugs Together ruled out decriminalization or legalization of any drug, for reasons given in Chapter 22 (see pp. 200–2).

Whatever policy is adopted against drug abuse – suppression, decriminalization, licensing or legalization – some measures considered in this chapter will be needed in any case to fight organized crime. These include steeply rising sentences for persistent criminals, including life meaning life for some of the more violent, sadistic or sexual crimes and for child abuse. For these and other crimes, we also need reliable measures for identification, preferably by means of machine-readable ID cards containing biometric data. Other measures to increase our ability to convict more of the guilty are also needed, including the preservation of the right to silence while also enabling juries to draw their own conclusions from refusal to answer questions; and the protection of juries and witnesses from corruption and intimidation.

The question of whether a more tolerant attitude to drug abuse would improve the situation will be discussed in Chapter 22.

22   Decriminalize? License? Legalize?

DECRIMINALIZATION

Decriminalization is roughly what the Dutch have done (described on pp. 149–52). Since 1976, possession of up to 30 gms of cannabis has been a misdemeanour, not a criminal offence; it is sold freely in 'hash cafés' in every town, 300 in Amsterdam alone. Police have strong powers against selling hard drugs but in 1985 they were instructed by the Ministry of Justice not to use them. Heroin and cocaine are sold openly on the streets. Addiction has *not* soared; it is lower, in proportion, than in Italy or the UK[1] but it does attract many 'drug tourists' from neighbouring countries, who either consume the drugs there or buy them to take home, at lower prices than in their own countries, but not all that much lower. Heroin and cocaine sell for about $75 per gm in Amsterdam compared with $100–20 in most EU countries.[2]

This is the main limitation of decriminalization; the saving in cost is only at the dealer end. The importers, and the exporters such as the Colombian cartels and Khun Sa in Myanmar, still make their full profit and therefore generate as much crime worldwide, though there may be less on the streets of the Netherlands. As the Dutch police happily say, 'it is right for us' but it does little to cut crime elsewhere.

Another disadvantage of decriminalization is that it encourages the idea amongst young Dutch people that there is nothing wrong with drug abuse. But the Dutch point out that the number of deaths caused by drugs is far less than those caused by alcohol and tobacco. By watching the street sales of heroin and cocaine the police can identify the users and guide them towards treatment before they become dangerously addicted, and they can keep most of the street dealers under discreet surveillance, detect their import channels and increase the number of seizures of smuggled drugs at the docks. They can also use the powers they have to arrest the larger scale importers if the trade shows signs of expanding.

In Britain, a number of local authorities have quietly adopted the Dutch *laissez-faire* policy at street level, by not prosecuting users in possession of small quantities of drugs. Instead, they devote their resources to warning them of the consequences if they continue drug abuse and providing plenty of treatment clinics and needle exchange facilities. For possession of small quantities for personal use, especially of cannabis but also of hard drugs within reason, the police throughout Britain usually caution rather than prosecute, for the same reasons as the Dutch do, and also in order to avoid filling up the cells with drug users and diverting police resources from fighting more serious crime. In Britain, however, drugs remain very expensive, so that the drug habit still generates a great deal of crime to fund it.

LICENSING

There are about 100 doctors in Britain licensed to prescribe addictive drugs[3] in the course of treatment to cure addiction in NHS Drug Dependency Units (DDUs). Relapse rates are high – of the order of 75 per cent.[4] There is a growing feeling, especially amongst police officers, favouring the idea of extending the issue of such licences, without either decriminalization or legalization. At the ACPO conference in 1993, the chairman of the Workshop on Drug Prevention Strategy,[5] Commander John Grieve, of the Metropolitan Police, said that it was

> fundamental in pursuing these issues that all of the agencies and the government should discover if this is what the community actually wants.

The thinking behind 'licensing' might be

(a) Certain problem drug users are supplied with a wide range of drugs based on medical opinion and delivery (these drugs include crack!). This is existing government policy.

(b) Are there some problem drug users (i.e. those who commit 5000 burglaries) who logically could be put into the category of (a) above?

(c) Would a consequence of (b) above be to undermine the economic base of organized crime via its acquisitive crime

> element and cut crime, in particular against the elderly
> and vulnerable?
> (d) Would the consequence of (b) and (c) above be a reduc-
>   tion in drug-related violence, in particular firearms crime?
> (e) What kind of research would explore these proposals?[6]

In the London Drug Policy Forum on 18 March 1994, Commander Grieve stressed the importance of a coordinated multi-
agency effort to combat drugs including:

• Enforcement especially video and undercover work
• Prevention, health education, current information
• Harm reduction, needle exchange, other facilities
• Education, teaching the teachers
• Research: some of the best has been by sixth formers
• Universities, parents, estate groups
• Cautioning, tackling personal causes
• Referral, involvement of street agencies
• Media strategy, ISDD media awards
• Joint training, police, health and safety, local agencies
• Intelligence, with Customs and Immigration
• International dimensions.[7]

The drugs prescribed by the current 100 licensed doctors in the
DDUs in Britain are imported through normal pharmaceutical
channels. Research as suggested above might result in a wider
extension of Home Office licences to distribute drugs to approved
consumers, including addicts undergoing compulsory treatment
in addition to those who volunteered. This would be an extension
of the present controlled and accountable network of DDUs, and
it would presumably be necessary to appoint more licensed
dealers to import the additional drugs. Imported and processed
commercially by the pharmaceutical industry, the cost of refined
heroin and cocaine would work out at about 3 per cent of the
street price (see p. 198). This cost would have to be met –
presumably by recovering the standard NHS prescription
charges, with provision for those on benefits and unable to pay.
The possibility of taxing drugs like alcohol is discussed later in the
context of legalization (see pp. 195–9).

Licensing on a large scale could greatly reduce the generation
of crime to finance addiction, and cut the huge profits to the

criminal gangs which export, import, distribute and retail drugs at clandestine street prices. On the other hand, short of full legalization, a hard core of users might prefer to buy all they wanted from the clandestine dealers without interference by 'do-gooders', the social services, the police and the health services. They would continue their massive theft, robbery and fraud to get the money. So the dealers and criminal gangs would still get most of it.

Then there is the worry that licensing might give the wrong impression to young people about the attitude of the community towards drug trafficking; it might also lead a larger number into trying drugs, of whom some would have their lives ruined by becoming hardened addicts.

LEGALIZATION UNDER LICENCE

Legalization is not the same as decriminalization, which is merely not prosecuting consumers or those in possession of small quantities of drugs for their own use. Legalization would treat drugs just as alcohol and tobacco are treated now; that is, drugs could be grown or manufactured under licence (like whisky, gin, wine and beer) and imported only by licensed importers. Under Customs supervision, imported drugs would be held in bonded warehouses, to be released to retailers only after payment of a heavy tax.

Like alcohol, drugs could be sold to the public only by retailers holding a licence to do so – the equivalent of hotels, pubs and shops holding an off licence. If licensed sellers abused their licence, for example, by selling to children, they would lose it, just as publicans do.

If legalization were to be attempted in Britain, it would best be introduced gradually by extending the licensing system already in force, whereby the pharmaceutical companies import drugs for the doctors in the DDUs for treatment of addicts, and for the hospitals and pharmacies for medicinal products containing derivatives of coca and opium and synthetic drugs such as barbiturates, for use as anaesthetics, relaxants, sedatives or stimulants. The natural retail outlet for wider distribution would therefore be the dispensers in high street pharmacies, who are already trained and licensed to handle and account for controlled and dangerous drugs for issue to the public on prescription. They are also accustomed to selling only limited quantities to any one customer of ordinary medicines of which an overdose could be dangerous, such as aspirin.

Because of the particular hazards of simultaneous consumption of alcohol with certain drugs, it would be best *not* to license hotels and pubs to sell drugs.

It would make sense, at any rate to start with, for each purchase of addictive drugs from a dispensary to be monitored and recorded on a database which would be programmed to draw attention to dangerous overindulgence by individuals, so that such drugs could thereafter be sold to that person only with a doctor's prescription. (This would be conditional on Britain introducing ID cards – see p. 186.) Some addicts would, of course, find ways of circumventing this, by getting others to buy for them, but, as with alcohol and tobacco, this would probably not be as widespread as some might expect.

The most important purpose of monitoring would be to prevent drug users from harming the community by, for example, driving under the influence or in the aftermath of a binge. This problem already exists with alcoholics, thanks to people who provide them with alcohol and then fail to keep them out of trouble thereafter. Much would depend on the alertness and sense of responsibility of the licensed dispensers, but computer technology is now available to back them up.

There now seems every likelihood of Britain introducing *machine-readable* ID cards (as described on pp. 186-7). The OCR date of birth on the card would enable dispensers to avoid selling drugs to juveniles, which is the most important of all the restrictions. If dispensers had a terminal with access to the NHS computer, or which had its own memory listing people barred from buying drugs without a prescription, this bar would be revealed by swiping the card through the slot within a few seconds. If there were no such bar, dispensers could, subject to their own discretion, sell within specified guidelines. Despite the risk of people buying for others, this system would deter and in most cases prevent abuse of drugs by children or chronic over-consumers.

To extend licensing in this way would require amendment of certain national laws and also of some of Britain's treaty obligations. These national and international laws already allow for legitimate medical use of drugs, including heroin, cocaine and crack for anti-addiction treatment in DDUs, so the changes would be a matter of getting agreement to extend these exception clauses.

The Misuse of Drugs Act 1971 is the British incorporation of the provisions internationally ratified in the UN Convention on Psychotropic Substances 1971 and later in the UN Convention against Illicit Traffic in Narcotic Drugs and Psychotropic Substances 1988.[8] Extension of Britain's licensing laws might also arouse some opposition from other EU countries in, for example, the European Committee to Combat Drugs (CELAD).[9]

Assuming that these legal and international problems could be resolved, another problem would be setting up a larger structure for purchasing and importing the drugs. Cocaine, heroin and cannabis might be bought direct from growers' associations in Latin America, Asia and elsewhere. Synthetic drugs could be bought by licensed importers direct from the factories in the Netherlands, Poland and Latvia or manufactured under licence in Britain. The most economical procedure would be to license commercial firms to develop a free market, like importers of coffee from Colombia or Kenya. It would be important to exercise sufficient control to prevent, say, Khun Sa or the Cali cartel from gaining surreptitious control of the market.

The safest way would be to follow the alcohol trade, where the manufacturing or importing is in the hands of reputable licensed firms (the whisky distilleries, brewers and wine merchants, large and small), keeping down prices by competition.

Legalization would apply only to licensed producers, importers and retailers, and to consumers. All other traffic in drugs would remain illegal, as with alcohol. Particularly firm action would be needed to prevent any drugs, hard or soft, from reaching children, who currently get alarming quantities through families and furtive traffickers in schools. With all lawful channels closed there would initially be intense pressure by some teenagers to find ways of getting drugs, at least until the habit could be made less fashionable. Children's thirst for alcohol seems to be well contained – better than their desire to show their sophistication with cigarettes. It would be necessary to retain all the laws to prohibit illicit manufacture, importing and selling of drugs and the powers to enforce them, including the severest punishments as discussed in Chapter 21, since the urge of teenagers to get hold of them regardless of cost will lead them to devote unlimited efforts to crime to raise the money. As approved licensing extended, the control would gradually become easier because the cartels and criminal gangs would be under cut by the licensed dealers and driven out of business.

If left to itself (untaxed), the retail price of licensed drugs would fall to around the price of those imported for use by the DDUs. The current street price of illicit heroin diluted to 40 per cent is now about £80 ($120) per gm. This means that the consumer is really paying £200 ($300) per gm of pure cocaine content. As compared with this, the cost to the NHS of pure heroin for the DDUs is £5.86, say £6 ($9) per gm,[10] that is, about 3 per cent of the true street price of pure heroin.

Alcoholic drinks are taxed according to the content of pure spirit they contain (e.g. 40 per cent alcohol in whisky or 10–12 per cent in wine). The tax works out at about 200 per cent of the value of the spirit. Heroin and cocaine should be almost as heavily taxed as alcohol, say about 150 per cent of the import price per gram; more than this might encourage too big a black market. Based on the current NHS cost, £6 per gm of pure heroin, the cost to a consumer after tax, distribution and wholesale and retail profits would work out at about £20 per gm of pure heroin. Diluted to 50 per cent heroin a quarter-gram dose would cost £2.50 (see Table 22.1). This is about the same price as a double tot of whisky in a pub.[11]

The final price of a quarter-gram dose of 50 per cent cut heroin in a dispensary would thus be about one-eighth of the street price of a quarter gram of 40 per cent cut heroin (£20). Cut cocaine and crack prices would be of the same order. Cannabis, amphetamines, MDMA and LSD would also carry a 150 per

Table 22.1   Possible Prices of Licensed Heroin

	Import cost	Duty (150%)	Distribution (VAT + profit)	Total
Pure heroin	£6	£9	£5	£20
50% cut heroin	£3	£4.50	£2.50	£10
Quarter gm dose of 50% cut heroin	£0.75	£1.125	£0.625	£2.50

cent tax. Manufactured commercially in bulk, they would be so cheap that an increasing number of drug users might forsake heroin, cocaine and crack in their favour.

The most powerful argument deployed by supporters of legalization is the experience of Prohibition of Alcohol in the USA in 1919. From 1919 to 1933 the consumption of alcohol climbed rapidly back to its previous levels but, being subject to no control, it was often dangerously strong (raw spirit) or adulterated, causing blindness or death – just as heroin can. As it was sold clandestinely, children were not protected from it. The bootleggers who emerged to meet the public demand for it developed into rival armed criminal gangs. With the enormous funds available, combined with mafia expertise and discipline, these became the foundation of the organized crime which has plagued the USA ever since. When Prohibition was repealed in 1933, alcohol consumption did *not* explode 'exponentially' as prohibitionists had predicted, but settled to a level probably lower than it had been during Prohibition ('probably' because estimates of clandestine consumption of illicit alcohol in the USA in 1919–33 are as variable and unreliable as those for drugs).

Legalization under licence of natural and synthetic drugs in the UK now would facilitate proper quality control, which is impossible so long as the trade is clandestine. Supply could be regulated and – like alcohol – sales to children would be enforceably illegal. So would selling of drugs to addicts whom the retailer perceived – or was informed – were unfit to receive them; retailers would risk losing their licence if they failed to show proper judgement.

The overall saving of cost by legalization under licence would be considerable. The current *additional* cost of Customs, police and prison services to combat illicit drug trafficking is of the order of £250 million ($375 million) per year.[12] The estimated annual cost to the community of drug-related theft is £2000 million ($3000 million). The motivation for this crime – funding clandestine addiction – would largely disappear. So would the need to recruit other addicts by the dealer/consumers (5 gm for the price of 4 gm) which is a substantial cause of the spread of drug addiction.

The money acquired from taxation and saved from Customs, police and prison service budgets would be available as first priority for education and government warnings of the consequences of misuse (on the lines of the successful drink-driving and tobacco health campaigns); also for expanding the DDUs and supporting organizations like ISDD, Narcotics Anonymous (NA) and Release which aim to cure people of addiction.

THE CASE AGAINST LICENSED LEGALIZATION

The chief danger of licensed legalization is that it might initially increase the number of drug users, especially by providing the weakest members of society with a cheaper way of escaping from the frustration and boredom of unrewarding lives or from despair over insoluble problems. With drugs more easily available, even more lives might be ruined than are ruined now. This must be set against the easing of the burden borne by the law-abiding majority in the form of violent crime, losses of billions of pounds from robbery, burglary, theft and fraud and of higher insurance premiums for everyone else. The experience of the repeal of Prohibition suggests that any increase in consumption might be only temporary.

There is also an unknown dimension in the possibility of new synthetic 'designer drugs' being developed in the laboratories – drugs which can bring new excitements and sensations to transcend the old ones. Research for these is continuous and new drugs come into fashion every year. It would be necessary for the licensing regulations to be sufficiently flexible to cope with a massive escalation in availability and demand for new and potentially dangerous synthetic drugs.

Then there are the moral questions. Should these weaker people be abandoned to their fate? Would legalization send the wrong signal to children?

Would legalization open the way for criminal monopolies to corner the markets, from the drug barons in Colombia and Myanmar to the criminal gangs in Britain? This should be preventable provided that the licensing system were as tight as it is for alcohol.

It can be argued that Third World countries would suffer from the loss of their massive inflow of drug money. This might apply particularly to Bolivia, though the current benefits to the economy may be outweighed by the fiscal distortion from illegal money and the violent crime and corruption generated by drug trafficking. The *campesinos* themselves should get just as much from licensed importers as they do from the barons' *traquateros*. So, with the arguable exception of Bolivia, the benefits (to Peru, Colombia, Myanmar, Pakistan, Afghanistan, Thailand, etc.) of cutting out the crime and corruption should outweigh any losses to their economies.

Legalizing drugs in isolation might make Britain (like the Netherlands on a larger scale) a haven for drug tourists and bargain hunters from neighbouring countries. This might cause resentment against Britain for once again opting out of international agreements which her partners have accepted. But Britain, as an island, is well placed to initiate a radical experiment of this kind. The relatively free availability of soft drugs and, though still expensive, of hard drugs in the Netherlands has not damaged her neighbours as much as her critics suggest. A British licensing system should be able to prevent large-scale re-export of drugs from Britain in bulk, so the chief need would be to step up the surveillance of ferry and Channel tunnel traffic, with extensive use of dogs, vapour sniffers and enhanced X-ray equipment, financed by taxes and by the money saved from present drug-enforcement measures. If legalization were introduced by a gradual process as proposed, and proved successful, neighbouring countries might be tempted to follow Britain's example.

The biggest problem about legalization might be the difficulty of reversing it if it were not working, or if it were causing intolerable strains on Britain's international relations. This should, however, be possible if it were carried out through a gradual extension of licensing. The pace of extension could be restrained to prevent it from getting out of control or upsetting Britain's neighbours; it could be done in a way which would allow for return to a more restricted form of licensing, or for reimposition of full-scale suppression if necessary. The measures proposed in Chapter 21 to suppress illicit drug trafficking should in any case be kept in force to counter the rise of a black market and they could be reapplied to all drug import and distribution if licensing were getting out of hand.

A radical proposal for legalization was made in 1993 by the Assistant Chief Constable of Hampshire, Mr G. W. Nelson.[13] He suggested that all drugs should be supplied under a government monopoly and sold to any adult on demand, subject to regulations on quantities. They would be purchased by a government agency direct from the growers or manufacturers and then sold under government contract by pharmacists. There would be severe penalties for anyone else trading in drugs outside the government-controlled outlets, with particularly severe punishments for providing drugs to children.

Nelson believed, however, that this would not work unless all the major countries agreed to adopt the same policy, which would therefore have to be initiated through the UN. He also ruled out the possibility of a gradual introduction or pilot schemes and said that the proposal would need to be implemented simultaneously as a complete package. He cited the Chinese proverb, 'one cannot cross a chasm in two bounds'.

In his paper, Nelson quoted in full the report of the International Narcotics Control Board (INCB) in Vienna in 1992, which refuted the idea of legalization in detail. This refutation was repeated in similar terms in the British government's Consultation Paper, *Tackling Drugs Together*, in 1994.[14]

The INCB report denied that law-enforcement strategies had failed, claiming that legal sanctions had helped to deter or delay potential abusers. It contended that legalization would expand the demand for drugs, particularly among young people. It argued that, since no community would accept making drugs available without restriction to all existing and potential abusers, including children, black markets and corruption would continue; while legislation might reduce crime to support personal abuse, crimes committed under the influence of drugs might increase. The INCB considered that supporters of legalization might underestimate the capacity of organized crime to adjust to changing conditions without loss of economic, political or social power. It also expressed concern over the effects of legalization on the control of potency and purity of drugs and the difficulties of enforcing age limits. The report quoted the experience of China in the nineteenth century after the Opium Wars, when the country was forced to accept free availability of opium, resulting in a drastic increase in the number of opium addicts to an estimated 20 million.

These arguments express the two extremes of the cases for and against legalization. There are, however, other more flexible means of change, and these should be debated during the British government's period of consultation to develop an anti-drug strategy. The main drawback to Nelson's proposal is his insistence that the entire package must be introduced in one bound, without trials or pilot schemes, and that all major countries must agree, through the UN, to adopt them simultaneously. There is very little chance of getting universal agreement on such a complex and controversial subject, when different countries have different problems and different perceptions. If there are to be any major changes in Britain, these would need to be introduced step by step, with safeguards for her neighbours.

THE CHOICE

Whatever we do, it is no good going on as we are. We are failing to check illicit drug consumption and the crime that it generates; we are allowing the drug habit to take root amongst teenagers; and we are financing crime, terrorism and corruption in the producing and transiting countries across the world.

Suppression, if it is to work at all, would need to be more ruthless, especially against the importers and distributors, with life meaning life sentences and steeply rising punishments for persistent offenders, needed in any case for other serious crimes. We would have to increase the rate of convicting the guilty without risk of convicting the innocent, with better means of identification and prevention of intimidation and corruption of witnesses and juries.

The Dutch government's open tolerance of cannabis dealing and tacit tolerance of some hard drug dealing, imprecisely described as decriminalization, might be an improvement on Britain's current policies. It would at least reduce domestic crime. Dutch importers, however, still pay as much for the drugs they buy from the barons and brokers in the producing countries, thereby still financing crime and corruption in the Third World. So the Dutch solution alone is not enough.

Britain should, however, take note of the lessons from the Dutch experience and from the experiments in *laissez faire* by some British local authorities, including measures to encourage more addicts to volunteer for treatment. Britain should also legitimize the widespread police practice of cautioning rather than prosecuting drug users and people found in possession of small quantities of drugs for their own use.

The extension of licensing could be pursued on an experimental basis. Licensing the purchase and issue of drugs by the NHS for treatment of addiction in DDUs might be extended to facilitate compulsory treatment of identified addicts, including those in prison. At the same time, there should be a detailed feasibility study, perhaps by a Royal Commission in conjunction with the CDCU strategy review, of the possibility of gradually bringing drugs on to the same basis as alcohol, that is, import and sale by licensed dealers only. It would remain a criminal offence for unlicensed dealers to import or sell drugs, as it is for alcohol.

Like wine merchants, the licensed importers would buy drugs directly from the producers, hold them in bond, pay a heavy tax and sell them to licensed retailers in the dispensaries of pharmacies who are accustomed to handling controlled substances. The sale price, even after 150 per cent tax, would be about one-eighth of the current street price of hard drugs, so the criminal network, from the drug barons through the trafficking gangs, would be driven out of business.

To do this it would be necessary to amend the Misuse of Drugs Act 1971 and extend the exception clauses in some of the UN and European Conventions which Britain has signed, to widen licensed dealing.

The money from taxation and saving on current suppression would be available for anti-drug education, advertising and treatment. In the early years of experiment, Customs and police resources would still be needed to prevent unlicensed import and sales, especially to children; also to prevent any flow of cheap drugs to mainland Europe.

In case the experiment were to fail due, for example, to large-scale smuggling to bypass the licensing system (especially by-passing the total ban on sales to juveniles under 18), it would be necessary at every stage to maintain the capability of suspending or reversing it. The draconian powers proposed in Chapter 21 should in any case be enacted to deal with other serious crimes, so that they would be available if ever required against illicit drug trafficking.

Part VIII
Conclusions

23 A War to be Won in the West

THE PRODUCERS

Despite the flow of Western money into the countries producing cocaine, heroin and cannabis, little benefit goes to the people as a whole or to their governments. Bolivia may be an exception but the price has been a long history of corruption at the top levels of government. Colombia has the highest kidnap rate in the world and 30,000 violent deaths each year. Afghanistan's warring tribes are financed by opium and so is Khun Sa in Myanmar. Though at least $2.5 billion in drug money comes into Peru per year from cocaine sales, only one-tenth of this goes to the *campesinos* who produce the cocaine paste; the other 90 per cent is swallowed up in corruption and has financed one of the most vicious terrorist movements in history.

Crop eradication and crop substitution will never be more than half-hearted, at best, so long as the citizens of affluent Western countries continue to pay hyper-inflated prices for drugs on their streets. For the peasant farmers, producing and consuming coca, opium and hashish are part of their culture and are much more profitable to grow than other crops. Few of the governments of underdeveloped countries are secure enough to risk the intense resentment which would result from total eradication and, in any case, most of the growing areas are too inaccessible for this to be practicable. It is up to the Western countries either to cut the demand or, in other ways, to cut the massive flow of money to the criminals who organize the supply and distribution.

There is, however, every reason to give incentives for cooperation by the producing countries in tracing the leads to the brokers in Bangkok, Hong Kong, South-west Asia, the Middle East, West Africa, East Europe, Latin America, the Caribbean and the USA. Whatever measures may be taken to cut demand or to license supplies, unlicensed traffic must continue to be treated as illegal, hunted down and interdicted.

The same approach must apply to the manufacture and distribution of synthetic drugs in countries such as the Netherlands, Latvia and Poland, and to illicit traffic in either natural or synthetic drugs through East Europe.

The essential is to cut out the financing of organized crime by removing the market for criminal supply of drugs, natural or synthetic. As well as the immediate damage, the prospects for the world in the long term, should we fail, are daunting. Of the $500 billion which pours every year into retail drug sales on the streets, at least $100 billion is likely to be invested for growth by the criminal gangs through the seemingly legitimate corporations which provide their cover, in property, stocks and financial undertakings. Their assets, already huge, will be growing a great deal faster than $100 billion a year. If we let this go on, by the end of the 1990 the drug barons will be in a position to offer bribes as big as are needed to buy the connivance of enough politicians, police officers, judges to gain virtual control of the government and judiciary in some countries, not only in Latin America and Asia but also through mafia-style gangs in Russia and East Europe. As a warning, *Cosa Nostra* by 1993 was in a dominating position in the two main political parties in Italy. The Cali cartel could, if unchecked, achieve total political control of Colombia.[1]

MONEY LAUNDERING

The legislation against money laundering, national and international, is good in principle but has so far yielded disappointing results in practice. The percentage of criminally acquired assets actually confiscated is very small.

The first essential is to cut out the fiscal havens and secret banking practices which enable money to be electronically transferred and retransferred between international banks without trace. This will be achieved only through concerted action by the big banks of the developed world – all the 12 countries which have signed the Basel Declaration of 1988 and as many as can be persuaded to participate of the 89 who signed the UN Vienna Convention of the same year. They should agree to boycott any banks anywhere in the world which fail to conform to a code to disclose the identity of clients and to permit inspection of their accounts, subject to international safeguards, when the courts judge that there is reasonable ground for suspicion that the money has been acquired by criminal means. The threat of isolation from the main stream of international banking transactions would carry decisive weight.

Irregularities will come to light only if there is confidence amongst bank employees that their own legal immunity and anonymity are guaranteed. This would be a matter for their employers backed by international agreement, and should be another condition for a bank being accepted into the international system.

In asking for judicial approval for access to bank records, police must present their case without indicating the identity of the informant, who must not be asked to appear personally as a witness, so the information must be used to lead the prosecution to other evidence from the bank's records and from witnesses who can appear in court. National police services with sufficient mutual trust should be free to exchange information under bilateral arrangements, with confidentiality guaranteed.

As with any intelligence activities, there must be sufficient oversight to ensure that, in the interests of acquiring more evidence, criminal irregularities are not knowingly allowed to continue. It was alleged that in both the Noriega case in Panama and in the BCCI scandal, intelligence services were aware of what was going on and that, in the BCCI case, innocent account holders suffered. This is a difficult area, requiring judgement and integrity, but ultimately intelligence chiefs, like others, must be answerable for the actions of those under them. But unless an intelligence officer can be proved to have personally committed indictable crimes, the identity of intelligence officers actually handling informants must not be divulged in case someone has seen them with the informants. Crime and terrorism can be prevented and detected only if informants have complete confidence in their own anonymity and security.

INTERNATIONAL ORGANIZED CRIME

The spread of international mafia-type activities, especially through Eastern Europe, is so serious that the international community should consider making 'association of a mafia kind' a crime in itself, as now defined in Italian law (see Chapter 16,

p. 131). To deal with cross-border criminals from Eastern Europe in the light of free movement across EU internal frontiers, it will be necessary to retain police powers to mount spot checks, with the right to require proof of identification, any time, anywhere within the EU.

For this purpose it is desirable to harmonize means of identification so that, say, a German police officer will be able to check and detect an illegal immigrant coming from France and claiming to be British. EU countries without ID cards, such as Britain, should follow the German lead in issuing machine-readable ID cards, later incorporating digital biometric data unique to the holder (which is far better than any photograph in preventing impersonation). In due course, offenders convicted of certain types of crimes should have DNA characteristics recorded on a databank, to be made accessible to other countries with which there are bilateral agreements. Also by bilateral arrangement offenders should be subject for trial, with automatic extradition, in the country in which the alleged offence was committed, according to that country's laws and judicial processes.

Criminal intelligence is too sensitive to be put in a pool, so information will normally be passed bilaterally only to the countries directly concerned, using the links between national PNCs. TREVI and Europol enable police and intelligence officers to get to know and trust each other and arrange such exchanges in cases where both sides wish it. Even at times of politically strained relations, professionals are usually ready to work together.

As already discussed in the context of money laundering, the identity of an informant must be known only to the handler and to the minimum number of others who need to know in their own police or intelligence service, probably only to the handler's immediate superior by name, and to others by a code name. Great care must also be taken not to reveal the informant's identity by the way the evidence is presented. These measures should increase the percentage of guilty criminals who are convicted without risk of convicting the innocent.

Within Britain, for the same purpose, provision should be made to protect jurors from intimidation and corruption. Trial judges should have the power, when they consider it necessary, to order that the jurors' anonymity be preserved by sitting them in a separate room or building, with five video screens showing the judge, accused, witness and the two counsel. In extreme circumstances, it may be necessary to provide similar anonymity to witnesses (see pp. 188–9).

Certain specified serious crimes, including some categories of murder, sadistic or sexual crimes with violence, child abuse and large-scale or persistent drug trafficking, should carry sentences of perpetual imprisonment – life meaning life with no remission – and this should be publicly known so that it is an effective deterrent. For all other serious crimes, there should be a sharply rising minimum sentences for subsequent offences – for example, first offence three years, second offence twelve years, third offence life meaning life. Offenders who have killed maliciously without extenuating circumstances, or have calculatedly and repeatedly ruined other people's lives in pursuit of personal gain, power or gratification, should for ever forfeit the right to be at large in a free society. There is a point at which rehabilitation of a criminal must give way to the need to protect future potential victims and to deter others from committing the same offence. Three repetitions is proof enough. To give prison officers the 'carrot and stick' they need to control such prisoners, prisons containing permanent lifers should operate three regimes, severe, standard and Special Security Units, as described in Chapter 21.

BRITAIN AS A TEST BED FOR RADICAL SOLUTIONS

Both in Britain and over all the rest of the world, present procedures for fighting drug trafficking are manifestly failing. Consumption of hard drugs, especially cocaine, is rising sharply, and so is the use of certain dangerous synthetic drugs. The prevalence of young people amongst new abusers and the prospect of new, more addictive and dangerous synthetic psychotropic substances being developed make it urgent that these trends are checked and reversed. And the crime generated by drug trafficking does more damage, both in Britain and worldwide, even than the drug abuse itself.

Most countries rely on suppression of supply and demand but, if this is to work, radical changes will be needed in the exercise of suppression of demand. There are three other alternatives, all of them equally radical: decriminalization, licensing and legalization under licence (that is, treating drugs like alcohol).

The measures for fighting organized crime proposed earlier in this chapter, and more fully described in Chapter 21 – ID cards, DNA databanks, extradition and trial, exchange of intelligence, protection of jurors and witnesses against intimidation and corruption, and sharply rising sentences, including life meaning life, for serious and persistent offenders – should have some effect on major drug traffickers.

The USA has applied suppression of drug trafficking more ruthlessly than any other large country except Turkey and Japan, whose methods would not be easy to apply in other countries. Results have been disappointing. Research and trials of other more radical alternatives should therefore be considered. Britain is ideally placed for conducting these trials. As an island state, she has greater control over access than others and better means of preventing undesirable effects of trials seeping into neighbouring countries.

Decriminalization of a kind has been tried by the Dutch, who have chosen not to enforce some of their laws. British police forces increasingly caution drug users rather than prosecuting them. There is much to be said for concentrating police resources on the importers and distributors and not wasting them on arresting and imprisoning the users. This does not, however, solve the problem of checking the flow of money into organized and international crime. Licensing of doctors in British DDUs to prescribe free drugs in voluntary treatment of addiction has had some success. These licences could be extended to cover compulsory treatment of addicts, including those in prison.

This could gradually be further extended towards legalization under licence, as is done with alcohol. Reputable licensed importers would buy the drugs at the lowest market price direct from the growers. From bonded warehouses they would be heavily taxed and distributed to licensed retailers, of whom the most suitable would be qualified dispensers in high street pharmacies. They, like the current dispensers of controlled drugs in DDUs, would be guided by strict regulations over what they sold, how much and to whom, to keep drugs out of the hands of children, and to sell to known over-consumers only with a doctor's prescription.

Licensing would *not* legalize unauthorized traffic in drugs. It could, however, even after 150 per cent tax, provide drugs at about 12 per cent of current street prices and that would undercut the criminal drug traffickers, from the Colombian cartels to the dealer in a London street, and drive them out of business.

The experience of ending Prohibition of Alcohol in the USA gives hope that licensing need not lead to the sharp rise in drug addiction that many people predict. Even if there were such an increase it would probably be temporary and would in any case do less harm than the crime now generated by drug trafficking, which it would largely cut out.

Nevertheless, it would be necessary to be prepared in case drug abuse did grow to an unacceptable degree. Extension of licensing would have to be gradual, keeping open always the possibility of reversing it and relying again on suppressive measures, most of which would in any case be in place to fight other serious crimes.

The first step should be to set up a Royal Commission to research the feasibility of the alternatives and the procedures for a trial period in 1995–8. This research and trial should run concurrently with the British government's review of anti-drug strategy set in motion by the CDCU Consultation Paper published in October 1994.[2] The trials would, if successful, lead to gradual extension of licensed legalization. Thereafter, an executive appointed by the Commission should monitor and control its implementation on behalf of Parliament.

As with any radical experiment, there would be hazards and some of these have been discussed in this book; for example, reconciliation with international conventions and obligations, the risk of a flow of cheap drugs to Britain's neighbours, attracting 'drug tourists' as Amsterdam has, and the dangers of undermining Britain's moral values regarding indulgence and unhealthy self-gratification – particularly amongst children. Those which have been foreseen can be countered but others will arise. Nevertheless, the wider problems of crime generated by illicit trafficking and the potential growth of drug abuse are too serious to allow us to do nothing.

Notes and References

After the first reference, a short title is normally used (see Bibliography).

1 Are We Losing the War?

1. The Economist, *World in Figures*, London, *The Economist*, 1994, p. 22
2. John Grieve, Paper presented to London Drug Policy Forum, 18 March 1994
3. *The Economist*, 13 November 1993, p. 38
4. Alison Jamieson, *Organized Crime and Drug Trafficking*, lecture to NATO Defence College, Rome, 27 January 1994
5. Ibid
6. CDCU (Central Drugs Coordination Unit), *Tackling Drugs Together* (Cm. 2678) Consultation Document, London, HMSO, October 1994.

2 The *Mistis* and the Shining Path

1. Simon Strong, *Shining Path*, London, Harper Collins, 1992, p. 49
2. Carlos Degregori, 'How Difficult it is to be God', *Critique of Anthropology*, London, Sage, 1991, 11 (3), p. 236
3. Hernando de Soto, *The Other Path*, London, Taurus, 1989, pp. 61 and 94–5
4. Enrique Obando, 'Subversion and Anti Subversion in Peru 1980–82', *Low Intensity Conflict and Law Enforcement*, London, autumn 1993, 2 (2)
5. Ibid, p. 319
6. Strong, pp. 25–6
7. Gustavo Gorriti, 'Shining Path's Stalin and Trotsky', in David Scott Palmer (ed) *Shining Path of Peru*, London, Hurst, 1992, p. 154
8. Ibid, pp. 154–5
9. Ibid, p. 156
10. Strong, p. 34
11. Ibid, pp. 35–6
12. Gorriti in Scott Palmer, p. 151
13. Obando, 'Subversion', p. 319

3 Coca Enters the War

1. *Annual of Power and Conflict (APC)*, London, Institute for the Study of Conflict, 1980–1 and 1981–2

214

2. Billie Jean Isbell, 'Shining Path and Peasant Responses in Rural Ayacucho', in Scott Palmer, p. 61
3. *APC*, 1981–2, pp. 88–92
4. Otto Guibovich, *Shining Path: Birth, Life and Death*, Camberley, Staff College, 1993, p. 18
5. Ibid
6. Strong, p. 174
7. Control Risks, *Briefing Book*, London, Control Risks, 1993
8. This 'substitution' procedure was vividly described by Nicholas Shakespeare in *The Vision of Elena Silves*, Harmondsworth, Penguin, 1991
9. Strong, p. 155
10. Obando, 'Subversion', p. 323
11. Guibovich, p. 23
12. Obando, 'Subversion', p. 323
13. Jose E. Gonzales, 'Guerrillas and Coca in the Upper Huallaga Valley', in Scott Palmer, pp. 113–18
14. Guibovich, p. 16

4 President Fujimori and the Capture of Guzman

1. Strong, pp. xvi–xvii, and Nicholas Shakespeare, 'Guzman Found', *Daily Telegraph Magazine*, 22 January 1994
2. This account is based on interviews by the author in Lima with General Vidal, head of DINCOTE, on 6 December 1991, 27 January 1994 and 4 February 1994; also with his successor, General Dominguez, in London on 13 July 1993 and again in Lima on 26 January 1994. These interviews were supplemented from John Simpson, *In the Forests of the Night*, London, Hutchinson, 1993, and Nicholas Shakespeare, 'Guzman Found', and an interview with Nicholas Shakespeare on 18 December 1993.
3. The Andean Commission of Jurists, *Andean Newsletter* (*ACJANL*) No. 91 June 1994, p. 5, reported that a further pointer to the involvement of Maritza and Inchaustigui was given in August 1992 by Luis Alberto Arana Franco, alleged to have been the SL logistic chief, who had been arrested in June 1992. After the Repentance Law (see pp. 34–6) was passed in August 1992, Arana was said to have given a tip-off that these two were respon-sible for the security of 'an important SL leader'. Arana was later freed in a safe area with a new identity. If this story is true, the Repentance Law may have played a part in Guzman's capture.
4. Richard Clutterbuck's *Riot and Revolution in Singapore and Malaya*, London, Faber & Faber, 1973, pp. 221–3 and pp. 253–5, and his *The Long Long War*, New York, Praeger, 1966; London, Cassell, 1967, pp. 95–111 give full accounts of the Malayan experience.

5. Alison Jamieson, *Collaboration: New Legal and Judicial Procedures for Countering Terrorism*, Conflict Studies No. 257, London, RISCT, 1993, and Richard Clutterbuck, *Terrorism, Drugs and Crime in Europe after 1992*, London and New York, Routledge, 1990, pp. 40–5

6. *APC*, 1980–1, p. 231

7. Obando, 'Subversion', p. 325

8. Clutterbuck, *Riot*, pp. 181–3

9. ACJANL, No. 81, August 1993

10. Author's visit to the Huallaga Valley, 28–9 January 1994

11. Control Risks, *Briefing Book*, July 1994

12. Shakespeare, 'Guzman', p. 24

13. The Peruvian presentation of conflict statistics is very different from that used in Northern Ireland where, in the 24 years 1969–93, 3133 people were killed, of whom 2175 (70 per cent) were listed as civilians and 938 (30 per cent) were uniformed soldiers and police officers (full time and part time). Of these 2175 civilians, just under 400 were believed to be republican and loyalist terrorists, so ·e of whom were killed by rival terrorist groups but most (about 375) by the army and police. Of the 2175, the remainder, about 1800, were all killed by terrorists, republican and loyalist. In proportion to the population, the average of 84 killed each year since 1977 out of 1.5 million people in Northern Ireland is about half the number in proportion to the population killed in Peru in recent years, 3000 per year out of 21.5 million, but the pattern of killing is very different.

14. Enrique Obando, 'The Power of the Armed Forces', *Peru Report*, August 1994, pp. 9–11

15. ACJANL No. 87, February 1994, p. 5

16. Obando, 'Armed Forces', p. 9

5 Cocaine Production in Peru

1. Rennselaar W. Lee III, *The White Labyrinth*, New Brunswick, NJ, 1990, p. 35

2. See, for example, the various issues of the Andean Commission of Jurists, *Drug Trafficking Update (ACJDTU)*, monthly 1992–4; and Lee, p. 35

3. Lee, p. 32

4. David Whynes, 'Illicit Drugs Policy in Asia and Latin America', in *Development and Change*, London, Sage, 1991, 22, pp. 475–96, supplemented by a visit by the author to the Huallaga Valley, 28–9 January 1994

5. Deborah Willoughby, *Cocaine, Opium, Marijuana: Global Problem, Global Response*, Washington, DC, US Information Service, 1988

6. Visit by the author to the Peruvian army in the Huallaga Valley, 28–9 January 1994

7. *ACJDTU* No. 45, January 1994
8. *ACJDTU* No. 47, March 1994, p. 7
9. *ACJDTU* No. 46, February 1994, p. 4
10. Obando, 'Armed Forces', p. 1
11. *World in Figures*, p. 22
12. Jamieson, NATO
13. *Statesman's Year Book*, London, Macmillan, 1993, p. 1087

6 Bolivia

1. Whynes estimates Bolivia's receipts at $2 billion; the *Stateman's Year Book* records the legitimate GDP as $7.8 billion
2. Jamieson, NATO
3. As with all illegal and clandestine operations, estimates vary wildly, from 'ten times more' to 'four times more', that is, 80 percent of the total exports; the second figure is probably nearer the truth

7 Colombia

1. Alison Jamieson, *Global Drug Trafficking*, Conflict Studies No. 234, London, RISCT, p. 15
2. Ibid
3. *Encyclopaedia Britannica* 1981, 4, p. 875
4. Control Risks, *Country Risk Service*, London, Control Risks, September 1994
5. Author's interview with the general manager of an oil project in Colombia in 1989
6. *ACJDTU* No. 44, December 1993, p. 2
7. James Adams, *The Financing of Terror*, London, New English Library, 1986, p. 219
8. Richard Clutterbuck, *Terrorism and Guerrilla Warfare*, London and New York, Routledge, 1990, pp. 205–6, gives a 'nightmare scenario' of how this might happen
10. Ibid, p. 94
11. This was in accord with a worldwide move to combat the laundering of drug money, initiated by the Basel Declaration and the UN Vienna Convention in December 1988; these and similar measures are discussed more fully in Chapter 13
12. Jamieson, CS 234, p. 34
13. Ibid, p. 15
14. Adams, p. 219
15. Jamieson, NATO
16. *ACJDTU* No. 47, March 1994
17. Jamieson, CS 234, p. 15
18. *ACJDTU* No. 46, February 1994, p. 3

19. Control Risks, *Briefing Book*, May 1994
20. *ACJDTU* No. 47, March 1994, p. 3
21. *ACJDTU* No. 48, April 1994, p. 3
22. Hor Lung, interview with the author in Malaya, 1967

8 Cocaine Distribution

1. Jamieson, NATO
2. Jamieson, CS 234, p. 20
3. *Observer Magazine*, London, 27 February 1994

9 Crack

1. Philip Bean (ed), *Cocaine and Crack: Supply and Use*, London, Macmillan; New York, St Martin's Press, 1993, p. 3
2. ISDD (Institute for the Study of Drug Dependence), *Cocaine and Crack*, London, ISDD, 1993, p. 4
3. John Reardon, 'Crack', *Observer*, 24 January 1988, p. 15
4. *The Times*, 10 August 1990
5. ISDD, *Cocaine*, p. 6
6. Reardon
7. Bean, p. 5
8. Jon Silverman, *Crack of Doom*, London, Headline, 1994, p. 99
9. Robert M. Stutman, New York DEA agent, lecture to ACPO Regional Drug Conference, Lancashire, 20 April 1989
10. Silverman, pp. 109–10
11. Ibid, p. 113
12 *The Times*, 10 August 1990
13. Silverman, pp. 1–35
14. Ibid, pp. 125–7
15. Ibid, p. 129

10 The Heroin Trail

1. Raymond Kendall, Secretary-General, Interpol, lecture to Europe 2000 Conference on Organized Crime, Berlin, 7–9 October 1993, p. 7
2. Willoughby, p. 7
3. ISDD, *National Audit of Drug Abuse in Britain*, London, ISDD, 1993, p. 59
4. *The Economist*, 17 April 1993, p. 36
5. Jamieson, CS 234, p. 10
6. Simon Baker, formerly Royal Hong Kong Police, interviews and correspondence with the author in 1994
7. Ibid

8. Gerald Posner, *Warlords of Crime: The New Mafia*, London, Macdonald Queen Anne Press, 1989, of which extracts were published in the *Observer Magazine*, 5 March 1989, p. 30
9. Simon Baker, interview
10. Kendall, p. 7
11. Alison Jamieson, *Drug Trafficking After 1992*, Conflict Studies No. 250, London, RISCT, April 1992, p. 3
12. Jamieson, CS 234, pp. 10–17

11 Cannabis and Synthetics

1. Willoughby
2. Jamieson, NATO
3. DEA (Drug Enforcement Administration), *Drugs of Abuse*, Washington DC, DEA, 1989, pp. 30 and 31
4. *Observer Magazine*, 27 February 1994
5. DEA, p. 40
6. *Observer Magazine*, 27 February 1994
7. DEA, pp. 30, 31 and 40
8 Martin Burton, 'ICE Cool in Honolulu', *Intersec*, London, March 1994
9. Jamieson, CS 250, p. 5
10. DEA, pp. 49–50
11. *Observer Magazine*, 27 February 1994
12. Jamieson, CS 250, p. 5

12 Money Laundering

1. Jamieson, CS 234, p. 4
2. Leon D. Richardson, 'The Urgency of Detergency, Part I', *TVI Journal*, winter 1986, pp. 12–22
3. Nicholas Dorn, Karin Mǔrji and Nigel South, *Traffickers: Drug Markets and Law Enforcement*, London and New York, Routledge, 1992, pp. 28–9
4. Adams, pp. 227–8
5. Jamieson, CS 250, p. 9
6. Jamieson, CS 234, p. 25
7. Ibid, pp. 26–8
8. Ibid, p. 27
9. Jamieson, CS 250, p. 32
10. R. T. Naylor, transcript of lecture, *Money Laundering*, Florence, 19 May 1989, based on his book *Hot Money*, London, Unwin, 1987
11. *Sunday Telegraph*, 14 July 1991
12. Richardson, p. 14
13. Ibid, p. 15

13 Countering Money Laundering

1. Dorn, p. 63
2. Jamieson, CS 234, p. 33
3. Ibid, p. 37
4. Jamieson, CS 250, p. 21
5. Ibid, pp. 19–20
6. Ibid, p. 20
7. Ibid, p. 17
8. Ibid, p. 2
9. Ibid, pp. 14–15
10. Ibid, p. 21
11. Silverman, p. 171
12. Jamieson, CS 250, p. 21
13. Dorn, p. 79
14. Jane Goodsir, 'Civil Rights and Civil Liberties Surrounding the Use of Cocaine and Crack', in Bean, p. 134
15. Dorn, p. 154
16. Jamieson, CS 250, p. 22
17. Ibid, p. 23
18. Jamieson, CS 234, p. 28
19. M. Gillard, 'BCCI: The Cocaine Cash Trail', *Observer*, 16 October 1988, quoted in Dorn, p. 71
20. *The Economist*, 3 August 1991
21. Jamieson, CS 250, p. 28
22. Dorn, p. 71
23. Jamieson, CS 250, p. 31
24. Ibid, p. 27
25. Ibid, p. 30
26. Ibid, p. 35
27. Ibid, pp. 35–6

15 The USA

1. Jamieson, NATO
2. DEA
3. Jamieson, CS 234, p. 20
4. *ACJDTU* No. 43, November 1993
5. Jamieson, CS 234, p. 20
6. Keesings Archives, 1987, 35486
7. Keesings Archives, 1988, 36089–91
8. *Guardian*, 15 August 1989
9. Jamieson, NATO
10. Whynes, pp. 475–96
11. Ibid, p. 491

12. 'The War on Drugs Should Begin at Home', *The Economist*, 7 June 1988, p. 38
13. Whynes, pp. 492–3
14. Dr Mark Gold, founder of the US National Cocaine Helpline, speaking at a World Ministerial Drugs Conference in London, 9–11 April 1990
15. Jamieson, CS 234, p. 32
16. *Sunday Telegraph*, 14 August 1994
17. *The Times*, 13 August 1994

16 The Italian Mafia

1. Alison Jamieson, *The Modern Mafia: Its Role and Record*, Conflict Studies No. 224, London, RISCT, 1989, p. 1
2. *Encyclopaedia Britannica* 1981, 6, p. 478
3. Alison Jamieson, 'Mafia and Political Power 1943–89', *International Relations*, 10 (1), May 1990
4. Jamieson, CS 224, p. 3
5. Giovanni De Gennaro, lecture to Europe 2000 Conference on Organized Crime and Terrorism, Berlin, 7–9 October 1993
6. Jamieson, CS 224, p. 10
7. Ibid, p. 26
8. Alison Jamieson, 'Mafia and Institutional Power in Italy', *International Relations*, 12 (1), April 1994
9. Jamieson, CS 257, p. 19
10. Ibid, p. 20
11. Control Risks, *Briefing Book*, May 1993

17 Russia and East Europe

1. For fuller details of these minorities in the former Soviet Union and East Europe, see Richard Clutterbuck, *International Crisis and Conflict*, London, Macmillan; New York, St Martin's Press, 1993, pp. 199–200
2. Kendall, p. 19
3. The author attended a security conference in Moscow in May 1990
4. Hagen Saberschinsky, President, Berlin Police, in a lecture to Europe 2000 Conference on Organized Crime and Terrorism, Berlin, 7–9 October 1993. An even higher figure was given by Christopher Ulrich, *The Price of Freedom*, Conflict Studies No. 275, London, RISCT, October 1994. He quoted 5700 criminal groups in Russia with a core strength of 100,000, of which 160 groups were operating internationally in 30 countries. Ulrich also estimated that organized criminals controlled almost 40,000 commercial

businesses and that 70–80 per cent of all businesses paid extortion or protection money to criminal groups or to corrupt government officials

5. General Gannady Chebotarev, second in command of the organized crime directorate in the Russian Ministry of the Interior, reported in *The Economist*, 9 July 1994
6. Report to the President of Russia in January 1994, reported in *The Economist*, 19 July 1994
7. *The Economist*, 9 July 1994
8. Ibid
9. Ibid. This figure may, however, be an exaggeration: it was given by a member of the Communist Party, who might wish to discredit attempts to develop a market economy
10. Kendall, p. 2
11. Ibid, p. 3
12. Russian Minister of the Interior, reported in *The Economist*, 9 July 1994
13. Kendall, p. 4
14. Jamieson, NATO
15. Kendall, p. 4
16. Ibid
17. Ibid, p. 7
18. Control Risks, *Briefing Book*, May 1993
19. Ibid
20. Ibid
21. *The Times*, 6 November, 1992
22. Hans Reermann, German Ministry of the Interior, lecture to Europe 2000 Conference on Organized Crime and Terrorism, Berlin, 7–9 October 1993
23. *Economist*, 30 July 1994
24. Police Chief Vavra, Prague Police, in a lecture to Europe 2000 Conference on Organized Crime and Terrorism, 7–9 October 1993
25. Jamieson, NATO

18 Italy, Germany and the Dutch Experiment

1. Control Risks, *Briefing Book*, May 1993
2. Jamieson, CS 250, p. 19
3. *ACJDTU* No. 51, July 1994, p. 6
4. BKA figured cited in Jamieson, CS 250, p. 19
5. Alison Jamieson, *International Dimensions of Italian Organized Crime*, lecture to Hans Seidel Stiftung, Wildbad Kreuth, 22–4 September 1993
6. *Sunday Telegraph*, 23 October 1994

7. ACJDTU No. 51, July 1994, p. 6
8. *The Economist*, 10 February 1990
9. Jamieson, CS 250, p. 13

19 Drug Trafficking in the UK

1. H. B. Spear and Joy Mott, 'Cocaine and Crack within the British System: A History of Control', in Bean, pp. 29–45
2. *The Independent*, 2 March 1994
3. ISDD, *National Audit of Drug Misuse in Britain*, London, ISDD 1993, pp. 20–1, and CDCU, *Tackling Drugs Together*
4. *Sunday Telegraph*, 5 June 1994
5. ISDD, *Audit*, pp. 22–6
6. *The Economist*, 13 November 1993, p. 38
7. Question Research and Marketing Strategists Report published in *Police Review* 26 (7), March 1994, p. 37
8. *The Independent*, 2 March 1994
9. Jamieson, CS 224, p. 29
10. Ibid
11. Silverman, pp. 211–18
12. Ibid, p. 220
13. Ibid, pp. 161–2
14. Frances Crook, director, Howard League for Penal Reform, interview with the author, 1 September 1993
15. Dorn, pp. 184–6
16. Silverman, pp. 155–61
17. Ibid, p. 165
18. Ibid, pp. 181–4
19. Dorn, pp. 50–2
20. Ibid, p. 49
21. Ibid, pp. 25–6
22. Ibid, pp. 21–4
23. Detective Superintendent David Brennan, head of Greater Manchester Police drug squad, quoted in Silverman, pp. 197–8
24. Dorn, p. 45
25. Silverman, p. 191
26. Ibid, pp. 190–3
27. Detective Sergeant Tony Brett, quoted in Silverman, pp. 194–5
28. Silverman, p. 196
29. Brennan, quoted in Silverman, pp. 197–8

20 Anti-Drug Enforcement in the UK

1. Dorn, p. 66. By contrast, the New York City Police Department in 1989 had 2700 full-time drug officers and made 90,000 drug arrests

in 1988 (Stutman, p. 14). A senior Metropolitan Police officer told the author in an interview in 1994 that he had fewer drug officers than the number of bandsmen in the Brigade of Guards

2. Dorn, pp. 78–80

3. *Police Review*, 27 September 1991

4. CDCU, p. 25

5. ACPO Report on Operational Intelligence, 1986, quoted by Dorn, pp. 157–8

6. Drug squad officer quoted by Dorn, p. 126

7. This technique can be compared with that used by the British in Malaya in the 1950s (see pp. 35 and 64–5), by the Italians against terrorists in 1980–83 and currently against the mafia (see pp. 135–6) and by the Peruvians under their Repentance Law (see pp. 34–6)

8. In Italy in 1976, in the interests of freedom of information, a law was passed enabling a magistrate investigating a case to ask for the intelligence file of any person connected with that case. Both the mafia and the terrorists soon learned how to find a corruptible magistrate. As a result, informants dared not come forward, and information from them virtually ceased until, after the kidnap and murder of former Prime Minister Aldo Moro in 1978, the Italian government had to change the policy. The subsequent success of the *pentiti* was described in Chapter 16

9. This happened in the case against Victor Agar in 1989. See Dorn, pp. 133–4

10. *Guardian*, 'Super for supergrasses', 15 February 1990

11. A. Jennings, P. Lashmar and V. Simpson, *Scotland Yard's Cocaine Connection*, London, Jonathan Cape, 1990, p. 32, cited in Dorn, p. 135

12. Richard Clutterbuck, *Terrorism in an Unstable World*, London and New York, Routledge, 1994, pp. 162–3

13. Goodsir in Bean, p. 135

14. Dorn, pp. 98–9

15. Ibid, pp. 181–3

16. Goodsir in Bean, p. 134

17. Ibid, p. 136

18. Notting Hill (London) police officer quoted in Dorn, p. 107

19. Dorn, pp. 108–10

20. Detective Superintendent John Jones, quoted in Silverman, pp. 64–76

21. Silverman, pp. 193–7

22. Ibid, pp. 8–22

23. Ibid, p. 1

24. A. Maden, M, Swinton and J. Gunn, 'A Survey of Pre-Arrest Drug Use by Sentenced Prisoners', *British Journal of Addiction*, 1992, 87 (1), pp. 27–33

25. Richard Stevenson, *Winning the War on Drugs: To Legalize or Not?*, Hobart Paper No. 124, London, Institute of Economic Affairs, 1994, p. 32
26. Home Office, *Bulletin of Statistics of Drug Addicts, 1993*, London, HMSO, 1994, reported in *The Independent* and the *Guardian*, 23 June 1993
27. Grieve, Forum
28. John Grieve, *Report of Workshop on Drug Prevention Strategy*, ACPO Conference, 1993

21 Could Suppression be Made to Work?

1. *The Economist*, 15 May 1993, p. 63
2. *The Economist*, 19 February 1994 and 15 May 1993
3. *Sunday Telegraph*, 5 June 1994
4. Attention was first drawn to this by Sir Robert Mark in his BBC Dimbleby Lecture in 1973
5. CDCU, p. 7
6. CDCU, pp. 68–9

22 Decriminalize? License? Legalize?

1. Stevenson, pp. 46–7. His figures differ from others but all figures from all sources agree that there is a lower percentage of addicts in the Netherlands than in Italy or the UK
2. *The Economist*, 10 February 1990
3. *Sunday Telegraph*, 5 June 1994
4. Stevenson, p. 48
5. At this workshop, nearly 50 percent of those taking part supported the idea of launching a major research project to investigate the feasibility and pros and cons of extending licensing
6. Grieve, *Workshop*, p. 32
7. Grieve, Forum
8. Jamieson, CS 234, pp. 35–6
9. Jamieson, CS 250, p. 2
10. Stevenson, p. 37
11. A tot of whisky (2.5 cl) contains 40 percent pure alcohol (2 cl). The price from the distillers ex bond is about £2.80 per 70 cl bottle (28 cl of pure alcohol) or 10 pence per tot. The duty on this (£5.54 per bottle or 20p per tot) works out at 200 percent. Adding profit and VAT, the bottle will cost about £11 at an off-licence shop. By the time the whisky gets to a pub, with further VAT, profit and the pub's overheads, it costs about £1.25 per tot or £2.50 for a double whisky

12. Stevenson, pp. 28–9: Customs £125–50 million, police £24 million, prison service £48 million
13. G. W. Nelson, *The War on Drugs: An Alternative Strategy*, London, Seaford House Papers, HMSO, 1993, pp. 35–51
14. CDCU, pp. 111–14

23 A War to be Won in the West

1. William Rees-Mogg, *The Times*, 15 September 1993
2. CDCU

Bibliography

BOOKS, ARTICLES AND LECTURES

	(Short Title)
ACPO (Association of Chief Police Officers), *Reports*, 1986–93	(ACPO)
ADAMS, JAMES, *The Financing of Terror*, London, New English Library, 1986	(Adams)
ANDEAN COMMISSION OF JURISTS, *Andean Newsletter*, Lima, monthly 1992–94	*(ACJANL)*
ANDEAN COMMISSION OF JURISTS, *Drug Trafficking Update*, Lima, monthly 1992–4	*(ACJDTU)*
Annual of Power and Conflict (APC), London, Institute for the Study of Conflict, 1980–1 and 1981–2	*(APC)*
BEAN, PHILIP (ed) *Cocaine and Crack: Supply and Use*, London, Macmillan; New York, St Martin's Press, 1993	(Bean)
BURTON, MARTIN, 'ICE Cool in Honolulu', *Intersec*, London, March 1994	(Burton)
CDCU (Central Drugs Coordination Unit), *Tackling Drugs Together* (Cm 2678), Consultation Document, London, HMSO, October 1994	(CDCU)
CLUTTERBUCK, RICHARD, *The Long Long War*, London, Cassell, 1967	(Clutterbuck, *Long War*)
CLUTTERBUCK, RICHARD, *Riot and Revolution in Singapore and Malaya*, London, Faber & Faber, 1973	(Clutterbuck, *Riot*)
CLUTTERBUCK, RICHARD, *Terrorism and Guerrilla Warfare*, London and New York, Routledge, 1990	(Clutterbuck, *Warfare*)
CLUTTERBUCK, RICHARD, *Terrorism, Drugs and Crime in Europe after 1992*, London and New York, Routledge, 1990	(Clutterbuck, *Europe*)
CLUTTERBUCK, RICHARD, *International Crisis and Conflict*, London, Macmillan; New York, St Martin's Press, 1993	(Clutterbuck, *Crisis*)

CLUTTERBUCK, RICHARD, *Terrorism in an Unstable World*, London and New York, Routledge, 1994 — (Clutterbuck, *World*)

Conflict Studies, Nos 224, 234, 250, 257, 275, see JAMIESON and ULRICH

CONTROL RISKS, *Briefing Book*, London, Control Risks, 1981–94 — (Control Risks, *Briefing Book*)

CONTROL RISKS, *Country Risk Service*, London, Control Risks, 1993–4 — (Control Risks, *Country Risk*)

DEA (Drug Enforcement Administration), *Drugs of Abuse*, Washington, DC, DEA, 1989 — (DEA)

DE GENNARO, GIOVANNI, lecture to Europe 2000 Conference on Organized Crime and Terrorism, Berlin, 7–9 October 1993 — (De Gennaro)

DEGREGORI, CARLOS, 'How Difficult it is to be God', *Critique of Anthropology*, London, Sage, 1991, 11 (3) — (Degregori)

DE SOTO, HERNANDO, *The Other Path*, London, Taurus, 1989 — (De Soto)

DORN, NICHOLAS, MUŘJI, KARIM, and SOUTH, NIGEL, *Trafficking: Drug Markets and Law Enforcement*, London and New York, Routledge, 1992 — (Dorn)

ECONOMIST, The, *World in Figures*, London, The Economist, 1994 — (*World in Figures*)

Encyclopaedia Britannica, 1981 — (EB)

EUROPE 2000, Collected papers from Conference on Organized Crime and Terrorism, Berlin 7–9 October 1993. See contributors DE GENNARO, KENDALL, REERMANN, SABERSCHINSKY and VAVRA — (E2000)

GILLARD, M., 'BCCI: The Cocaine Cash Trail', *Observer*, 16 October 1988 — (Gillard)

GONZALES, JOSE E., 'Guerrillas and Coca in the Upper Huallaga Valley', in SCOTT PALMER — (Gonzales in Scott Palmer)

GOODSIR, JANE, 'Civil Rights and Civil Liberties Surrounding the Use of Cocaine and Crack', in BEAN — (Goodsir in Bean)

GORRITI, GUSTAVO, 'Shining Path's Stalin and Trotsky', in SCOTT PALMER — (Gorriti in Scott Palmer)

GRIEVE, JOHN, *Report of Workshop on Drug Prevention Strategy*, ACPO Conference, 1993 — (Grieve, *Workshop*)

GRIEVE, JOHN, Paper presented to London Drug Policy Forum, 18 March 1994 — (Grieve, Forum)

GUIBOVICH, OTTO, *Shining Path: Birth, Life and Death*, Camberley, Staff College, 1993 — (Guibovich)

HOME OFFICE, *Bulletin of Statistics of Drug Addicts, 1993*, London, HMSO, 1994, quoted in *The Independent* and the *Guardian*, 23 June 1994 — (Home Office *Bulletin*)

ISBELL, BILLIE JEAN, 'Shining Path and Peasant Responses in Rural Ayacucho', in SCOTT PALMER — (Isbell in Scott Palmer)

ISDD (Institute for the Study of Drug Dependence), *Cocaine and Crack*, London, ISDD, 1993 — (ISDD, *Cocaine*)

ISDD, *National Audit of Drug Misuse in Britain*, London, ISDD, 1993 — (ISDD, *Audit*)

JAMIESON, ALISON, *The Modern Mafia: Its Role and Record*, Conflict Studies No. 224, London, RISCT, September 1989 — (Jamieson, CS 224)

JAMIESON, ALISON, 'Mafia and Political Power 1943–89', *International Relations*, 10 (1), May 1990 — (Jamieson, Mafia 1990)

JAMIESON, ALISON, *Global Drug Trafficking*, Conflict Studies No. 234, London, RISCT, September 1990 — (Jamieson, CS 234)

JAMIESON, ALISON, *Drug Trafficking After 1992*, Conflict Studies No. 250, London, RISCT, April 1992 — (Jamieson, CS 250)

JAMIESON, ALISON, *Collaboration: New Legal and Judicial Procedures for Countering Terrorism*, Conflict Studies No. 257, London, RISCT, January 1993 — (Jamieson, CS 257)

JAMIESON, ALISON, *International Dimensions of Italian Organized Crime*, lecture to Hans Seidel Stiftung, Wilbad Kreuth, 22–4 September 1993 — (Jamieson, Hans Seidel)

JAMIESON, ALISON, *Organized Crime and Drug Trafficking*, lecture to NATO Defence College, Rome, 27 January 1994 — (Jamieson, NATO)

JAMIESON, ALISON, 'Mafia and Institutional Power in Italy', *International Relations*, 12 (1), April 1994 — (Jamieson, Mafia 1994)

JENNINGS, A., LASHMAR, P. and SIMPSON, V., *Scotland Yard's Cocaine Connection*, London, Jonathan Cape, 1990 — (Jennings)

KENDALL, RAYMOND, Secretary-General, Interpol, lecture to Europe 2000 Conference — (Kendall)

230   *Bibliography*

on Organized Crime and Terrorism, Berlin,
7–9 October 1993

KEESINGS ARCHIVES, 1987, 35486   (Keesings, 1987)

KEESINGS ARCHIVES, 1988, 36089–91   (Keesings, 1988)

LEE III, RENNSELAAR W., *The White*   (Lee)
Labyrinth, New Brunswick, NJ, 1990

MADEN, A, SWINTON, M. and GUNN, J.,   (Maden)
'A Survey of Pre-Arrest Drug Use by Sentenced Prisoners', *British Journal of Addiction*,
1992, 87 (1) pp. 27–33

NAYLOR, R. T., *Hot Money*, London, Unwin,   (Naylor)
1987

NELSON, G. W., *The War on Drugs: An*   (Nelson)
Alternative Strategy, Seaford House Papers,
London, HMSO, 1993

OBANDO, ENRIQUE, 'Subversion and Anti (Obando, 'Subversion')
Subversion in Peru 1980–82', *Low Intensity
Conflict and Law Enforcement*, London, autumn
1993, 2 (2)

OBANDO, ENRIQUE, 'The Power of the   (Obando, 'Armed
Armed Forces', *Peru Report*, August 1994,   Forces')
pp. 9–11

POSNER, GERALD, *Warlords of Crime: The*   (Posner)
New Mafia, London, Macdonald Queen
Anne Press, 1989

REARDON, JOHN, 'Crack', *Observer*, 24
January 1988, p. 15 (Reardon)

REERMANN, HANS, German Ministry of   (Reermann)
the Interior, lecture to Europe 2000 Conference on Organized Crime and Terrorism,
Berlin, 7–9 October 1993

RICHARDSON, LEON D., 'The Urgency of   (Richardson)
Detergency, Part I', *TVI Journal*, winter
1986, pp. 12–22

SABERSCHINSKY, HAGEN, President, Ber-   (Saberschinsky)
lin Police, lecture to Europe 2000 Conference
on Organized Crime and Terrorism, Berlin,
7–9 October 1993

SCOTT PALMER, DAVID (ed) *Shining Path*   (Scott Palmer)
of Peru, London, Hurst, 1992

SHAKESPEARE, NICHOLAS, *The Vision of* (Shakespeare, *Vision*)
Elena Silves, Harmondsworth, Penguin, 1991

SHAKESPEARE, NICHOLAS, 'Guzman   (Shakespeare,
Found', *Daily Telegraph Magazine*, 22 Janu-   'Guzman')
ary 1994

SILVERMAN, JON, *Crack of Doom*, London, Headline, 1994 — (Silverman)

SIMPSON, JOHN, *In the Forests of the Night*, London, Hutchinson, 1993 — (Simpson)

SPEAR, H. B. and MOTT, JOY, 'Cocaine and Crack within the British System: A History of Control', in BEAN — (Spear and Mott in Bean)

Statesman's Year Book, London, Macmillan, 1993 — (*Statesman's YB*)

STEVENSON, RICHARD, *Winning the War on Drugs: To Legalize or Not?*, Hobart Paper No. 124, London, Institute of Economic Affairs, 1994 — (Stevenson)

STRONG, SIMON, *Shining Path*, London, Harper Collins, 1992 — (Strong)

STUTMAN, ROBERT M., New York DEA agent, *Crack: Its Effects on a City and Law Enforcement Response*, lecture to ACPO Regional Drug Conferences, 20 April 1989 — (Stutman)

ULRICH, CHRISTOPHER, *The Price of Freedom*, Conflict Studies No. 275, London, RISCT, October 1994 — (Ulrich)

VAVRA, Chief, Prague Police, lecture to Europe 2000 Conference on Organized Crime and Terrorism, Berlin, 7–9 October 1993 — (Vavra)

WHYNES, DAVID, 'Illicit Drugs Policy in Asia and Latin America' *Development and Change*, London, Sage, 1991, 22, pp. 475–96 — (Whynes)

WILLOUGHBY, DEBORAH, *Cocaine, Opium, Marijuana: Global Problem, Global Response*, Washington, DC, US Information Service, 1988 — (Willoughby)

JOURNALS AND NEWSPAPERS

Andean Commission of Jurists, *Andean Newsletter (ACJANL)*
Andean Commission of Jurists, *Drug Trafficking Update (ACJDTU)*
British Journal of Addiction
Conflict Studies
Critique of Anthropolgy
Daily Telegraph
Daily Telegraph Magazine
Development and Change
The Economist

Guardian
The Independent
International Relations
Intersec
Low Intensity Conflict and Law Enforcement
Observer
Observer Magazine
Peru Report
Police Review
Sunday Telegraph
The Times
TVI Journal

Index

Where acronyms are shown in the list of abbreviations (pp. xiii–xv) the acronym rather than the full title is normally used in this index.